Miss Vickie's

real food, real fast

Pressure Cooker Cookbook

Miss Vickie's

real food, real fast

Pressure Cooker Cookbook

Vickie Smith

PHOTOGRAPHY BY JASON WYCHE

WILEY

John Wiley & Sons, Inc.

This book is printed on acid-free paper. ♾

Cover design by Suzanne Sunwoo
Published by John Wiley & Sons, Inc., Hoboken, New Jersey.
Published simultaneously in Canada.

For general information on our other products and services, or technical support, please contact our Customer Care Department within the United States at 800-762-2974, outside the United States at 317-572-3993 or fax 317-572-4002.

Wiley publishes in a variety of print and electronic formats and by print-on-demand. Some material included with standard print versions of this book may not be included in e-books or in print-on-demand. If this book refers to media such as a CD or DVD that is not included in the version you purchased, you may download this material at http://booksupport.wiley.com. For more information about Wiley products, visit www.wiley.com.

Library of Congress Cataloging-in-Publication Data

Smith, Vicki (Vicki L.), 1947–
Miss Vickie's pressure cooker, real food real fast / Vickie Smith ; photography by Jason Wyche.
p. cm.
Includes index.
ISBN 978-0-470-87342-7 (pbk.); ISBN 978-1-118-11065-2 (ebk.); ISBN 978-1-118-11066-9 (ebk.);
ISBN 978-1-118-11067-6 (ebk.)
1. Pressure cooking. I. Title.
TX840.P7.S654 2013
641.5'87—dc23

2012017464

Printed in The United States of America

10 9 8 7 6 5 4 3 2 1

contents

introduction

All over America, cooks are once again rediscovering the benefits of modern pressure cookery. Today's advanced pressure cookers are a far cry from our grandmothers' unreliable vintage models. These new time-saving appliances are completely reengineered, completely safe, and ultra-reliable—in short, "goof-proof." They are designed to appeal to busy cooks with hectic schedules, demanding jobs, active families, and little spare time for cooking. The modern pressure cooker is the perfect solution for anyone looking for healthier recipes and faster, economical ways to prepare nutritious home-cooked meals.

A tremendous variety of different foods and types of recipes can be cooked in just minutes in the pressure cooker. In this book I've included more than two hundred recipes for everything from breakfast to dessert, from quiches to cakes. There are family-friendly one-pot stews, roasts, and casseroles as well as multicourse feasts for company. There are also "shortcut recipes," nutritious and superfast versions of kitchen staples like chicken soup, mac and cheese, and tuna casserole. And there are recipes for snacks, starters, sides, and sauces.

So forget about Grandma's stories of exploding pressure cookers and those old tales about dinner decorating the kitchen ceiling or family dinners consisting of mush. The old-style, noisy, hissing pressure regulators have become a distant memory, a relic of bygone days. Say goodbye also to hot ovens and standing in front of a stove, constantly watching and stirring a pot. It's time to take a good look at today's new pressure cooker. Join the many happy people who are discovering—or rediscovering—the completely safe and very easy-to-use modern pressure cooker.

pressure cooker tips, techniques, and equipment

All pressure cookers operate by the same principle. The pot is an enclosed system. Heat builds steam, which produces the pressure needed to cook the food faster. The pressure is controlled by adjusting the heat. Safety devices are designed to vent off excess pressure, and the pressure must be released before opening the lid. That's it in a nutshell.

Getting Started

Be sure to thoroughly read the owner's manual to familiarize yourself with the basic principles, new terminology, and techniques associated with pressure cookery. Keep the manual in a safe place for quick reference. If you have lost the original owner's manual that came with your cooker, replacements are often available at little or no cost by contacting the manufacturer.

BEFORE YOU BEGIN

You should carefully inspect your pressure cooker prior to each and every use. Make sure that it is clean inside and out. Lift or turn the pressure valve to make sure it moves freely, and check the housing assembly or connecting screw to see that it is secure. Examine the vent pipe if your cooker uses the classic jiggle-top pressure regulator, making sure it's clean and open. Check the handles on the pot and the lid to confirm that they are firmly attached, tightening the screws as necessary. The gasket and other replaceable rubber or silicone seals should be in good condition, with no signs of tears or other deterioration such as gumminess or brittleness. Replace the parts if there are any suspicious areas or other signs of deterioration. The gasket should fit snugly in its place in the lid.

FOLLOW RECIPE DIRECTIONS

Always use a pressure cooker recipe for the correct timing and release method. Don't rely on guesswork when it comes to pressure cooking. A mistake in choosing the proper cooking method, timing, or release method will yield unsatisfactory results in short order.

ADDING LIQUID TO THE PRESSURE COOKER

Before starting to cook anything in a pressure cooker, there must be some sort of liquid inside the pot to generate enough steam to pressurize the cooker. The minimum amount of water or liquid required depends on two factors: (1) the length of cooking time, and (2) the cooking method; it does not depend on the amount of food in the pressure cooker. Modern pressure cookers can use as little as less than ½ cup of water or other cooking liquids, but check the owner's manual for the minimum amount as recommended by the manufacturer. This amount of liquid recommended is usually sufficient for about 15 minutes of pressure-cooking time, and longer cooking times will require correspondingly more liquid.

FILLING THE PRESSURE COOKER

Never exceed the maximum fill level on any pressure cooker. Some units have these maximum fill levels conveniently marked on the inside of the pot. Do not exceed the two-thirds full level for most ingredients. The exceptions are foods that are mostly liquids, and foods that foam, froth, or expand during cooking (see page 3), in which case the maximum is only half full.

PRESSURIZING THE COOKER

Place the pressure cooker on the correct size burner, which means one that is no larger, or is slightly smaller, than the diameter of the cooker base. Do not use a burner that is larger or a super-high BTU heating element. Set the heat on high initially, to rapidly pressurize the cooker. Once high pressure (15psi) is reached, as shown by the pressure indicator, immediately lower the heat to the lowest possible setting that will stabilize and still maintain pressure. Now it's time to begin actually timing the cooking according to the recipe directions.

Cooking and Timing

If using a model with the classic pressure regulator, or jiggle top, it should rock three to five times per minute. If it is in constant motion, the heat is too high and it needs to be adjusted to a lower setting. As with any other cooking method that uses high heat, such as frying, broiling, or grilling, the pressure cooker should not be left unattended. Always—let me repeat that—always use a timer. A digital timer is preferred because it can be carried with you on a lanyard, clipped on a belt, or pocketed so you will never forget about the pressure cooker. When the cooking time is up, remove the pressure cooker from the heat source and proceed with the release method recommended in the recipe.

RELEASING PRESSURE

Before the lid can be removed from the pressure cooker, the pot must be depressurized. This is an important element of pressure cooking, and the choice of pressure release methods can have a great impact on the food inside the cooker. There are three methods (see page 6) for releasing the pressure in a modern stovetop pressure cooker: (1) the natural release method, (2) the quick release method, and (3) the cold water release method. Using the correct pressure release method is the final phase of pressure cooking and affects the successful outcomes of most recipes. Individual recipes will indicate which release method to use at the end of the cooking process.

OPENING THE COOKER

As a matter of routine safety, be certain the cooker is completely depressurized before unlocking and removing the lid. The pressure indicator will have dropped, but a simple test of moving or lifting the pressure valve or regulator will verify that the cooker has depressurized, if there is no sound of escaping steam. When you have verified that the cooker is completely depressurized, open the lid, tipping it away from you to avoid coming into contact with the escaping hot steam.

Pressure Cooker Safety

Modern pressure cookers have more safety features than ever, making them completely safe and reliable. Today's pressure cooker has a lid-locking system that prevents the lid from being removed until the pressure inside has returned to normal. Top-quality brands will have a total of five, or even six, safety features. Be sure to read and follow the directions in your owner's manual, and even more important, understand how the pressure cooker operates and become familiar with all the terms and methods used.

Ten Golden Rules of Pressure Cookery

Regardless of the type of pressure cooker you own, these basic safety rules apply to all brands and models.

1. Check to see that the vent or valve systems are clean and in good working order before using the pressure cooker.
2. Never use less than the minimum amount of liquid as recommended by the manufacturer, or as required for the length of cooking time.
3. Do not exceed the two-thirds full level for most recipes. The exception are foods that are mostly liquids, and foods that foam, froth, or expand during cooking, in which case half full is the maximum fill level.
4. Use high heat to establish the desired pressure, immediately reduce the heat to the lowest possible level to stabilize and maintain that pressure, and then begin timing.
5. For best results, always use a recipe, carefully following the directions for the proper cooking technique, amount of liquid, cooking time, and pressure release methods.
6. Always set a timer, and, as with any other kitchen appliance that cooks rapidly and uses high temperatures, do not leave the pressure cooker unattended.
7. Never use more than ¼ cup of fats or oils or exceed the maximum as recommended by the manufacturer.
8. Use the natural release method (see page 7) for foods that are mostly liquids or that foam, froth, or expand, or for foods with a skin or peel, and for most cuts of meat.
9. When using the cold water release method (see page 6), do not allow water to run directly over the vent or valve system.
10. Always be sure that the pressure has dropped back to normal before opening the locking lid on a pressure cooker.

Five Formulas for Foods that Foam, Froth, or Expand

When using a pressure cooker for foods that foam, froth, or expand, there are additional safety rules that apply. Examples of these types of foods include dried beans or peas, pasta, rice and grains, and some varieties of fruit.

1. Always use a pressure cooker that is 5 quarts in size or larger.
2. If necessary, adjust the recipe, but do not exceed the half-full level.
3. To minimize foaming, use 1 or 2 tablespoons of cooking oil.
4. Pay careful attention to adjusting the heat to the lowest possible setting immediately after the cooker comes to pressure to avoid scorching problems.
5. Depressurize the cooker by using either the natural or the cold water release method (see pages 6, 7).

CHECK YOUR PRESSURE COOKER BEFORE AND AFTER EACH USE

Do a visual inspection before using the pressure cooker. Pay close attention to the lid with its gasket, vents, and valve systems, to be sure everything is clean and in good working order. On pressure cookers that use the old-style, jiggling pressure regulator, hold the lid up to the light and look through the vent pipe to be sure it's clear. Check the overpressure plug on a jiggle-top cooker, looking for any cracking in the rubber, and be sure that the little metal rod is loose and moves up and down freely. On the newer, modern pressure cookers that use a pop-up, spring valve pressure regulator, be sure the pop-up button or rod moves up and down without sticking. On the pressure cookers using a dial or knob setting, be sure that the mechanism rotates easily.

Ten-Point Safety Checklist

Before purchasing or using any new pressure cooker (or trying to use the one you discovered in Granny's attic), make sure can it pass this Ten-Point Safety Checklist. To protect your investment and for obvious safety reasons, all questions require a "yes" answer.

1. Can you identify the manufacturer, and is the company still in business?
2. Can you identify the model number or name, and is that unit still being manufactured?
3. Are replacement parts and accessory items easily available from more than one source?
4. Is an owner's manual included, or can a replacement copy still be obtained from the manufacturer?
5. If used, is the pressure cooker in good condition and free of pitting or signs of undue wear or misuse?
6. Are the handles well attached and free of cracks or nicks, and does the manufacturer still offer replacements?
7. Are all the necessary parts available, and can they still be obtained from the manufacturer?
8. If the pressure cooker has a gauge, has it been tested for accuracy to make sure it is actually able to maintain pressure as indicated?
9. Are there any stains or discoloration caused by leaks around the lid or valve fittings that may indicate the lid does not seal properly?
10. Does the pressure cooker have at least three safety features, including an interlocking lid, an overpressure valve or vent, and a gasket release slot in the lid?

Pressure: Getting It, Keeping It, Releasing It

The modern pressure cooker is easier to operate than the old-time versions, which required constant attention to keep the pressure adjusted properly. The heavy encapsulated base and modern spring valves have solved the mystery of pressure cooking. Some novice pressure cooker users are under the impression that they must only use recipes specially designed just for their particular brand. Not true! As long as a pressure cooker meets the 15psi standard, virtually all recipes designed for pressure cooking can be used.

HOW TO ACHIEVE AND MAINTAIN PRESSURE

All pressure cookers use heat to generate pressure. Center the pressure cooker on a burner that is slightly smaller than the diameter of the base. Do not use any oversized heating element or a super-high BTU setting when pressure cooking. The cooker is brought to high pressure (15psi) over high heat until the pressure indicator shows that it is pressurized. Once pressure is achieved, immediately lower the heat to the lowest possible setting that will stabilize and then maintain that pressure. Begin timing at this point, and set a timer for the length of time indicated in the recipe.

Depending on your pressure cooker, there may be more than one pressure setting available, generally corresponding with 5, 10, and 15psi. At 5 pounds, the internal temperature is 228°F; at 10 pounds, it's 240°F; at 15 pounds, it's 250°F. The standard of 15psi is the most important setting because it is used in most recipes. Read the owner's manual to find out the pressure settings of your particular brand. To complicate matters, some nonstandard pressure cookers operate at a maximum setting ranging from 11psi to 13psi, which means that recipes will need to be adjusted for increased time to compensate for the lower pressure setting.

A modern pressure cooker has a three-ply base for even heat distribution. Once the heat is properly adjusted to maintain a stable pressure during the cooking process, it will require very little heat, and no further heat adjustments should be necessary.

Tips for Using Pressure Cookers on Glass-Top Stoves

Induction or glass-top stoves use an electromagnetic coil beneath a ceramic cooking surface that creates a magnetic field. This magnetic field passes through the cooking surface to ferrous (iron or steel) cookware, heating the pan and cooking the contents, so cookware used on these stoves needs to have magnetic properties. Nonmagnetic metal such as aluminum cannot be used on induction ranges. These stoves tend to cook at a very high heat, cycling on and off repeatedly—even as frequently as every few seconds—but the only heat generated is to the cookware itself; the cooktop remains relatively cool.

Be sure to read the owner's manual for your stove. Although most glass-top stove manufacturers approve of stainless-steel cookware, it's a good idea to check with the company about which pressure cookers are safe for use. A two-step method is useful; set one heating element to high and the second one to medium or low. Bring the pressure cooker to 15psi on the burner with the high-heat setting. As soon as the cooker is pressurized, move it to the second heating element with the lower temperature and begin timing. If you are having problems with food burning on your glass-top stove, despite your best efforts to lower or adjust the heat, then call for service and have the heat calibrated and adjusted.

Tips for Using Pressure Cookers on Electric Stoves

If you are using an electric stove, it will be somewhat more difficult to adjust the pressure cooker, because electric burners are notoriously slow to respond to temperature-control changes. As with glass-top stoves, it will help to heat two elements, one set to high and the second set to medium or low. Bring the pressure cooker to 15psi on the first burner using the high-heat setting. As soon as the cooker is pressurized, move it to the second heating element with the lower temperature and begin timing.

Tips for Owners of Electric Pressure Cookers

Unlike modern stovetop pressure cookers, the digital or electronic appliances are limited in their capabilities. They aren't practical to use for recipes or foods that require very short cooking times, or with the cold water release method (see page 6). In addition, some of the more advanced pressure-cooking techniques, such as the interrupted cooking method (see page 10), may prove to be quite challenging with many of these models.

There is no generally accepted standard among the makers of electric pressure cookers, so choose carefully and select a unit that adheres to the 15psi standard pressure setting, or to a corresponding temperature setting. Operating instructions vary widely, even between models made by the same manufacturer, so it's important to follow the directions in your owner's manual for basic operating instructions. In general, you can use the "brown" setting to do the initial sautéing and browning. Program the appliance for high pressure and set the timer for the amount of time recommended in the recipe. If the recipe calls for a cold water release, use the quick release mechanism instead, keeping in mind that the results may be less than expected or desired. Use the "brown" setting to do any final cooking after pressure is released.

Pressure Cookers with a Weighted Regulator, or Jiggle Top

If your pressure cooker uses a pressure regulator weight, or the old-style jiggle top, then it's necessary to expel the air from the inside of the cooker before placing the weight on the vent pipe. Set your heat at high and wait until you see steam flowing from the vent pipe. Now place the pressure regulator weight on top. Continue cooking at high heat until the regulator weight begins to rock rapidly and lots of steam is escaping. You may see some water droplets escaping from under the weight, and hissing and spitting is normal for this type of pressure cooker. Now is the time to immediately lower the heat on your stove appropriately. At this point, the pressure regulator should be rocking three to five times per minute and there will be a slight hissing of escaping steam during cooking. If the regulator is rocking continuously, the heat setting is too high and must be lowered. Once pressure has been achieved and you have lowered the heat, use a timer set for the length of time indicated in your recipe. It may be necessary to make several small adjustments to the heat setting over the length of the cooking time to maintain the desired pressure.

RELEASING PRESSURE

There are three methods for releasing the pressure in a modern stovetop pressure cooker. Recipes will indicate which release method to use at the end of the cooking process.

Cold Water Release Method

This is the fastest method to stop the cooking process by lowering the temperature and the pressure. This method is often used for foods with very short cooking times, or when it is essential to stop the cooking process as quickly as possible. Use this method for serving fresh, tender-crisp vegetables or delicate seafood. The pressure cooker is carried to the sink and tilted at a slight angle to allow cold water to run over the outer edge of the lid so that it runs down the side of the pot and across the top of the lid, but not directly over the vent or valve. If your faucet is too short to allow water to run over the top of the cooker, then use the sprayer attachment, if available. Otherwise, sit the pressure cooker in the sink filled with a couple of inches of cold water until the pressure drops.

When using the cold water release method, there are a couple of safety concerns to keep in mind. All modern pressure cookers should have two handles for easier lifting and carrying, but always be careful when carrying any large, heavy pot full of hot food. Always check to see that you have a clear path with nothing underfoot, such as children or pets. People of small stature, or those with physical limitations, may find it easier to slide the pressure cooker along the countertop from the stove to the sink.

Never run water directly over the pressure release vent or valve when using the cold water release method. Remember those old schoolroom physics demonstrations that created a vacuum by condensation? If you inadvertently run water directly over the venting mechanism during the cold water release, you may have a real-world demonstration of physics in action, much as I did. Once—and only once—I didn't pay attention and allowed water to run straight over the pressure regulator on a stainless-steel cooker. I heard a *POP* and the lid suddenly caved in—the metal was left with a depression in the middle that made it completely unusable. When a pressure cooker is heated, the air inside expands. When the cooker is removed from heat, the air molecules inside begin to cool and contract rapidly. If the vent or valve opening is blocked by a stream of water, the air molecules cannot get inside the cooker fast enough to replace the volume and there will be less air pressure inside the pot than outside. Those condensing air molecules then start pulling a vacuum, creating a powerful suction that can actually cause the lid, or the weakest area of the cooker, to collapse. If the vacuum is strong enough, it can actually pull the metal down into the pot. Usually there is no warning before this occurs; even in my case there was only a popping sound as a result of the lid caving in.

Quick Release Method

People often confuse the quick release with the cold water release, but these are two distinctly different methods. The quick release mechanism is found on modern pressure cookers, and while not as fast as the cold water release, this special valve rapidly releases pressure with just the turn of a knob or the push of a button. The quick release is used to drop the pressure without lowering the temperature of the food. This method is suggested if you wish to interrupt the cooking process to add some further ingredients or check food for doneness. When you're finished, the pressure cooker can be returned to pressure very quickly.

Do not use the quick release method for foods that increase in volume, or that froth or foam, or for those that are mostly liquids, like soup or broth. The quick release method may cause foods that have a tendency to foam to boil up and vent through the release valve. This happens when the pressure drops rapidly, and you can actually hear the food begin to boil when the temperature drops back to the normal boiling point.

Natural Release Method

This is the slowest, and the most often used, method of releasing pressure. The pressure cooker is removed from the heat source and the pressure is allowed to subside naturally. This gradual drop in pressure and temperature allows the food to finish cooking throughout the slow cool-down process. Use this method for most cuts of meat and for foods like beans, potatoes, or apples that have a skin or peel that you wish to remain intact. The natural release method is preferred for foods that increase in volume, and that froth or foam, and for those that are mostly liquids, like soup or broth, to prevent them from clogging the valve system.

There is no hard-and-fast rule to determine how long the cooling process will take before the cooker is depressurized. Factors such as the construction of the cooker and the volume and type of foods being cooked will affect the amount of time it takes for the pressure to drop. Be patient; an appropriate length of time should be about 15 minutes. After that, if you are in a hurry or can't wait any longer, then use the cold water release method to completely drop the remaining pressure.

Pressure-Cooking Techniques in This Book

Many people never go beyond learning one or two basic pressure cooker techniques, but there are several different ways of using moist heat for steaming, boiling, poaching, stewing, braising, and more.

INFUSION PRESSURE COOKING

There is no secret to infusion cooking; all pressure cookers infuse flavors if food is placed directly into a well-seasoned, flavorful broth or marinade rather than just plain water. The tasty combination of herbs, spices, and seasonings along with flavor-enhancing liquids are forced into the food. In using the infusion method, or super marinating, the cooking liquid will penetrate deep inside foods, not just sit on the outside, and create a richer-tasting sauce or gravy. Infusion cooking is appropriate for thinner cuts of meat like chicken pieces, chops, steaks, cut fruits and vegetables, and even polenta and risottos, but it is not as effective on thicker cuts of meat, like roasts.

STEAMING IN A PRESSURE COOKER

Steaming is the most often used method in pressure cooking, and not surprisingly, it is one of the healthiest ways to cook because no additional fat is necessary for cooking. The pressure cooker excels as a first-class steamer, and by using a rack, fats drain away from food. Pressure cooker steaming takes only a few minutes for most foods, minimizing the loss of nutrients while preserving the vibrant colors and textures of even the most delicate foods. Steaming is often used for Asian recipes; fluffy rice and other grains; fresh, tender-crisp vegetables; and delicate fish or seafood. Serve up everything from hot, buttery garlic bread to traditional English molded puddings by using this method. In all cases, plain water is used to produce steam, and foods are elevated above the water line.

STEWING IN A PRESSURE COOKER

Stewing, not to be confused with a recipe for a stew, is a moist-heat cooking method much like infusion cooking, except that, generally, plain water is used instead of a flavoring liquid, although it's certainly possible to use any combination of liquids that will enhance or complement the food. Stewing is the ideal cooking method for small cubes of meat from the toughest cuts of beef, such as the round, flank, plate, and shank. Stewing is also used for vegetables like stewed tomatoes and fruits such as stewed prunes. A rack is not typically used in this cooking method, and the liquid should cover the ingredients.

BOILING IN A PRESSURE COOKER

Boiling is the cooking method of choice to turn otherwise inedible bones, such as a turkey carcass, into a rich, nutrient-dense broth or stock. Boiling tough meats such as tongue and heart, or smoked, salt-cured, or brined or pickled meats makes them more palatable and digestible. It takes longer to bring the cooker to pressure when using the boiling method. A rack may be used as desired, and the meat is covered with plain water and any appropriate seasonings.

PACKET PRESSURE COOKING

Similar to PIP cooking (see page 9) and also used in tiered pressure cooking (see page 10), this method is quick and easy but is used primarily for preparing individual servings, or for separating small amounts of individual foods without intermingling flavors, and even reheating foods that might dry out in an oven. In packet cooking, the ingredients are centered on a square of heavy-duty aluminum foil, and then the foil is tightly sealed and placed on a rack above the water level for steaming. Several layers of packets can be stacked or layered in this manner.

BRAISING IN A PRESSURE COOKER

You may be familiar with braising from regular stovetop cooking recipes for dishes like the classic osso buco. This moist-heat cooking method is often used to cook tough cuts of meat, and sometimes fish, seafood, or vegetables. The pressure cooker teams up beautifully with braising recipes, turning out very tender dishes with full-bodied sauces.

In braising, meats and vegetables are usually cut into larger serving-size portions, rather than small cubes as in stewing. Meats can be dusted with seasoned flour, which will thicken the sauce, and then browned in a small amount of hot fat in the pressure cooker. The amount of liquid, which can be anything from water or stock to wine, beer, or tomato juice, covers only about half of the food to be braised. At the end of cooking, the braising vegetables can either be removed and discarded or pureed and incorporated into the sauce.

PRECOOKING IN A PRESSURE COOKER

A pressure cooker can really be a timesaver in the kitchen when used to precook large cuts of pork, beef, lamb, chicken, ham, or turkey that would normally take hours to cook by traditional means. Precook a "roast" chicken in the pressure cooker, and then pop it in a hot oven with a glaze, or baste with butter to brown and crisp the skin. Use a pressure cooker to precook roasts, and then use the meat for shredded barbecue sandwiches, tacos, fajitas, burritos, pita bread fillings, or salads. For falling-off-the-bone, tender barbecued ribs, precook them in the pressure cooker and finish them up on the grill or under the broiler. Precook several pounds of chicken wings in the pressure cooker, brush on your favorite barbecue sauce, and put them in the oven for a party-size platter of hot wings.

POACHING IN A PRESSURE COOKER

Poaching allows certain foods to retain their natural tenderness, texture, and delicate flavor. The pressure cooker does an outstanding job with this very healthy cooking method because no additional fat is required. Always use small or thin cuts of food for poaching so that they can finish cooking very quickly. Foods are cooked directly in a small amount of liquid; water is used most often but other ingredients may be added to provide additional flavor. When the poaching process is completed, the liquid can be saved as a broth for later use, or it can be reduced to intensify the flavors and then served with the poached food.

PIP (PAN IN POT) PRESSURE COOKING

A PIP recipe calls for placing food in a separate pan and then inserting that pan into the pressure cooker, leaving sufficient space between the insert and the side of the cooker to allow steam to move freely. This method has the added benefit of eliminating any accidentally burned or scorched foods. It is an excellent way to prepare casseroles, one-pot meals, a perfect bowl of rice, or even a scrumptious cheesecake.

When using PIP recipes, do not fill the insert pan more than two-thirds full, or more than half full for foods that foam, froth, or expand. Use the natural release method (see page 7), and avoid the sudden drop in temperature caused by using the quick or cold water release methods (see pages 6, 7), which may cause the foods to boil over.

Many pressure cookers already come with an assortment of inserts such as steamer baskets, trays, and other stackable pans. Acceptable substitutions may be found right in your kitchen, or accessory items can be ordered from any manufacturer, as long as the diameter will fit loosely inside your pressure cooker. A rack is necessary with this cooking method, and plain water is used to produce steam. Foil helper handles (see page 11) make it easier to position the insert and remove the pan from the cooker.

INTERRUPTED PRESSURE COOKING

In this method, the longest cooking ingredients are started first, and then the cooking is interrupted to add shorter cooking ingredients using the quick release method (see page 7) to drop the pressure rapidly without losing heat. The modern pressure cookers with the quick release mechanisms make it easier than ever to use the interrupted cooking method to prepare more recipes than ever before.

When making beef stew, for example, the beef takes 15 minutes to cook, but the vegetables need only 5 minutes. Many cooks will add everything to the pressure cooker at the same time, only to end up with mushy vegetables. The correct method is to partially cook the meat for 10 minutes, remove the pot from the heat, and use the quick release to drop the pressure without lowering the temperature. The lid is then removed, the shorter-cooking vegetables are added, and the pressure lid is then locked back in place. The pressure cooker is returned to pressure for the last 5 minutes of cooking time for tender meat and perfectly cooked vegetables. It's quite possible to use the interrupted cooking method more than once in preparing a recipe that uses several different ingredients with varying cooking times.

TIERED PRESSURE COOKING

This advanced pressure-cooking method is a variation of the PIP cooking technique, using more than one pan inside the pressure cooker to cook several different foods, or even an entire two- or three-course meal at the same time. The secret of this method is to select foods or recipes with the same, or very close, cooking times and have a pressure cooker of a large enough size to accommodate everything on your menu. Alternatively, this technique can be combined with the interrupted cooking technique for foods with very different cooking times.

A trivet or rack is used to raise the insert pans above the water level. The bottom tier is for meat or the longest-cooking ingredient, with the side dish(es) placed on top. Depending on the size of your pressure cooker, pans can be stacked in two or more tiers. Stainless steel, aluminum, or tightly sealed aluminum foil packets can all be used inside the pressure cooker. Glass, ceramic, or other clay-fired bowls are the least acceptable, as they require extra cooking time because of their poor heat-conducting properties.

STEAM ROASTING OR BAKING IN A PRESSURE COOKER

Steam roasting is a moist-heat cooking method that results in tender and flavorful meats; moist breads and cakes; fluffy "baked" potatoes; and delectable casserole-type dishes. It is different than oven roasting in that there is less moisture lost and meats do not shrink as much. Meats should be seared in hot fat and quickly browned on all sides before steam roasting. Foods are placed on a rack or steaming basket well above the water level and are cooked in superheated steam.

Accessory Items

If your cooker does not come with any accessories, it's quite all right to use products from a different manufacturer as long as the diameter is slightly smaller than the inside of your pressure cooker. Search your kitchen; you may already have several pans or dishes on hand that can be used inside the pressure cooker. Look around the cooking section of local stores and on the Internet for additional items such as mini Bundt pans, small springform pans, mini loaf pans, ramekins or custard cups, pudding basins and molds, tube pans, and small cake pans. Metal pans are preferable because of their superior heating properties. In the early days of pressure cookery, resourceful cooks gathered a collection of wide, short, and tall empty food cans that could be easily arranged inside the cooker. Boston brown bread, for example, an old-time pressure cooker recipe, is traditionally made in a can.

THE MATERIAL DIFFERENCE

Any type of heatproof dish can be used in the pressure cooker; remember that the inside temperature at 15psi is 250°F, well below that of an oven. Some materials heat better than others, and choosing just the right dish for use as a PIP (Pan in Pot) insert can affect the cooking time as well as the results of the finished recipe.

Metal containers will heat faster than any other material, and they may also provide a slight amount of browning to make a more appealing presentation. Glass or ceramic containers will absorb heat more slowly and heat unevenly, which means foods will take longer to cook. When using nonmetallic dishware, plan to increase the cooking time by 5 to 10 percent to allow for the extra thickness and slower heating properties. Avoid using fired clay bowls, especially foreign imports, because the applied glazes may not be food-safe.

RACKS AND TRIVETS

Most modern pressure cookers come with an indispensable stainless-steel or aluminum rack or trivet. In a pinch, use canning rings, or a heavy heatproof ceramic, stoneware, or earthenware saucer, bowl, or small plate. You can purchase a round, seven-inch wire cake rack in most kitchen shops, or you can use a collapsible stainless-steel steamer basket in place of a rack. Extra racks can be purchased from most pressure cooker manufacturers, and they are easily interchangeable between brands as long as the diameter does not exceed the width of your cooker.

The main purpose of a rack is to raise foods or pan inserts above the waterline for steaming. By raising foods off the bottom of the cooker, you can minimize the chance of scorching foods. A rack may also be used when several items need to be stacked or arranged in layers. When using individual custard cups, for example, a rack is placed on the bottom of the cooker to elevate the ramekins, and then a second rack is placed on top of the first layer to serve as a stable platform for the second tier of cups. Racks can also be used to separate foods, such as a three-course meal of pork chops, baked potatoes, and stuffed apples, making it easier to remove each component when the cooking process is completed. Finally, a rack can also be placed on top of bulky foods like greens or cabbage to keep them away from the underside of the lid as they quickly wilt and diminish in volume.

LIDS FOR INSERT PANS

Some recipes will require a dish with a lid, turning the covered dish into a miniature oven inside the pressure cooker. A lid might be used to contain the steam in the dish, transferring heat from the steam vapor, both inside and outside the dish, to the food. A lid can also protect the food from condensation that may drip from the lid during the cool-down phase. Some accessory pans, like a pudding mold, come with a convenient lid, but a square of aluminum foil, tightly crimped over the top of the pan, makes a reasonable substitute. Use cooking spray, or lightly butter the inside of the pan as well as the inside of the lid or foil covering, to prevent food from sticking.

FOIL HELPER HANDLES

To make a foil helper handle, tear off a length of heavy-duty aluminum foil long enough to center the dish, and fold the ends over the top of it. Begin by folding the sheet of foil in half lengthwise, and then fold it in half again, ending up with a long, double-folded narrow strip of foil. With the dish placed in the center of the strip, bring the ends up over the top of the dish to use as a helper handle. Now the insert can be easily lowered into the pressure cooker; just fold or tuck the ends down so they will not interfere with the lid. When the dish has finished cooking, use the handy helper handles to lift the hot dish out of the cooker. Use two helper handles with large cuts of meat like roasts and whole chicken or for lifting heavy dishes.

Tips and Tricks

When the pressure cooker is filled at or near the maximum two-thirds capacity, it will take longer to reach full pressure. This may be a problem when cooking thick sauces or stews and may cause scorching on the bottom. To reduce the time it will take to pressurize the cooker, start simmering the liquid while chopping the rest of the ingredients. Bring it to a boil, stirring occasionally, and then lock the lid in place.

When cooking breads or puddings with a leavening agent (baking powder, baking soda), remember that it must have room to rise, so do not fill the mold more than two-thirds full.

If you don't have a suitable insert pan, simply use a bowl of the appropriate size to shape a double layer of heavy-duty aluminum foil into a bowl. Leave the top of the foil bowl open, unless stated otherwise in the recipe. Always place the foil bowl on a rack and not in direct contact with the bottom of the cooker. Make sure to leave enough space between the bowl

Pan Sizes and Volume

Pan Size	Approximate Volume
ROUND PAN	
5″ × 2″	2⅔ cups
6″ × 2″	3¾ cups
7″ × 1¼″	2 cups
8″ × 1½″	4 cups
CASSEROLE DISH	
1 quart	4 cups
1½ quarts	6 cups
2 quarts	8 cups
2½ quarts	10 cups
SPRINGFORM PAN	
8″ × 3″	6 cups
BUNDT PAN	
7″ × 3″	6 cups

Pan Size	Approximate Volume
CHARLOTTE MOLD	
6″ × 4¼″	7½ cups
CUSTARD CUP	
2¾″ × 1½″	½ cup
3″ × 1¼″	⅝ cup
LOAF PAN	
5½″ × 3″ × 2½″	2 cups
6″ × 4½″ × 3″	3 cups
TUBE PAN OR RING MOLD	
7½″ × 2″	4 cups
7½″ × 3″	6 cups
8″ × 3″	9 cups

Quick Guide to Accessories and Their Heat Conduction Properties

Metal Type	Heat Properties	Notes
BEST CHOICES FOR HEAT CONDUCTION		
Copper: bowls, molds, pans, pudding basins, Bundt pan	Accepts heat faster than any other metal; heats evenly; loses heat quickly	Best are coated or lined with tin; can be reactive with some foods; not very durable
Aluminum: trivets and racks, bowls; molds; tube, small cake, springform, mini loaf and Bundt pans; steamers; separators or dividers; pudding basins; egg poachers	Heats quick and evenly	Can discolor easily, but easily cleaned; reacts with some foods; hand washing required for some
Stainless: trivets and racks, steel bowls, molds, pans, steamers, separators or dividers, pudding basins, pasta steamer baskets	Heats quickly	Durable and nonreactive
SECOND CHOICE FOR HEAT CONDUCTION		
Recycled substitutes: disposable aluminum pans, foil packets or shaped bowls, 1-pound coffee cans, cookie tins, assorted empty food cans	Heats quickly	Readily available, toss after use, no cleanup; foil can be shaped for small or odd shapes; aluminum reacts with some foods
Wood: trivets, bamboo steamer baskets, skewers	Does not transfer heat when wet	Inexpensive; must be soaked before using; porous; may be difficult to clean; not very durable
THIRD CHOICE FOR HEAT CONDUCTION		
Ceramics, vitrified ceramic, porcelain, other heatproof glassware: ramekins, custard cups, pudding basins, soufflé dishes, mini Bundt pans, quiche, tart, and flan pans, Corningware, Pyrex	Heats slowly and unevenly; matte finishes increase heat absorption slightly; retains heat extremely well	Can chip or break; may be the only choice available with certain shapes or sizes
Stoneware, Earthenware, fired clay: ramekins, custard cups, pudding basins, soufflé dishes	Heats slowly and evenly, but retains its temperature for a long time	Avoid glazes that are not food-safe: follow manufacturer's guidelines for allowed safe uses and care

and the sides of the pressure cooker for steam to circulate freely.

When chopping foods to be cooked together, be sure the pieces are of similar size so that they will cook in the same amount of time.

You can always cook small items in a large pressure cooker, but not the reverse. Never exceed the maximum fill rules, and always use at least the minimum amount of liquid as recommended by the manufacturer and required by the length of cooking.

Do not allow the liquid to touch the food when steaming or the food will boil and overcook.

When cooking in tiers, place meats, fish, or juicy foods in the bottom tiers so they cannot drip onto foods below. Place the larger or longer-cooking foods on the bottom, where they are closest to the heat source. Foods cooked in upper tiers cook slower because they are farther away from the heat, so plan ahead and place the most delicate ingredients on top. Always leave space around the insert pans to allow steam to circulate and cook more efficiently.

When cooking whole potatoes, use the natural release method to keep the skin intact. To make it easier to peel the skin after cooking, use the cold water release method.

Foods that rise, such as cakes and puddings, require a preliminary steaming period before the cooker is pressurized. There are several methods to use: (1) For pressure cookers with a spring valve, use a regular lid or leave the pressure lid ajar and not in the locking position. (2) For a pressure cooker with a removable or weighted regulator, simply remove it from the vent pipe and let the steam escape freely, or leave the pressure lid ajar and not in the locking position.

Kitchen Shortcuts and Frugal Tips

Frozen foods can really cut down the prep work and get you out of the kitchen in record time. Frozen chicken, for example, comes in a wide variety of choices; I stock up on large bags of boneless and skinless chicken breasts and thighs. If you don't want to go to the trouble of cutting up a round steak, then by all means buy the precut stew meat.

If you don't have time for all that peeling, chopping, and dicing when it comes to preparing fresh vegetables, or you don't have all the fresh vegetables called for, then by all means substitute frozen vegetables.

Many fresh vegetables can be quickly prepared and frozen in convenient serving portions. Take advantage of sales to stock up on fresh vegetables and herbs like onions, celery, carrots, carrots, and my favorite, cilantro. After a little slicing and dicing, just measure them out in convenient amounts, seal them up in a plastic freezer bag, and tuck them into the freezer for use whenever needed.

Fresh herbs are available all year long, and they are a quick way to transform ordinary meals into extraordinary meals. As a general guideline when exchanging fresh herbs for dried for use in a pressure cooker, use three times as much of the fresh variety as you would use of a dried herb. Herbs are great to have on hand, but they do not keep. The good news is they freeze rather well, and in the process the flavor and aroma intensifies. To freeze fresh herbs, wash, drain, and pat dry with paper towels. Fill the sections of an ice-cube tray about half full with chopped herbs, cover with water, and freeze. Transfer the frozen cubes to a freezer bag, and then they are ready to drop into soups, stews, and sauces as needed. Be aware that frozen herbs are not suitable for garnish, as they become wilted and darker in color after thawing.

Be a frugal cook and save and freeze vegetable trimmings, meat and bone scraps, and other leftover ingredients that might otherwise be tossed for making a great pot of free stock.

To remove the last bit of fat from stew or broth, drop a lettuce leaf in the pot to absorb excess grease.

Twenty-Five Important Dos and Don'ts

1. Pressure cooking is really fairly simple once you become familiar with how the cooker operates. The best place to start is always the owner's manual. Do read it thoroughly and make sure you understand all the new terms and processes for this exciting method of cooking.
2. Do not use oils, fats, or grease in any quantity beyond ¼ cup or exceed the amount recommended by the pressure cooker manufacturer.
3. Do not cook thick sauces, such as spaghetti or pasta-type sauces, without thinning them first with ½ cup of liquid for every 2 cups of sauce. Thick sauces take much longer to heat up, and that means the pot takes longer to pressurize, increasing the possibility of scorching the sauce.
4. Do not overcook; remember that pressure cooker timing depends on the size of the individual pieces of food, not the quantity.
5. As a general rule, do not add milk, cream, cheese, or other dairy products at the beginning of pressure cooking because they tend to scorch, and high heat causes the milk solids to separate and curdle.
6. Do not add too much salt when pressure cooking. Everyone has personal or dietary preferences for the amount of salt used in their food; wait until the food is cooked and then adjust to taste.
7. Do read the recipe from start to finish before you began. Make sure you understand the cooking processes and methods used. Make sure that you have all the necessary ingredients and equipment required to complete the recipe.
8. Do not use a pressure cooker without setting a timer.
9. Do not use a pressure cooker as a pressure fryer. Never, ever. There are special pressure fryers available specifically for that purpose, which operate with much lower pressure than a standard pressure cooker, and the two appliances are not interchangeable.
10. Just as you would not leave a broiler or grill unsupervised, do not leave your pressure cooker unattended.
11. When combining several different ingredients with slightly different cooking times, do cut foods that cook more quickly into slightly larger pieces, and cut those that cook with longer cooking times into smaller pieces.
12. Do cut the same foods into pieces of uniform size to promote even cooking.
13. Do remember to brown meats first. This important step not only improves the visual appearance but also adds increased flavor and improves the taste.
14. When a recipe calls for frozen vegetables, do not allow them to thaw before putting them in the pressure cooker. Thawing

will affect the cooking time and result in the vegetables being overcooked.

15. When a recipe calls for frozen vegetables, break up any solid clumps to assure uniform cooking, but again, do not allow them to thaw.

16. Do not add thickeners such as flour or cornstarch at the start of pressure cooking, because they can thicken the sauce to the point where it begins to burn. Instead, wait until the pot is pressurized and then thicken the sauce as desired.

17. To minimize foaming and frothing, do add a spoonful of cooking oil.

18. Do not use less cooking liquid than the minimum amount recommended by the manufacturer.

19. To mingle the flavors of different foods in a pressure cooker, do let them come into contact with the cooking liquid, which will distribute the flavors.

20. To keep the flavors of different foods separate in a pressure cooker, do place the foods on a rack or steamer basket well above the water level. Steam does not transmit, blend, or mix flavors.

21. When pressure cooking breads or cakes that contain a leavening agent such as baking powder or baking soda, a 15-minute period of steaming is required to allow the recipe to rise before the cooker is pressurized. With a pressure cooker that uses a removable regulator, just remove the weight for the steaming. For a modern pressure cooker with a spring-loaded valve, use a regular lid instead of the locking pressure lid. Check the water level, replenishing with boiling water if necessary, before locking the lid in place.

22. A pressure cooker with a three-ply base is the best defense against scorched foods. One old-fashioned trick is to layer the ingredients in such a way that foods with high sugar or starch content are not placed near the bottom of the cooker.

23. Do not alter the cooking times when multiplying or dividing a recipe. The amount of food in the pressure cooker has no bearing on the cooking time. For example, a dozen pork chops will cook just as quickly as one.

24. If using a pressure cooker with an electric or glass-top stove, do set one burner on high heat and a second one on a lower heat. Bring the cooker up to pressure on the high-heat burner, and then move it to the second burner for the rest of cooking.

25. Do remember to perform routine maintenance on your pressure cooker, and periodically check the screws that hold handles and valve assemblies in place, tightening them as needed.

breakfast

bacon, potato, and tomato frittata

Think of frittatas as open-faced omelets, or as a quiche sans crust. Sometimes they're plain, but usually they include fillings like cheese and vegetables. This frittata is perfect by itself or with some fresh fruit for a Sunday morning breakfast or brunch. It's also versatile enough to serve as a complete meal for a quick weeknight dinner with a crisp green salad and some crusty bread. • SERVES 4

- 2 medium russet potatoes, scrubbed and halved
- 1 tablespoon butter, softened, for greasing the insert pan
- 1 small Roma tomato, thinly sliced
- 6 strips bacon, cooked until crisp and crumbled
- ⅓ cup chopped scallions
- 3 large eggs
- ¼ cup heavy cream
- Salt and coarsely ground black pepper to taste
- Dash of Louisiana-style hot sauce
- ½ cup shredded sharp cheddar cheese
- Prepared salsa, for serving

Place the cooking rack in the bottom of the pressure cooker and add ⅔ cup water. Put the potatoes in the pressure cooker. Lock the lid in place. Bring to 15psi over high heat and immediately reduce the heat to the lowest possible setting to stabilize and maintain that pressure. Cook for 10 minutes. Remove from the heat and use the natural release method before opening the lid. When cool enough to handle, peel the potatoes and chop them into small pieces.

Butter a metal or silicon insert pan that will fit within your pressure cooker. Make an even layer of chopped potatoes in the insert pan. Layer some of the tomatoes, bacon, and scallions evenly over the potatoes. Repeat the layering with the remaining potatoes, tomatoes, bacon, and scallions.

In a small bowl, beat together the eggs, cream, salt and pepper, and hot sauce. Pour the mixture over the top of the potato layers, shaking the pan to distribute it throughout.

(continued)

Tightly crimp a square of aluminum foil over the top of the insert pan. Use foil helper handles under the insert pan to place the covered insert pan on top of the cooking rack. Lock the lid in place. Bring to 15psi over high heat and immediately reduce the heat to the lowest possible setting to stabilize and maintain that pressure. Cook for 10 minutes. Remove from the heat and use the quick release method before opening the lid.

Lift the insert pan out of the pressure cooker and immediately remove the foil cover. Sprinkle the cheese on top and put the lid back on the pressure cooker again, but leave it ajar and do not lock it in position. Wait about 3 minutes or until the cheese melts. To serve, spoon a portion of the frittata on each dinner plate and top with salsa as desired.

Variation:

HAM, POTATO, AND TOMATO FRITTATA

Omit the bacon and substitute 1 cup fully cooked or leftover diced ham.

southwest sausage frittata

Think of a frittata as an inside-out omelet without all the fussing and folding. How simple could it be? Just mix the ingredients together and cook it for a few minutes in the pressure cooker. If you're cooking for a crowd, fill as many stacked insert pans as will fit inside your pressure cooker, taking care not to exceed the one-third full rule. Use the same ingredients in each pan or something completely different for more variety. Frittatas are easily customized, so if you don't feel like shopping, improvise with what you have on hand and use up all those odd bits of leftover vegetables. • **SERVES 4**

2 medium russet potatoes, scrubbed
1 tablespoon butter, softened, for greasing the insert pan
8 ounces chorizo sausage, cooked, crumbled, and well drained
3 scallions, white and green parts sliced separately
½ cup thawed frozen corn kernels
1 cup grated pepper Jack cheese
3 large eggs, beaten
Salt and coarsely ground black pepper to taste
1 cup prepared salsa
1 avocado, pitted, peeled, and sliced

Place the cooking rack in the bottom of the pressure cooker and add ⅔ cup water. Put the potatoes in the pressure cooker. Lock the lid in place. Bring to 15psi over high heat and immediately reduce the heat to the lowest possible setting to stabilize and maintain that pressure. Cook for 10 minutes. Remove from the heat and use the natural release method before opening the lid. When cool enough to handle, slice the potatoes about ⅛ inch thick.

Butter a metal or silicon insert pan that will fit within your pressure cooker. Make a layer of sliced potatoes in the insert pan. Add a layer of crumbled sausage, some of the white scallion slices, and a layer of corn. Sprinkle on a layer of cheese. Repeat with the remaining potatoes, sausage, scallions, and cheese, ending with a layer of cheese. Pour the eggs over top, shaking the pan to distribute throughout. Sprinkle with salt and pepper. Cover the insert pan with a square of aluminum foil, crimping it tightly around the rim. Use foil helper handles to place the insert pan in the pressure cooker. Lock the lid in place. Bring to 15psi over high heat and immediately reduce the heat to the lowest possible setting to stabilize and maintain that pressure. Cook for 10 minutes. Remove from the heat and use the quick release method before opening the lid. Lift the insert pan out of the pressure cooker and immediately remove the foil covering.

Spoon a portion of the frittata on each dinner plate and top with a spoonful of the salsa. Sprinkle some of the green scallion slices on top and then add a couple of the avocado slices. Pass the remaining salsa at the table.

soft-cooked eggs with accompaniments

When I was growing up, soft-cooked eggs were a regular breakfast item in my family. I get all nostalgic remembering how my mother always did meals with great style and pizzazz, so there were starched table linens—I still loath ironing!—set with her pretty blue Delft breakfast plates and matching eggcups with the absurd little "baby spoons" for eating the custardy white and yolk. We had special antique egg scissors, where one blade is like a guillotine to lop the top off the eggshell and expose the yummy contents. There was a blue Delft toast caddy, too; a contraption that keeps the slices of buttered toast separate so they stay crisp. The house rule was to take a piece of toast, cut it into narrow strips, and then position your "soldiers" around the eggcup, ready for dipping into the soft yolk.

If you don't have an eggcup to cradle your egg, a shot glass is a fine substitute, or use anything in your kitchen that will hold the egg upright, or just scoop the egg onto a piece of toast. You don't even need the nifty little egg scissors with a chicken on them, my dears, now that you can buy round gadgets that will remove the end of the eggshell with perfect surgical precision. Or you can easily DIY by gently tapping around the top of the egg with a spoon to get to the hidden gold inside. I like to break my soft-cooked eggs into a ramekin and then add a knob of butter, some salt and pepper, and perhaps a little hot sauce, and then use my "soldiers" to dip out the yolk, followed by a spoon to get what's left. • **SERVES 2 TO 4**

4 large very fresh eggs
4 slices whole wheat toast, for serving

Optional Garnishes

- 3 tablespoons minced fresh chives
- 2 strips bacon, cooked until crisp and crumbled
- 2 tablespoons butter, softened
- 3 tablespoons hot heavy cream
- Hot sauce

Gently wash the eggs. Place the cooking rack in the bottom of the pressure cooker and add ½ cup water. Place the eggs in a perforated steaming basket so they are well above the water line. Lock the lid in place. Bring to 15psi over high heat and immediately reduce the heat to the lowest possible setting to stabilize and maintain that pressure. Cook for 1 minute (yes, 60 seconds) for soft-cooked eggs with delicious molten yolk centers to accompany bread soldiers for dipping. Cook for 1½ minutes (90 seconds) for medium-cooked eggs, if you prefer to tuck in with a spoon. Remove from the heat and use the quick release method before opening the lid. Serve immediately with the toast and the garnishes of your choice.

polenta with asparagus tips and shirred eggs

At one time, shirred eggs were on everyone's brunch repertoire. Served in individual ramekins, they looked elegant at a posh luncheon, but they are so quick and easy to prepare that they make a great light supper as well. I love the colors of this dish, with the white of the cream, the gold from the yolk and the polenta, and the green of the asparagus. The different colors and textures all combine to please the palate as well as the eye. • **SERVES 4**

Step One: THE POLENTA

1½ cups boiling water
2 tablespoons butter
1 tablespoon minced garlic
Salt and coarsely ground black pepper to taste
1½ cups chicken broth
1 cup polenta or stone-ground coarse cornmeal
1½ cups shredded Gruyère cheese
2 scallions, minced

Place the cooking rack in the bottom of the pressure cooker and add ½ cup water. Place a 1½-quart metal insert bowl on the rack and pour the boiling water into the bowl. Add the butter, garlic, and salt and pepper to the bowl. Add the broth. Gradually sprinkle the polenta into the bowl while stirring continuously with a wire whisk. Lock the lid in place. Bring to 15psi over high heat and immediately reduce the heat to the lowest possible setting to stabilize and maintain that pressure. Cook for 5 minutes. Remove from the heat and use the natural release method before opening the lid. The polenta may look thin but it will thicken as it cools. Stir the cheese and scallions into the polenta and move the bowl to a low oven to keep warm. Rinse out the pressure cooker and proceed with step two.

Step Two: THE ASPARAGUS AND SHIRRED EGGS

2 tablespoons butter
8 large eggs
Salt and coarsely ground black pepper to taste
4 tablespoons heavy cream
Hot paprika to taste
1 pound thin asparagus spears, tips only

Place the cooking rack in the bottom of the pressure cooker and add ½ cup water. Grease 4 (6-ounce) ramekins with the butter. Break 2 large eggs into each ramekin and sprinkle with salt and pepper. Slowly pour 1 tablespoon cream over each dish of eggs and dust lightly with paprika. Cover each ramekin with a small square of aluminum foil. Arrange the ramekins on the cooking rack. Place the asparagus tips in a steamer basket and set it on top of the ramekins. Lock the lid in place. Bring to 15psi over high heat and immediately reduce the heat to the lowest possible setting to stabilize and maintain that pressure. Cook for 3 minutes. Remove from the heat and use the quick release method before opening the lid.

Step Three: TO SERVE

Stir the polenta just before serving. Spoon a portion on the side of each dinner plate. Add a portion of asparagus tips on top of the polenta. Remove the foil from the ramekins and place a ramekin on each plate. Finish by grinding some black pepper over the top if desired.

COOK'S NOTE: Scrape any remaining polenta into a greased loaf pan, cover, and refrigerate. When chilled and firm, the polenta may be fried or toasted and served with butter and syrup, honey, or jam. Frugal cooks will chop up the remaining asparagus stalks and freeze them for later use in soups or for making stock.

---

upside-down swiss chard quiche

If you've never tried fresh Swiss chard or kale, you're missing the mild, slightly sweet taste of these beautiful and delectable leafy greens. Both of them are lovely to look at: The kale is deep green with ruffled leaves, and some varieties of Swiss chard sport an explosion of colorful stalks with a rainbow of colors from lemon yellow and bright orange to cherry red and fuchsia pink. In this quiche, the cheesy cornmeal crust is on top so that it will rise a little and not absorb the liquid from the layer of vegetables hidden underneath. Serve hot as the star attraction for brunch or a light supper, or chill and cut into bite-size squares for an appetizer. • **SERVES 4**

Step One: THE GREENS

1 bunch Swiss chard, kale, or spinach

Examine the chard leaves and cut away any blemished or discolored parts. If using spinach, remove the stems and tear the larger leaves into smaller pieces. For kale or chard, remove the tough stalks and cut away the bottom third of each leaf. Roll up the remaining leaves into a long cigar shape and cut them into 1-inch-wide strips.

Place the cooking rack in the bottom of the pressure cooker and add ⅔ cup water. Put the chopped leaves in the pressure cooker. The leaves will take up a lot of space until they start to wilt. Lock the lid in place. Bring to 15psi over high heat and immediately reduce the heat to the lowest possible setting to stabilize and maintain that pressure. Cook for 2 minutes. Remove from the heat and use the quick release method before opening the lid. Immediately drain the leaves in a colander set in the sink. Remove the cooking rack, rinse out the pressure cooker, and proceed with step two.

Step Two: THE FILLING

2 tablespoons butter plus 1 tablespoon butter, softened, for greasing insert pan
⅓ cup minced onion
2 cloves garlic, minced
½ cup chopped red bell pepper
2 large eggs
¼ cup milk
½ teaspoon Louisiana-style hot sauce, or to taste
1 tablespoon all-purpose flour
1 teaspoon salt

Heat the 2 tablespoons butter in the pressure cooker over medium-high heat. Add the onion and garlic, and cook, stirring, until softened, about 4 minutes. Add the bell pepper and drained chard and cook, stirring, until they are soft and wilted.

In a mixing bowl, beat together the eggs, milk, hot sauce, and flour, then stir in the salt and the chard mixture. With the softened butter grease a metal or silicon insert pan that will fit within your pressure cooker. Spread the filling mixture in the pan, pressing it flat and smooth.

Step Three: THE CRUST

- 1 (8-ounce) package corn muffin mix
- ⅔ cup shredded Swiss cheese
- ½ cup thawed frozen corn kernels, drained
- 1 large egg
- ¼ cup milk
- 2 tablespoons butter, melted

In a mixing bowl, beat together the muffin mix, cheese, corn, egg, milk, and butter until just moistened. Spread the corn muffin batter evenly over the chard mixture in the insert pan. Cover the insert pan with a square of aluminum foil. Place the cooking rack in the bottom of the pressure cooker and add ½ cup water. Use foil helper handles to set the insert pan in the pressure cooker. Lock the lid in place. Bring to 15psi over high heat and immediately reduce the heat to the lowest possible setting to stabilize and maintain that pressure. Cook for 12 minutes. Remove from the heat and use the natural release method before opening the lid. Lift out of the pressure cooker and cool for 5 minutes before cutting into wedges.

COOK'S NOTE: The frugal cook will chop up all the Swiss chard ribs and freeze them for later use in soups.

---

savory fresh tomato and squash tart

With vivid red tomatoes and yellow squash, this savory tart is as beautiful to look at as it is to eat. It's simple, pretty, and truly delicious as a dazzling dish for brunch, lunch, or a light supper. Serve hot with a cup of soup or chilled with a bowl of fresh fruit. • **SERVES 4 TO 6**

Step One: THE CRUST

1½ cups dry bread crumbs
¼ cup grated Parmesan cheese
2 tablespoons butter, melted
½ teaspoon dried Italian herb blend

In a small bowl, combine the bread crumbs, cheese, butter, and herb blend. Coat a round metal insert pan that will fit within your pressure cooker with nonstick cooking spray and then press the crumb mixture over the bottom and partway up the sides. Use the back of a spoon to create a smooth surface. Chill in the refrigerator while you prepare the filling.

Step Two: THE FILLING

3 large eggs
½ cup heavy cream
2 tablespoons chopped fresh basil
1 clove garlic, minced
½ teaspoon sea salt
½ teaspoon Louisiana-style hot sauce
1 cup shredded mozzarella cheese
2 or 3 ripe Roma tomatoes, sliced ¼ inch thick
1 small summer squash, sliced ¼ inch thick
2 scallion tops, chopped

In a medium bowl, whisk together the eggs, cream, basil, garlic, salt, and hot sauce. Layer the fillings in the chilled crust in the following order: Spread ½ cup of the cheese over the crust, then pour about one-third of the egg mixture over the top. Decoratively arrange the tomato and squash slices in a single layer, forming concentric circles, and then add half of the remaining egg mixture. Top with the remaining cheese and pour the remainder of the egg mixture over all, shaking the pan to settle the contents.

Cover the insert pan with a lid or tightly crimp a square of aluminum foil over the top. Place the cooking rack in the bottom of the pressure cooker and add ½ cup water. Use foil helper handles to lower the insert pan into the pressure cooker. Lock the lid in place. Bring to 15psi over high heat and immediately reduce the heat to the lowest possible setting to stabilize and maintain that pressure. Cook for 10 minutes. Remove from the heat and use the quick release method before opening the lid. Top with the scallions before serving.

COOK'S NOTE: For an attractive variation on this recipe, use other varieties of fresh tomatoes and squash in differing colors depending on the seasonal vegetables that are available in your market.

---

ham and potato hash

This easy breakfast hash goes perfectly with eggs. Let me clarify that: Not only is this a tasty breakfast or brunch dish with eggs, but you should also try it for lunch with some homemade fresh salsa or as dinner entree served with a green salad. • **SERVES 6**

2 tablespoons olive oil
1 small onion, diced
½ cup chicken broth
1 tablespoon Worcestershire sauce
1 teaspoon Louisiana-style or Mexican hot sauce
1 teaspoon salt
¼ teaspoon freshly ground black pepper
2 cups diced cooked ham
5 cups diced peeled potatoes
2 cups chopped seeded tomatoes
1 green bell pepper, seeded and chopped
1 cup shredded sharp cheddar cheese

Heat the oil in the pressure cooker over medium-high heat. Add the onion, and cook, stirring, until softened, about 4 minutes. Stir in the broth, Worcestershire sauce, hot sauce, salt, and black pepper. In the following order, add the ham, potatoes, tomatoes, and bell pepper; do not stir. Lock the lid in place. Bring to 15psi over high heat and immediately reduce the heat to the lowest possible setting to stabilize and maintain that pressure. Cook for 6 minutes. Remove from the heat and use the quick release method before opening the lid. Stir the contents and simmer, uncovered, over low heat to cook off any excess liquid. Taste and adjust seasonings as needed. Spoon the hash mixture onto a serving plate and sprinkle the cheese on top. Serve immediately.

Variation:
SAUSAGE AND POTATO HASH

Substitute 8 ounces bulk sausage for the ham. Brown the meat in the pressure cooker until it is crumbled and no longer pink. Pour off any grease. Continue with the recipe as directed.

country-style fried potatoes

These fried potatoes are a weekend favorite at my house because they don't need to be peeled, and they make the perfect companion for a big breakfast of bacon and eggs. While you should never use the pressure cooker for pressure frying, we can use it to precook the potatoes so that they need much less time to fry, and that makes for perfect home fries. To get that crispy outer skin and soft, tender middle, the oil must be very hot, so it's important to choose oil with a high smoke point, such as peanut oil. If you have a frying thermometer, look for a reading of about 350°F, or test it by carefully dropping a sliver of potato into the oil; it should start to bubble vigorously. • **SERVES 4**

4 medium thin-skinned potatoes, such as white or red rose or Yukon gold, scrubbed
Peanut oil, for frying
Salt, freshly ground black pepper, spice blend of your choice, or seasoned salt to taste

Place the cooking rack in the bottom of the pressure cooker and add ½ cup water. Put the potatoes in the pressure cooker. Lock the lid in place. Bring to 15psi over high heat and immediately reduce the heat to the lowest possible setting to stabilize and maintain that pressure. Cook for 8 minutes. Remove from the heat and use the natural release method before opening the lid. When cool enough to handle, cut the potatoes into slices, chunks, wedges, or sticks.

Pour about ½ inch peanut oil into a heavy cast-iron skillet and set over medium-high heat. The oil must be very hot to fry just the surface of the precooked potatoes to a crispy golden brown. Use a slotted spoon to carefully add some potatoes to the hot oil. Fry them in small batches and don't overcrowd the pan or the temperature will drop. The frying should take only about 3 minutes, or just until the potatoes are lightly browned. Alternatively, if using a deep fryer, follow the manufacturer's directions. Drain the fries on paper towels. Keep warm in a low oven while frying the remaining batches. Season with salt and pepper, your preferred spice blend, or seasoned salt. Serve hot.

breakfast roundup

This was always a popular breakfast and brunch dish at my house. I like to get everyone involved in the cooking process, and a weekend breakfast is a good time to get rest of the family involved with routine kitchen tasks like chopping the vegetables and grating the cheese. While this dish cooks in the pressure cooker, you'll have just enough time to make some scrambled eggs and set the table. • **SERVES 4**

1 pound bulk breakfast sausage
1 small onion
4 russet potatoes, peeled and sliced a ¼ inch thick
1 green bell pepper, seeded and chopped
2 Roma tomatoes, seeded and chopped
Salt and coarsely ground black pepper to taste
1 cup shredded sharp cheddar cheese

In the pressure cooker over medium heat, brown the sausage meat, breaking it up and stirring until it is crumbled and no longer pink. Add the onion and cook, stirring, until softened, about 4 minutes. Pour off any extra grease. Add the potatoes in loose layers and scatter the bell pepper and tomatoes on top. Add ½ cup water. Lock the lid in place. Bring to 15psi over high heat and immediately reduce the heat to the lowest possible setting to stabilize and maintain that pressure. Cook for 6 minutes. Remove from the heat and use the natural release method before opening the lid. Add salt and black pepper to taste, and then gently stir the contents to mix. Use a colander to drain off any extra liquid. Spoon the mixture onto a serving plate and sprinkle the cheese on top. Serve immediately.

oat groats

Oat groats are the least processed of all the edible forms of oats, and they are a nutritious addition to your table. They are not an instant convenience food, but oat groats taste like what you've always wanted oatmeal to taste like. They're nutty and chewy with a firm texture, and unlike rolled oats, the oat grains stay intact, making them much more interesting than a bowl of typical oatmeal. The oat groats will continue to swell and absorb liquid, and you will probably need to add additional liquid to any leftovers; besides milk or cream, try fruit juices. Top the cooked groats with any type of sweetener, including honey, maple syrup, or brown sugar; a little dribble of molasses is good too. Stir in a splash of milk, add a sprinkling of crunchy toasted nuts if you like, and set out fresh or dried fruit to finish this hearty breakfast off quite nicely. • **SERVES 2 TO 4**

1 cup oat groats
1 teaspoon ground cinnamon (optional)
Sweetener of your choice, for serving (optional)
Milk, for serving (optional)

Place the cooking rack in the bottom of the pressure cooker and add 1 cup water. Add 3 cups water and oat groats to an insert bowl that will fit within your pressure cooker. Position the insert bowl inside the pressure cooker using foil helper handles. Lock the lid in place. Bring to 15psi over high heat and immediately reduce the heat to the lowest possible setting to stabilize and maintain that pressure. Cook for 16 minutes for a chewy texture or 20 minutes for a smoother consistency. Remove from the heat and use the natural release method before opening the lid. Stir the oat groats and add the cinnamon, if desired. To serve, spoon into cereal bowls and let each person add sweetener and milk as desired.

sweet-and-spicy old-fashioned oatmeal

When you say "oatmeal," do your kids curl their lips and roll their eyes? Yeah, I remember those days, too, so this is my version of oatmeal, and it's something that your kids will actually like because it tastes good—no, really! It's not only hearty, but also flavorful, with a hint of orange juice, a little brown sugar, and cinnamon. The black pepper adds to the spiciness. First off, I will tell you that the secret to making a great bowl of oatmeal is to start with high-quality old-fashioned rolled oats. Premium oat flakes are much bigger and thicker than the bottom-shelf variety found in your supermarket, so they cook up with a heartier, more substantial texture than that gluey glob of ordinary oatmeal that makes your kids snarl at their breakfast. You can find these lovely old-fashioned oats in smaller 1-pound packages in the hot cereal section of many supermarkets, or in bulk bins like at my favorite market. • **SERVES 2**

1 cup premium-quality old-fashioned rolled oats
⅔ cup fresh orange juice
½ cup chopped dried fruit, such as dates, raisins, or apricots
⅓ cup packed dark brown sugar
1 teaspoon ground cinnamon
½ teaspoon salt
Coarsely ground black pepper to taste
Sweetener of your choice, for serving (optional)
Cold milk, for serving (optional)

Place the cooking rack in the bottom of the pressure cooker and add ½ cup water. In a 1-quart stainless-steel insert bowl, mix the oats, orange juice, dried fruit, sugar, cinnamon, salt, pepper, and 2¼ cups water. If necessary, use foil helper handles to place the insert pan into the pressure cooker. Lock the lid in place. Bring to 15psi over high heat and immediately reduce the heat to the lowest possible setting to stabilize and maintain that pressure. Cook for 3 minutes. Remove from the heat and use the natural release method before opening the lid. Carefully lift the insert pan out of the pressure cooker, and stir the oatmeal to evenly mix the ingredients. Spoon the oatmeal into serving bowls and add sweetener and a splash of cold milk if desired.

sweet buttermilk cornbread

Every family in America has their own cherished cornbread recipe, and in my house cornbread was just as likely to be cooked in a pressure cooker as in the oven. My mom was a frugal woman and nothing went to waste in our house, so in the morning she would toast any cornbread left over from dinner, crumble it into a bowl and add milk and maybe some fruit, and that was her breakfast. Any way you serve it, cornbread is a great accompaniment for all kinds of soups, stews, beans, and chili . . . and even breakfast. • **SERVES 4 OR 5**

2 tablespoons butter, softened, for greasing the insert pan
2 large eggs
¼ cup bacon drippings or ½ cup (1 stick) butter, melted and cooled to room temperature
1 cup buttermilk
1⅓ cups cornmeal
⅔ cup all-purpose flour
⅔ cup sugar
2 teaspoons baking powder
2 teaspoons baking soda
1 teaspoon salt
Butter, for serving

Generously butter a stainless-steel insert pan that will fit within your pressure cooker. In a small bowl, whisk the eggs until lightly beaten, and then blend in the bacon drippings and buttermilk. In a large bowl, mix together the cornmeal, flour, sugar, baking powder, baking soda, and salt. Add the liquid ingredients to the dry ingredients and stir until just barely blended. The batter should look a bit lumpy. Pour the batter into the prepared pan, only filling to about two-thirds full to allow room for it to rise. Cover the cornbread pan with a lid or crimp a square of aluminum foil over the top to make a tight seal. Add ⅔ cup water to the pressure cooker and put a cooking rack in the bottom. Use foil helper handles to place the pan on top of the rack. Lock the lid in place. Bring to 15psi over high heat, then immediately reduce the heat to the lowest possible setting to stabilize and maintain that pressure. Cook for 14 minutes. Remove from the heat and use the natural release method before opening the lid. Remove the insert pan from the cooker and let it cool on a wire rack for about 5 minutes. Then run a small, sharp knife around the edge to loosen the sides before inverting the cornbread on a plate. Cut into wedges and serve with lots of butter.

Variations:

This recipe can accommodate all kinds of personal touches, so feel free to add about 1 cup of extras, like grated sharp cheddar cheese, or mix and match from a choice of sliced scallions, corn kernels, chopped jalapeño chiles, cooked sausage, or crumbled bacon. I like a combo of cheese and jalapeños.

(continued)

COOK'S NOTE: Some pressure cookers are available with a choice of insert pans. You can also use any flat-bottomed, round metal or silicone baking pan that will fit inside your pressure cooker. Use any tight-fitting lid or a square of aluminum foil crimped tightly over the top of the pan to create a mini oven within the pressure cooker to bake the cornbread. The lid also acts as a shield against condensation droplets than can occur as the cooker cools down during the natural release.

blueberry scones with lemon-vanilla glaze

This recipe was inspired by my grandma's old scone recipe that dates from the World War II era, when food supplies were rationed and staples like flour, sugar, butter, eggs, and milk were in short supply. You'll find no eggs here, and part of the flour has been replaced with cornmeal to cope with the shortages, and I held true to those ingredients. There is a little more butter and milk—a luxury in those days—in my version, and I've used plump blueberries rather than the prunes in Grandma's original recipe. I've also added a glaze because it appeals to my sweet tooth and because the combination of the sweet blueberries and the tangy lemony glaze is fantastic! These scones are really easy to make, but be warned, they're also very addictive. I generally serve these scones as a weekend brunch treat, with a pot of tea or hot coffee. • **MAKES 8 SCONES**

Step One: THE SCONES

⅓ cup cold butter, diced, plus 2 tablespoons butter, softened, for greasing cake pans
1½ cups all-purpose flour
½ cup cornmeal
⅓ cup sugar
1 tablespoon baking powder
½ teaspoon salt
⅔ cup milk
⅔ cup frozen blueberries

With the softened butter grease and flour two round metal or silicone cake pans that will fit inside your pressure cooker. In a large mixing bowl, combine the flour, cornmeal, sugar, baking powder, and salt. Using a pastry blender or fork, work the cold butter into the dry ingredients until it looks like coarse crumbs. Make a well in the center of the mixture and pour in the milk. Fold the ingredients together until just mixed. Fold the blueberries into the dough, taking care not to overwork the dough or mash the berries. Turn the dough out onto a floured surface and flour your hands, as the dough will be quite sticky. Divide the dough in half and gently pat each half into a ½-inch-thick circle about the diameter of your insert pans. Carefully move the dough to the prepared insert pans and cut each into 4 wedges. Tightly crimp a square of aluminum foil over the top of each insert pan. If your pressure cooker is large enough to accommodate two stacked insert pans, both pans of scones can be cooked at the same time. Alternatively, the scones can be cooked in batches, or in two separate pressure cookers. Place the cooking rack in the bottom of the pressure cooker and add ½ cup water. Use foil helper handles to lower the pan into the pressure cooker. Lock the lid in place. Bring to 15psi over high heat and immediately reduce the heat to the lowest possible setting to stabilize and maintain that pressure. Cook for 20 minutes. Remove

(continued)

from the heat and use the quick release method before opening the lid. Lift the insert pans out of the pressure cooker and invert the scones onto a wire cooling for about 5 minutes. Invert the scones onto a serving plate.

Step Two: THE LEMON-VANILLA GLAZE

⅔ cup confectioners' sugar
2 tablespoons butter, melted
2 tablespoons fresh lemon juice
1½ teaspoons vanilla extract
¼ cup milk

Place the sugar in a small bowl and stir in the butter. Add the lemon juice, vanilla, and milk, and stir the glaze until it is smooth and lump-free. Drizzle the glaze over the scones. Slice the scones into wedges along the existing cut lines and serve immediately while they are still warm. Pass the remaining glaze at the table.

COOK'S NOTE: Instead of the glaze, these scones may be served with jam or honey.

Variation: CRANBERRY OR DRIED CRANBERRY SCONES

Substitute ⅔ cup frozen cranberries or frozen raspberries for the blueberries.

Variation: RAISIN OR CRANBERRY SCONES

Substitute ½ cup raisins or dried cranberries for the blueberries.

Variation: PRUNE SCONES WITH ORANGE-VANILLA GLAZE

Substitute ½ cup chopped and pitted prunes for the blueberries. Soak the chopped prunes in ½ cup hot orange juice for about 15 minutes. Pour off the orange juice and set it aside. Prepare the scones as directed. To make the Orange-Vanilla Glaze, replace the lemon juice with the reserved orange juice.

breakfast blueberry corn cake with lemon glaze

I remember my grandma telling stories about the lean years of the Great Depression and the food rationing of World War II. She would laugh, patting her ample stomach, as she told us about the strange recipe concoctions she came up with. So when I rediscovered her old recipe for corn cake, I knew I had to give it a try. I've updated the original version to use more modern ingredients (no lard!). I included the blueberries one day when I wanted something sweeter to serve with tea. Mix up the glaze while the cornbread cake is cooking. This is a PIP recipe, and you will need a metal or silicone cake pan that will fit within your pressure cooker. • **SERVES 4 OR 5**

Step One: THE CAKE

2 large eggs
1 cup buttermilk
½ cup applesauce
2 tablespoons fresh lemon juice
1⅓ cups cornmeal
1 cup all-purpose flour
⅔ cup sugar
1 teaspoon baking powder
1 teaspoon baking soda
½ teaspoon salt
1½ cups frozen blueberries
2 tablespoons butter, softened, for greasing the insert pan

In a small bowl, whisk the eggs until lightly beaten, and then blend in the buttermilk, applesauce, and lemon juice. In a large bowl, mix together the cornmeal, flour, sugar, baking powder, baking soda, and salt. Add the liquid ingredients to the dry ingredients and stir until just barely blended. The batter should look lumpy. Gently fold in the blueberries.

Generously butter a stainless-steel insert pan that will fit within your pressure cooker. Pour the batter to the prepared pan, filling it about two-thirds full to allow room for it to rise. Cover the insert pan with a buttered lid, or crimp a square of buttered aluminum foil over the top of the pan to make a tight seal. Add ⅔ cup water to the pressure cooker and put a cooking rack or trivet in the bottom. Use foil helper handles to place the pan on top of the rack. Lock the lid in place. Bring to 15psi over high heat and then immediately reduce the heat to the lowest possible setting to stabilize and maintain that pressure. Cook for 15 minutes. Remove from the heat and use the natural release method before opening the lid. Remove the insert pan from the pressure cooker and let it cool on a wire rack for about 5 minutes. Run a small, sharp knife around the edge of the cake to loosen the sides before inverting the cornbread onto a serving plate.

(continued)

Step Two: THE LEMON GLAZE

⅔ cup confectioners' sugar
2 tablespoons butter, melted
¼ cup milk
2 tablespoons fresh lemon juice

In a small bowl, blend the sugar with the butter. Add the milk and lemon juice and stir until the glaze is smooth and lump-free. Drizzle some of the glaze over the top of the warm corn cake, and pass the remaining glaze at the table.

COOK'S NOTE: Instead of the glaze, the cake may be served plain with lots of butter, jam, or honey.

---

snacks, starters, and salads

chunky pinto bean dip

Everyone loves bean dip, but those little store-bought cans are pricey, and there's never enough to go around. So let's cut the costs and make a fabulous homemade bean dip for a crowd that is loaded with all kinds of extra goodies. This is a perfect dip for a party, or a summer barbecue, or for a lazy afternoon of snacking in front of the TV. • **MAKES ABOUT 6 CUPS**

Step One: THE BEANS

2 cups dried pinto beans, picked over and rinsed
1½ cups shredded Mexican cheese blend or pepper Jack cheese
6 to 8 cloves garlic, roasted (see page 252)
1½ teaspoons ground cumin
1 tablespoon chili powder
1 teaspoon Mexican hot sauce, or to taste
1 teaspoon salt, or to taste

Place the beans in the pressure cooker and add enough water to cover by 2 inches. Lock the lid in place. Bring to 15psi over high heat and immediately reduce the heat to the lowest possible setting to stabilize and maintain that pressure. Cook for 45 minutes. Remove from the heat and use the natural release method before opening the lid. Thoroughly drain the beans in a colander. Use a food processor to pulse the beans in small batches, leaving some of chunks of bean mixed in with the creamier mashed beans. Put the mashed beans in a large bowl and stir in the cheese while the beans are still hot. Add the garlic, cumin, chili powder, hot sauce, and salt. Stir to blend, and then cover and allow the mixture to cool slightly in the refrigerator before adding the remaining ingredients.

(continued)

Step Two: THE GOODIES

4 Roma tomatoes, seeded and diced
½ cup finely chopped fresh cilantro
1 medium onion, diced
1 (4-ounce) can mild diced green chiles
Corn tortilla chips, for serving

Add the tomatoes, cilantro, onion, and chiles to the bean mixture, and stir to mix. Taste and adjust seasonings as desired. Serve at room temperature with your favorite brand of tortilla chips.

COOK'S NOTE: Use any leftovers to replace the refried beans in the Shortcut Beef and Bean Burritos (page 166).

---

loaded potato skins

Potato skins are a pretty pricey appetizer at most restaurants, but they are easy to make at home, and you even get a bonus potato dish (see Cook's Note). Use the pressure cooker to quickly precook the potatoes and then pop them into the oven to crisp before adding your favorite toppers. These potatoes are great appetizers, but don't stop there: Serve them as a side dish with barbecued chicken or ribs. Select Idaho or russet potatoes because their thicker skins will help hold the potato's shape. Medium potatoes are best for finger foods that are held in the hand; avoid larger potatoes, as they tend to bend or break more easily under the weight of the toppings.

• **SERVES 4**

4 medium russet or Idaho potatoes, scrubbed
¼ cup olive oil
1 teaspoon salt
½ teaspoon freshly ground black pepper
½ teaspoon garlic powder
¼ teaspoon hot smoked paprika or chili powder
1½ cups shredded sharp cheddar cheese
8 strips bacon, cooked until crisp and crumbled
1 cup finely chopped fresh chives or scallions
1 (16-ounce) bottle blue cheese or ranch-style salad dressing or sour cream

EXTRA TOPPINGS (OPTIONAL)

1 cup finely chopped bell peppers in assorted colors
½ cup minced fresh cilantro
⅓ cup toasted sunflower seeds
1 cup prepared guacamole or chopped avocado
1 (16-ounce) container prepared salsa
1½ cups Pico de Gallo (page 45)

Place the cooking rack in the bottom of the pressure cooker and add 1 cup water. Add the potatoes. Lock the lid in place. Bring to 15psi over high heat and immediately reduce the heat to the lowest possible setting to stabilize and maintain that pressure. Cook for 8 minutes. Remove from the heat and use the natural release method before opening the lid. Transfer the potatoes to a wire rack until cool enough to handle.

Preheat the oven to 475°F. Cut the potatoes in half lengthwise and scoop out the insides, leaving a shell about ¼ inch thick. Brush each potato half, inside and out, with the oil. In a small bowl, mix together the salt, black pepper, garlic powder, and paprika, and season both sides of the potatoes with the spice blend. Place the potatoes cut side down on a baking sheet. Bake in the oven for about 8 minutes, watching closely as the skin starts to crisp. Turn the potatoes over and continue baking for another 8 minutes.

(continued)

Turn off the oven and add some cheese and crumbled bacon to the empty potato skins. Close the oven and wait for 2 minutes or until the cheese melts. Transfer the potato skins to a serving tray and top with the chives and a generous grinding of black pepper.

To serve, place the blue cheese dressing in a small bowl and set on the tray in the middle of the hot skins. Serve the extra toppings in small bowls alongside, as desired, so everyone can pick and choose their favorites.

COOK'S NOTE: The scooped-out potato flesh should be tightly covered and refrigerated for use within 2 days. Use them for mashed potatoes (see page 258) or a brunch frittata (see page 19).

---

mini herbed feta cheesecakes

These yummy little savory—yes, my dears, I said savory—cheesecakes make elegant appetizers. This is party fare that will impress your guests. Spread the cheese on crackers or toast points, or make tiny finger sandwiches—if you're old enough, you might remember those, if not, just start munching—and include an assortment of tasty toppings from the list below if you like. • **SERVES 6**

Step One: THE CRUST

1/3 cup fine dry bread crumbs
1/4 cup ground salted peanuts
1 teaspoon butter, softened

Spray 6 (6-ounce) ramekins with nonstick cooking spray. Combine the bread crumbs, peanuts, and butter in a small bowl and mix well. Spoon about 1 tablespoon of the crumb mixture into the bottom of each ramekin, pressing it smooth with a small glass.

Step Two: THE FILLING

8 ounces cream cheese, softened
4 ounces feta cheese, crumbled
1/3 cup finely minced fresh herbs of your choice, such as basil, oregano, chives, dill, and/or sage
1 large egg
4 to 6 cloves garlic, roasted (see page 252) and mashed
1/2 teaspoon hot sauce
Crackers, for serving

OPTIONAL TOPPINGS

Sliced black or green olives
Capers
Halved cherry tomatoes
Thin cucumber slices
Chopped pimientos
Slivers of smoked salmon or halibut
Chopped prosciutto
Crumbled cooked bacon

In the bowl of a stand mixer fitted with the paddle attachment, blend the cream cheese and feta together. Beat in the herbs, egg, garlic, and hot sauce until smoothly blended. Divide the mixture evenly between the ramekins.

Cover each ramekin with a small square of aluminum foil, crimping it tightly around the rim. Place the cooking rack in the bottom of the pressure cooker and add 1/2 cup water. Arrange the ramekins in two layers, offsetting the top layer so as not to completely cover the bottom layer. Lock the lid in place. Bring to 15psi over high heat and immediately reduce the heat to the lowest possible setting to stabilize and maintain that pressure. Cook for 6 minutes. Remove from the heat and use the natural

(continued)

release method before opening the lid. Carefully transfer the ramekins to a wire rack to cool for about 30 minutes.

Run a small, thin knife blade around the sides of each ramekin to loosen the cheesecakes. Leave the mini cheesecakes in the ramekins, cover with plastic wrap, and refrigerate for several hours to chill and allow the flavors to blend.

To serve, invert each cheesecake onto a plate and surround it with an assortment of crackers. Set out the desired toppings in small bowls. Use a knife to spread a little of the cheesecake on a cracker and then add the toppings of choice.

chicken quesadillas with fresh pico de gallo

Chicken quesadillas are easy to make, with many choices for the filling. A quesadilla can be filled with just about anything—beef, pork, seafood, cheese, or a host of vegetables—and this is a good way to use up those little bits of leftovers. So be sure to experiment with your own favorite ingredients, or just use whatever you may have on hand. Add the fresh and flavorful taste of homemade pico de gallo, and this dish becomes versatile enough to serve for a nice brunch, a quick lunch, a super weekend snack, or even a light dinner. If you're looking for something simple and delicious, this is much better than anything on the local fast-food menu. • **SERVES 4 OR 5**

Step One: THE FRESH PICO DE GALLO

- 3 large Roma tomatoes, seeded and diced
- 1 medium onion, finely chopped
- 1 small bunch fresh cilantro, leaves only, finely chopped
- 1 small jalapeño chile, seeded and minced
- 1 mild chile, such as Anaheim, pasilla, or poblano, seeded and diced
- Juice of 2 small limes
- Salt to taste

To develop the maximum flavor, prepare this several hours before serving, or even a day ahead. A food processor is very useful in prepping the vegetables, but process each ingredient separately in short bursts to avoid turning them into puree. Combine the chopped ingredients, lime juice, and salt in a glass or other nonreactive bowl and mix well. Cover the bowl and refrigerate, stirring occasionally as the juices to come out to blend the flavors. Stir before serving.

Step Two: THE CHICKEN

- 1 tablespoon vegetable oil
- 2 large skinless, boneless chicken breasts or thighs
- 1 small bell pepper, seeded and cut into strips
- 1 small onion, sliced
- 1 mild chile, such as Anaheim, pasilla, or poblano, seeded and cut into strips

Heat the oil in the pressure cooker over medium heat and brown the chicken on both sides. Add the bell pepper, onion, chile, and ½ cup water to the pressure cooker. Lock the lid in place. Bring to 15psi over high heat and immediately reduce the heat to the

(continued)

lowest possible setting to stabilize and maintain that pressure. Cook for 4 minutes. Remove from the heat and use the quick release method before opening the lid. Transfer the chicken to a cutting board and cut the meat into thin strips. Divide the meat and the peppers and onions into four portions.

Step Three: THE TORTILLAS

- 2 to 3 tablespoons butter, melted, or olive oil
- 8 (12-inch) flour tortillas
- 1½ cups shredded pepper Jack or sharp cheddar cheese, divided into 4 portions
- Sliced avocado or guacamole, for garnish (optional)
- Crema agria (Mexican-style sour cream), for garnish (optional)

Brush a small amount of the butter on each side of the tortillas. Heat a large heavy skillet over medium-high heat. Place 1 tortilla in the hot skillet. Lightly brown one side of the tortilla and flip it over when air pockets begin to form; adjust the heat as need to avoid burning the tortillas. Quickly sprinkle one-half of one portion of the cheese evenly over half of the tortilla. Spread one portion of the chicken mixture evenly over the cheese on the tortilla and top with the remaining portion of cheese. Fold the tortilla in half and cook until the cheese is sufficiently melted and the tortilla is crisp and lightly browned on both sides. Remove from the pan and cut into wedges. Repeat with all the tortillas. Serve warm with the pico de gallo on the side and include other toppings like avocado and crema agria, if desired.

Variation: TURKEY QUESADILLAS

Substitute 1 pound skinless, boneless white turkey meat for the chicken, and cook as directed above.

Variation: BEEF QUESADILLAS

Substitute 1 pound sirloin steak for the chicken. Cut the beef into very thin strips, about 2 inches long by ¼ inch thick, and cook as directed above.

chipotle hot wings with creamy cilantro dipping sauce

Chicken wings are probably one of the cheapest meats you can make, and this Mexican-inspired hot wing recipe will taste way better than an expensive restaurant appetizer. It's a great party dish or halftime snack in front of the TV on the weekend, but don't limit it to just finger food. Serve these wings for lunch with fries, potato salad, or coleslaw. Try them for dinner, served with fluffy rice and a crisp salad; it's a big favorite at my house. To prepare the recipe, I'm using the pressure cooker to precook the wings, shaving as much as 45 minutes off the cooking time, so they only need to be grilled or broiled for a few minutes to crisp the spicy glaze. Oh, and maybe you'd better double the dipping sauce. • **SERVES 4 TO 6**

Step One: THE DIPPING SAUCE

16 ounces sour cream
1 cup packed minced fresh cilantro
½ cup crumbled feta cheese
½ cup mayonnaise
2 tablespoons fresh lime juice
Salt and coarsely ground black pepper to taste

Combine the sour cream, cilantro, cheese, mayonnaise, and lime juice in a small glass or other nonreactive bowl. Mix thoroughly until all the ingredients are well blended. Taste and season with salt and pepper as desired. Cover tightly with plastic wrap and refrigerate for several hours to allow the flavors to blend. This may be prepared the day before if it's more convenient.

Step Two: THE WINGS

3 to 4 pounds chicken wings, whole or shoulder drumettes
1 (15-ounce) can tomato sauce
½ cup honey
⅓ cup chipotle hot sauce or adobo sauce canned chipotles in adobo, or more to taste
3 tablespoons fresh lime juice
2 teaspoons grated lime zest
2 teaspoons ground cumin
1 teaspoon garlic powder

Wash the chicken parts thoroughly. If using whole wings, use kitchen scissors or a sharp knife to separate the mini drumstick end of the wing, slicing between the joints to separate. Cut off the unwanted wing tips and freeze for later use in making chicken broth or stock for soups and stews. Place the cooking rack in the bottom of the pres-

(continued)

sure cooker and add ½ cup water. Add all the wings. Lock the lid in place. Bring to 15psi over high heat and immediately reduce the heat to the lowest possible setting to stabilize and maintain that pressure. Cook for 4 minutes. Remove from the heat and use the quick release method before opening the lid.

Meanwhile, mix together the tomato sauce, honey, hot sauce, lime juice, lime zest, cumin, and garlic powder in a deep bowl, blending well. Taste and adjust the seasoning as desired, adding more hot sauce if more heat is wanted.

Using tongs, add a few wings to the sauce, turning several times to coat evenly. Repeat until all the wings have been covered in sauce.

Preheat a grill or the broiler. Grill the wings as desired, turning and basting just until the sauce begins to caramelize and brown. Or place them in a roasting pan, spaced apart so they are not touching. Position the pan about 6 inches from the heat source. Turn and baste the wings until the sauce begins to caramelize, watch closely to avoid burning. Serve hot with plenty of the dipping sauce on the side.

creamy creole potato salad

When I was in college, one of my favorite places to visit was New Orleans. The little cafés served giant po' boy sandwiches with this wonderfully creamy, yellow potato salad that had a bold and spicy mustard dressing. At the first bite, there are all these little crunchy explosions of different flavors in your mouth, and then the tangy taste of the dressing, all blended in with the creamy potatoes. There are no big chunks of cold potatoes in this potato salad because the ingredients are all diced very small, with nothing larger than a lentil. Back in those days, all that dicing and slicing had to be done by hand, but with a food processor this prep work is done in just a few minutes. I like that, and it's a lot less work than the traditional chunky-style potato salad we're all familiar with.

The trick to making any potato salad is to start with right type of potato. You'll want to choose one of the thin-skinned, waxy potatoes that can better withstand boiling—or steaming for our purposes—such as the white or red rose or the Yukon gold. Using the pressure cooker we'll cook the potatoes whole, with the skin, and then use the quick release method to cause the skins to split in the rapid pressure change. This will make it easy to quickly pull the skins off in big sheets. Like all potato salads, this gets better if chilled for several hours before serving. • **SERVES 8 TO 10**

Step One: THE POTATOES

6 medium thin-skinned potatoes, such as white or red rose or Yukon gold, scrubbed

Place the cooking rack in the bottom of the pressure cooker and add ½ cup water. Arrange the potatoes on the rack. Lock the lid in place. Bring to 15psi over high heat and immediately reduce the heat to the lowest possible setting to stabilize and maintain that pressure. Cook for 6 minutes. Remove from the heat and use the quick release method before opening the lid. Set aside until cool enough to handle, and then remove the skins. Coarsely chop the potatoes and then use a food processor in on-off pulses to chop the potatoes into tiny pieces (about the size of a lentil, but take care not to overdo it). Put the potatoes in a large bowl and chill in the refrigerator.

(continued)

Step Two: THE EXTRAS

4 large hard-cooked eggs (see page 59)
½ cup diced sweet onion
3 scallions, thinly sliced
1 cup diced celery
4 radishes, diced
1 dill pickle, diced

Slice 2 of the eggs, pull out the 3 perfect center slices from each, and set aside in the refrigerator to use as a garnish. Dice up rest of the sliced and whole eggs and add them to the potatoes. Add the cut-up vegetables to the potatoes.

Step Three: THE DRESSING

¾ cup salad dressing of your choice (not mayonnaise)
3 tablespoons Creole mustard (look for it in the international foods aisle or use the recipe below)
2 tablespoons dried Italian parsley
1 tablespoon dried dill weed
1 teaspoon celery seeds
2 tablespoons white wine vinegar (optional)
Salt and coarsely ground black pepper to taste
Paprika, for garnish

In a bowl, blend the salad dressing, mustard, parsley, dill weed, and celery seeds to a smooth consistency. Add vinegar if the dressing is not tangy enough. Once the dressing is satisfactory, pour it over the potato mixture and fold together, stirring until the ingredients are thoroughly blended. Season with salt and pepper and refrigerate for at least several hours to allow the flavors to blend.

Just before serving, decorate the top of the potato salad with the perfect egg slices and sprinkle lightly with a dusting of paprika.

creole mustard

½ cup grainy brown mustard
2 tablespoons finely minced shallot
1 tablespoon molasses
2 tablespoons white wine vinegar
½ teaspoon Louisiana-style hot sauce, or to taste

Combine all the ingredients in a small bowl and stir until well blended. Refrigerate until ready to use.

marinated mayocoba bean salad with tuna and creamy italian dressing

Mayocoba beans have thin skins, which allows them to readily absorb flavors, but they also have a buttery soft and creamy texture and hold their shape well when cooked. They are considered the "king of beans" by many Latino chefs because they can be used in so many different recipes in place of pinto beans, great Northern beans, and cannellini beans. Look for this popular bean in the aisle with other dried beans or in bulk bins in the produce section of some supermarkets, and also packaged in the Hispanic foods section. It is also labeled under several different names, including peruano, canary, Peruvian, and Inca beans. Alternatively, these beans can be cooked plain (see Step Two) and then added to a spicy sauce for barbecued beans. • **SERVES 4 TO 6**

Step One: THE CREAMY ITALIAN DRESSING

½ cup mayonnaise
⅔ cup extra-virgin olive oil
½ cup red wine vinegar
2 tablespoons fresh lemon juice
2 teaspoons dried oregano
1 teaspoon crushed dried rosemary
1 teaspoon salt
½ teaspoon coarsely ground black pepper
⅓ cup grated Parmesan cheese

Prepare the dressing several hours or up to a day in advance of serving, to allow time for the flavors to blend. Measure the mayonnaise into a small glass bowl. Slowly whisk in the oil until the mixture is thoroughly blended. Add the vinegar, lemon juice, oregano, rosemary, salt, and pepper and continue to whisk until the ingredients are well blended. Stir in the cheese. Taste and adjust seasonings as desired. Cover tightly and refrigerated until needed.

Step Two: THE BEANS

1½ cups dried mayocoba beans, picked over and soaked in water for 8 hours or overnight
1 tablespoon olive oil

Drain and rinse the soaked beans and put them in the pressure cooker with enough water to cover by 2 inches. Add the oil. Lock the lid in place. Bring to 15psi over high heat and immediately reduce the heat to the lowest possible setting to stabilize and maintain that pressure. Cook for 16 minutes. Remove from the heat and use the

(continued)

natural release method before opening the lid. Thoroughly drain the beans in a colander. Place the cooked beans in a mixing bowl and add half the dressing, tossing to mix. Cover the bowl with plastic wrap and refrigerate for at least 4 hours to marinate the beans. Toss the beans occasionally so they marinate in the dressing evenly.

Step Three: THE SALAD

- 2 (6-ounce) cans solid white albacore tuna in olive oil, drained and flaked
- 1½ cups cherry tomatoes, halved
- 1 cup chopped cucumber
- ½ cup chopped fresh cilantro or Italian parsley
- ½ cup sliced scallions
- ½ cup sliced radishes
- ½ cup chopped pitted kalamata olives
- ½ cup crumbled feta cheese
- ⅓ cup drained capers, chopped
- 1 small bunch fresh spinach

In a large mixing bowl, blend the tuna, tomatoes, cucumber, cilantro, scallions, radishes, olives, feta, capers, and the remaining dressing. Add the beans and any dressing from the bowl and gently stir to mix. Remove the stems from the spinach and tear larger leaves into bite-size pieces. Divide the spinach leaves among salad plates. Add a mound of the bean mixture on top and serve.

COOK'S NOTE: When cooking plain beans without any seasonings, I like to double the amount of beans and then divide the extra quantity into 2-cup portions to freeze for later use. Beans freeze very well, and when packed into resealable plastic freezer bags and frozen flat, they thaw quickly. This will save you several hours the next time you want to make a recipe that calls for dried beans. When using frozen beans in soups, there is no need to thaw—just remove the packaging and place the block of frozen beans near (but not directly on) the bottom of the pressure cooker. The cooking time for your soup recipe remains the same.

---

five-spice chicken salad

Hot summer days, chilled salads . . . and a pressure cooker? Sure! I often remind visitors to my website that their pressure cookers should be working just as hard during the warm weather months as they do the rest of the year. Five-spice powder is popular in Asian cookery, as it is said to create a harmonious balance in the yin and yang of food. The mixture of spices includes sweet, sour, bitter, pungent, and salty tastes. Look for tamari in the Asian foods section of most supermarkets. It's a type of soy sauce made with little or no wheat and using a different fermentation process that makes it a bit sweeter than the ordinary variety. The combination of flavors certainly gives a powerful boost to the chicken that stars in this delicious salad. Serve this with my Chipotle Hot Wings (page 47) and make a double batch of the Asian Five-Spice Dressing to use as a dipping sauce. • **SERVES 4**

Step One: THE ASIAN FIVE-SPICE DRESSING

⅓ cup honey
½ cup mayonnaise
3 cloves garlic, minced
3 tablespoons rice wine vinegar
2 tablespoons minced fresh ginger
2 teaspoons Dijon mustard
½ teaspoon sesame oil
½ teaspoon Chinese five-spice powder

Blend all the dressing ingredients together in a glass or other nonreactive bowl. Taste and adjust the seasonings as desired. Cover the bowl tightly with plastic wrap and refrigerate for at least 2 hours before serving. Stir before using.

Step Two: THE FIVE-SPICE CHICKEN

⅓ cup tamari
¼ cup rice wine vinegar
1 teaspoon sesame oil
1 teaspoon Chinese five-spice powder
2 large skinless, boneless chicken breasts
3 cloves garlic, minced
2 tablespoons minced fresh ginger
⅓ cup honey
Salt to taste (optional)

Mix the tamari, vinegar, oil, and five-spice powder together in the pressure cooker. Add the chicken breasts, turning several times to coat. Add the garlic and ginger. Lock the lid in place. Bring to 15psi over high heat and immediately reduce the heat to the lowest possible setting to stabilize and maintain that pressure. Cook for 4 minutes. Remove from the heat and use the natural release method before opening the lid.

(continued)

Transfer the chicken to a cutting board and cut into bite-size pieces. Heat the sauce in the pressure cooker over medium-high heat and cook until reduced by half. Stir in the honey, reduce the heat, and continue cooking, stirring often to prevent burning, until the sauce thickens. Add the chicken pieces to the sauce and stir to coat each piece. Taste and add salt, if needed. Remove from the heat and allow to cool.

Step Three: THE SALAD

- 1 head Asian cabbage, such as napa or bok choy, shredded
- 1 head butter lettuce, torn into bite-size pieces
- 2 cups sliced cherry tomatoes
- 1 (11-ounce) can mandarin oranges, drained
- 1 medium red bell pepper, seeded and cut into strips
- 1 cup packed chopped fresh cilantro leaves
- 1 cup diced cucumber
- ½ cup matchstick-cut carrots
- 5 radishes, sliced
- 4 scallions, sliced
- Toasted sesame seeds, for serving (optional)

Toss all the salad ingredients, except for the sesame seeds, in a large bowl and divide among individual serving plates. Divide the chicken pieces among the plates, arranging them on top. Sprinkle with the sesame seeds, if desired. Pass the dressing at the table.

COOK'S NOTE: If you're in a hurry and want to skip the prep work, use packaged salad greens, Asian slaw mix, and other precut vegetable mixes and a bottled Asian-style dressing.

BONUS RECIPE

five-spice chicken with perfect white rice

Prepare the Five-Spice Chicken as directed and put the breast pieces in the bottom of the pressure cooker. Prepare Perfect White Rice on page 269. Place the insert pan of rice on top of the chicken. Lock the lid in place. Bring to 15psi over high heat and immediately reduce the heat to the lowest possible setting to stabilize and maintain that pressure. Cook for 4 minutes. Remove from the heat and use the natural release method before opening the lid. Transfer the rice to a serving dish and fluff up with fork. Set the chicken aside, but do not cut it up (or cut each breast in half). Finish cooking the sauce as directed, and when it's thickened, return the chicken to the pressure cooker and turn to coat with the sauce. Skip the salad step. To serve, spoon a mound of rice on each serving plate and place a chicken breast beside it. Spoon any remaining sauce over the chicken.

SERVES 2 TO 4

---

california chicken salad

This is a lovely recipe. The flavors are as fresh as the ingredients, and it's great for a hot weather lunch or a light dinner. I'm always reminding pressure cooker users to keep using them throughout the year and not to give them the summer off. Besides all the roasts and soups and stews that everyone loves in the cold weather months, don't forget to use your pressure cooker for easy meals in the summer months when it's too hot to cook. • **SERVES 4**

Step One: THE CHICKEN

3 skinless, boneless chicken breast halves
½ cup chicken broth
2 tablespoons soy sauce
3 sprigs fresh basil
Juice of 1 lemon
1 teaspoon grated lemon zest

Place the chicken in the pressure cooker. Add the broth, soy sauce, basil, lemon juice, and lemon zest. Lock the lid in place. Bring to 15psi over high heat and immediately reduce the heat to the lowest possible setting to stabilize and maintain that pressure. Cook for 8 minutes. Remove from the heat and use the quick release method before opening the lid. Transfer the chicken to a cutting board to cool while making the dressing. Reserve the broth if desired, freezing it for later use in other recipes.

Step Two: THE CHICKEN SALAD

½ cup sour cream
½ cup mayonnaise
1½ teaspoons fresh lemon juice
Salt and coarsely ground black pepper to taste
1 stalk celery, minced
½ cup minced red onion
¼ cup chopped fresh basil
¼ cup toasted sunflower seeds

Combine the sour cream, mayonnaise, and lemon juice in a small bowl and stir until smooth. Taste and add salt and pepper as desired. When the chicken is cool enough to handle, dice it into small pieces. Combine the chicken, celery, onion, basil, and sunflower seeds in a bowl and toss gently to coat. Cover and chill.

Step Three: THE SALAD

8 cups torn mixed salad greens of your choice
2 large tomatoes, each cut into 8 wedges
2 avocados, pitted, peeled, and sliced

Divide the salad greens evenly between 4 plates. Arrange alternating tomato and avocado slices in a star pattern on top of the greens. Pack the chicken salad into a 1-cup measuring cup. Carefully invert the chicken salad onto the plate at the center of the star pattern. Serve immediately.

BONUS RECIPE

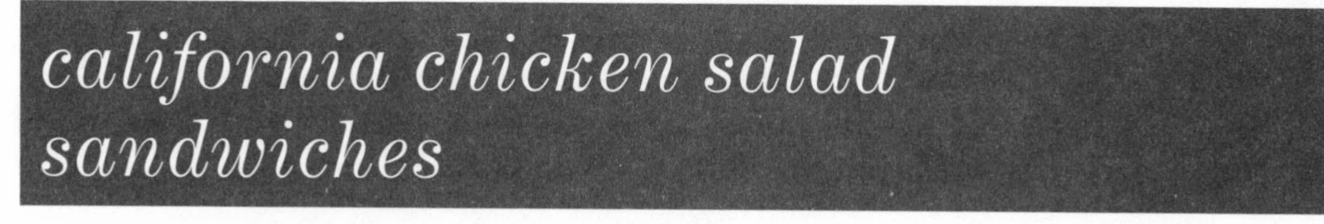

california chicken salad sandwiches

4 ounces cream cheese, softened
4 croissant rolls, split
1 avocado, pitted, peeled, and mashed
1 large tomato, thinly sliced
5 ounces alfalfa sprouts
4 leaves lettuce

Prepare the chicken salad as directed. Spread the cream cheese onto one side of the croissant rolls, and spread the mashed avocado onto the other half. Arrange the tomato slices over the cream cheese and add a mound of the chicken salad. Top with alfalfa sprouts and then a lettuce leaf. Serve immediately.

SERVES 4

supreme chicken and pasta salad

This chilled pasta salad is an easy and colorful light summer meal. Serve with garlic bread or crunchy Italian bread sticks. • **SERVES 4**

Step One: THE CHICKEN AND PASTA

2 tablespoons olive oil
2 skinless, boneless chicken breasts
3 cups penne, rotini, or fusilli (rainbow mix if available)
2 tablespoons fresh lemon juice

Heat the oil in the pressure cooker over medium-high heat and brown the chicken on all sides. Add the pasta and lemon juice. Add only enough water to barely cover the ingredients. Lock the lid in place. Bring to 15psi over high heat and immediately reduce the heat to the lowest possible setting to stabilize and maintain that pressure. Cook for 5 minutes. Remove from the heat and use the quick release method before opening the lid. Transfer the chicken to a cutting board. The pasta will be al dente. Immediately drain the pasta in a colander and then rinse under cold running water; set aside until thoroughly drained. Cut the chicken into bite-size pieces.

Step Two: THE SALAD

4 cups assorted cut vegetables, such as broccoli florets, carrots, red onions, bell peppers, radishes, and/or cherry tomatoes
1 (8-ounce) bottle Italian salad dressing or your own homemade dressing
2 teaspoons dried Italian herb blend
Salt and coarsely ground black pepper to taste
½ cup sliced green olives with pimientos
½ cup crumbled feta cheese

Place the chicken into a sealable container and add the drained pasta, vegetables, dressing, herb blend, and salt and pepper. Toss gently to coat. Cover tightly and refrigerate for at least 4 hours or until ready to serve.

Add the olives and cheese and toss again just before serving. Taste and adjust seasonings as desired.

perfect hard-cooked eggs for salads, deviled eggs, and more

Don't you just hate it when you try to cook hard-boiled eggs and they come out cracked, or with an ugly discoloration around the yolk, and they're just impossible to peel? Well, the pressure cooker is the solution for perfect hard-cooked—not boiled—eggs with beautifully centered, bright yellow yolks that are so easy to peel that the shell slips off in one piece. Hard-cooked eggs are so handy to have around for healthy after-school snacks and for egg salad sandwiches for lunch, chef's salads for dinner, or a plate of deviled eggs for your weekend barbecue. Select only the freshest large eggs with absolutely no cracks or those shadowy "fault lines" that may ruin your perfect eggs.

Any number of large eggs, from 1 egg to any amount that will fit in a single layer in your pressure cooker

If cooking 1 egg or just a few eggs, place the eggs on a doubled square of aluminum foil and then shape it loosely around the eggs to hold them steady so they don't roll around and possibly break while they cook. For a larger number of eggs, place them in a perforated steaming basket in the bottom of the pressure cooker. Add enough water to cover the eggs halfway. Lock the lid in place. Bring to 15psi over high heat and immediately reduce the heat to the lowest possible setting to stabilize and maintain that pressure. Cook for 4 minutes. Remove from the heat and use the cold water release method before opening the lid. Immediately cool the eggs in a bowl of ice water. Remove the shells if the eggs are to be used right away. Unpeeled hard-cooked eggs may be stored in the refrigerator for about 1 week.

salpicón de res: shredded beef salad

When I was growing up, we lived in Spain for a time, and my mom soon introduced the flavorful local cuisine to our dinner table. The food carries an aromatic spiciness introduced by the Moors, which we found similar to many of the Latin American foods we were familiar with in our permanent home in California. Salpicón de res is a shredded beef salad that was a popular lunchtime meal when I lived in Spain, and there were many variations of this dish served at all the little sidewalk cafés. The beef brisket is braised in a heady mix of spices until fork-tender, and then the meat is shredded into a concentrated sauce for maximum flavor. The spicy and piquant beef tops the salad, adding contrast to the cool, crisp lettuce and all the juicy vegetables. The vinagreta dressing is well seasoned to complement the other ingredients, but use your own favorite blend if you prefer something different. • **SERVES 6**

Step One: THE VINAGRETA

½ cup extra-virgin olive oil
1 hard-cooked egg (see page 59)
¼ cup drained capers
¼ cup red wine vinegar
1 small shallot, minced
2 cloves garlic
1 tablespoon chopped fresh oregano
½ teaspoon sea salt
½ teaspoon freshly ground black pepper

Place the oil, egg, capers, vinegar, shallot, garlic, oregano, salt, and pepper in a blender and process until smooth. Prepare the dressing several hours in advance and refrigerate the mixture in a tightly sealed jar to allow the flavors to meld. Shake well before using.

Step Two: THE BEEF

1 cup beef broth
½ cup dry red wine
1 onion, minced
6 large cloves garlic, minced
2 tablespoons sweet smoked Spanish paprika (pimentón de la Vera)
¼ teaspoon cayenne pepper, or to taste
2 bay leaves
1 to 1½ pounds beef brisket
Salt and coarsely ground black pepper to taste

Mix the broth, wine, onion, garlic, paprika, cayenne pepper, and bay leaves in the pressure cooker. Season the beef on both sides with salt and black pepper, then place it in the pressure cooker. Lock the lid in place. Bring to 15psi over high heat and immediately reduce the heat to the lowest possible setting to stabilize and maintain that pressure. Cook for 45 minutes. Remove from the heat and use the natural release method before opening the lid. Check for doneness; the meat should easily shred with a fork. Lock the lid in place and return to pressure for an additional 5 minutes or until the meat is fork-tender. Use the natural release method before opening the lid.

Transfer the beef to a cutting board and shred it into small pieces. Meanwhile, skim the visible fat from the surface of the broth. Bring the broth to a boil, uncovered, and continue cooking until the liquid is reduced and concentrated down to about 1 cup. Return the shredded meat to the pressure cooker, lower the heat, and continue cooking, stirring frequently, until the liquid begins to thicken. Spoon the meat into a covered container and refrigerate until the meat is cool, but not chilled cold.

Step Three: THE SALAD

- 6 cups romaine lettuce, torn into 1-inch pieces
- 3 cups chopped Roma tomatoes
- 1 cup diced red onions
- 1 small bunch fresh cilantro, leaves only, finely minced
- 2 avocados, pitted, peeled, and cut into chunks
- ½ cup crumbled queso fresco or feta cheese
- ½ cup sliced pitted black olives
- 12 corn tortillas

In a large serving bowl, toss together the torn lettuce, tomatoes, onions, and cilantro. Add the vinagreta, avocado chunks, queso fresco, and olives, tossing gently to mix. Heat the tortillas in the microwave until soft and pliable; stack 6 tortillas at a time and heat for 45 to 60 seconds on High.

To serve, portion a mound of the salad mixture on a serving plate and top with a portion of the cooled shredded beef. Pass the tortillas at the table, filling as desired with the shredded beef and salad mix. Either fold the tortillas over the filling, or roll them up like a wrap.

COOK'S NOTE: This well-seasoned, shredded beef can be used in many other dishes, so do customize it for other uses, such as a topping for tostadas or in shredded beef sandwiches.

BONUS RECIPE

tapas, a spanish-style bruschetta

In Spain, dinner was usually served between 9 p.m. and 11 p.m. for the grown-ups, but all of us children ate at the earlier American dinner hour and were fast asleep long before the main meal was laid out in the big dining room. Sometimes when dinner guests were expected, tapas were served, and we were invited to share in that treat. Tapas is the name of a wide variety of appetizers or snacks that are very popular in Spanish cuisine; they are small servings of practically anything that can be served either hot or cold.

1 crusty baguette or loaf of similar narrow bread
10 cloves garlic, roasted (see page 252; 1 for each slice of bread)
½ cup extra-virgin olive oil

Start by preheating the broiler and slicing the bread on the diagonal into ½-thick-inch slices (you want to get about 10 slices). Mash the garlic and blend it in a small bowl with the oil. Brush one side of the bread with the olive oil mixture and arrange the slices on a baking sheet. Place under the broiler and watch closely as they begin to brown and crisp. Top each slice of bread with some of the shredded beef and then top with some of the salad mixture. Don't pile on too much or your tapas will be difficult to bite into. Arrange the tapas on a platter and serve as a fun starter.

MAKES 10 TAPAS

soups, stews, and chilis

richer chicken stock

Homemade chicken stock should be added to your to-do list because it's healthy and very economical. Use this basic recipe as a guide, but customize it as you like to use the ingredients you have on hand to produce remarkably full-flavored stocks. It couldn't be easier to make your own chicken stock from scratch, and you can control the flavor, as well as the fat and salt content, and freeze it in convenient portions to use later in recipes.

Significantly more flavor is extracted from the chicken parts in this method because of the higher temperature in the pressure cooker. That combination of higher temperature and pressure produces a deep, rich, golden brown stock. Use a 6-quart or larger pressure cooker when making stocks to get the maximum yield for your efforts. • **MAKES ABOUT 3 QUARTS**

- 4 pounds mixed chicken parts, such as backs, wings, necks, and feet
- 2 medium onions, quartered
- 1 celery heart, the whole stalks and innermost leaves only, or 2 stalks celery with leaves, chopped
- 1 carrot, peeled and halved lengthwise
- ½ bunch fresh Italian parsley
- 6 cloves garlic, crushed
- 1 teaspoon whole black peppercorns
- 1 teaspoon dried thyme
- 1 teaspoon dried marjoram
- 2 bay leaves
- 2 teaspoons salt

Add all the ingredients to the pressure cooker. Pour in 3 quarts cold water or whatever amount will fill the pressure cooker two-thirds full. Lock the lid in place. Bring to 15psi over high heat and immediately reduce the heat to the lowest possible setting to stabilize and maintain that pressure. Cook for 45 minutes. Remove from the heat

(continued)

and use the natural release method before opening the lid. Strain the stock through a fine-mesh wire strainer or a colander lined with a double layer of cheesecloth. Repeat if necessary to clarify the stock. Discard the solids. To defat the stock, use a fat-separator cup, or preferably refrigerate the stock overnight so the fat will rise to the top and solidify for easier removal. Use the stock within 3 days, or freeze in convenient portions (1-quart and 1-cup containers are useful) for later use.

essential smoked meat broth for dried beans

Did your mama tell you that dried beans are bland? It's true, but that's why beans are so versatile, because they can literally go with anything. Beans lend themselves well to all kinds of added flavors, and that's where this meaty broth comes in. Cooking dried beans in a tasty soup is usually a two-step process: First you need to prepare the broth with meats that typically take a long time to cook. After the delicious broth is ready, then the soaked beans and other vegetables are added to finish making the soup. Try this essential meat broth to add much needed flavor to your next bean soup. • **MAKES ABOUT 2 QUARTS**

1 medium onion, quartered
6 cloves garlic, crushed
1 large meaty ham bone or 2 pounds smoked meat, such as pork hocks or neck bones, or smoked turkey legs or wings
1 jalapeño chile, seeded and halved
4 dried ancho chiles or similar mild dried chiles, seeded and chopped
1 small bunch fresh cilantro (about 20 sprigs), leaves and stems finely chopped
2 bay leaves
1 teaspoon liquid smoke

Add the onion, garlic, ham bone, jalapeño, dried chiles, cilantro, and bay leaves to the cooker. Add enough cold water to cover all the ingredients completely. Lock the lid in place. Bring to 15psi over high heat and immediately reduce the heat to the lowest possible setting to stabilize and maintain that pressure. Cook for 40 minutes. Remove from the heat and use the natural release method before opening the lid. Strain the broth through a colander into a large bowl. Pick the meat from the bones. Discard all the leftover vegetables, bones, and pieces of fat. Skim off any excess fat from the surface of the broth, return the meat to the broth, and stir in the liquid smoke. The meaty broth is ready to use for your dried bean recipe or to freeze for later use.

roasted garlic broth

Garlic, they say, has legendary medicinal properties. I wouldn't know about that, but I can attest to the useful culinary properties of this great-tasting garlic broth. This deceptively simple broth has the delicately mild sweetness of the roasted garlic, but still a powerful garlic flavor that will complement many dishes. While it's really a base for other soups or stews, this broth may also be served on its own . . . and maybe even ward off a vampire or two. • **MAKES 6 CUPS**

20 large plump cloves garlic, roasted (see page 252)
10 fresh sage leaves
1 teaspoon whole black peppercorns
1 large onion, quartered
10 sprigs fresh cilantro
1 celery heart with stalks and leaves

Do not peel the garlic cloves; use the meat mallet that's been hiding in the back of your utensil drawer and give each one a good whack to open them up . . . don't be nice, you're going to toss them out later. To bruise the sage, stack the leaves and then use that mallet again until you can smell the aroma and the leaves look like assault victims. To crack the peppercorns, put them in a plastic sandwich bag and lay a kitchen towel over it. Grab that mallet again and use the flat side to smack the peppercorns once or twice so they are cracked but not crushed.

Place the smashed garlic, the onion, cilantro, celery, cracked peppercorns, and the poor sage leaves in the pressure cooker. Pour in 6 cups water. Lock the lid in place. Bring to 15psi over high heat and immediately reduce the heat to the lowest possible setting to stabilize and maintain that pressure. Cook for 12 minutes. Remove from the heat and use the natural release method before opening the lid. Strain the broth through a wire strainer or a colander lined with a double layer of cheesecloth. Press the solids with the back of a spoon to get the last bit of the liquid. You should end up with slightly more than 6 cups. Refrigerate the broth in a tightly closed container and plan on using it within 3 days. Alternatively, divide the garlic broth into 1- or 2-cup portions and freeze for up to 6 months.

sweet corn stock

Making something from nothing takes skill and planning, but to make it delicious . . . you need a pressure cooker. From an early age, I can remember my grandma preaching about thriftiness. She raised a family during the Great Depression, and after Gramps died, she managed the farm like a commanding general. Woe betide the hapless grandchild who tossed out a single corncob. Never let something useful go to waste; that was her motto, and fresh corncobs are like kitchen gold to a frugal cook like me. Yes, I'm a victim of my grandma's thriftiness, and I compulsively freeze bits of fresh corn and corncobs in the summer to make stock in the winter. Corncob stock imparts an intense corn flavor to soups, stews, risotto, or any recipe with corn as an ingredient. • **MAKES ABOUT 2 QUARTS**

- 8 ears fresh or frozen sweet corn on the cob
- 1 large sweet onion, diced
- 2 stalks celery with leaves, diced
- 2 carrots, peeled and diced
- 6 sprigs fresh thyme or 1 teaspoon dried thyme
- 2 bay leaves
- 10 whole black peppercorns
- Salt to taste

If using fresh corn, cut the corn kernels from the cob and either refrigerate them for use within a day or two or freeze them for later use. (If using frozen corn, the kernels are not worth saving for later use.) "Milk" the cobs by scraping them with a heavy spoon. Add the liquid to the pressure cooker. Cut the cobs into 3-inch sections and add them to the pressure cooker along with the onion, celery, carrots, thyme, bay leaves, and peppercorns. Add enough water to cover the ingredients by 3 inches. Lock the lid in place. Bring to 15psi over high heat and immediately reduce the heat to the lowest possible setting to stabilize and maintain that pressure. Cook 15 minutes. Remove from the heat and use the natural release method before opening the lid. Line a wire strainer or colander with a double layer of cheesecloth and carefully strain the stock into another large pot. Discard the solids and taste the stock, adding salt as needed. Plan on using this corn stock within 2 days, or portion into containers and freeze.

quick and easy tomato soup

These simple ingredients are almost always on hand, so who needs the condensed stuff? My mother used to make this soup all the time, and it was a big family favorite on wintry weekends when we had all been playing out in the snow. Nothing warms you up faster than a mug of hot soup. Add grilled cheese sandwiches and you have the perfect combination for lunch or a light supper. • **SERVES 4 OR 5**

3 tablespoons butter
1 medium onion, finely chopped
3 stalks celery, thinly sliced
4 carrots, peeled and thinly sliced
1 teaspoon smoked paprika
Pinch of red pepper flakes, or to taste
1 teaspoon dried basil
1 tablespoon minced garlic
Salt and freshly ground black pepper to taste
1 cup beef broth or 1 teaspoon beef bouillon granules mixed with 1 cup water
1 cup dry white wine
2 cups water
1 (28-ounce) can tomato puree
1 (28-ounce) can diced tomatoes with juice

Heat the butter in the pressure cooker over medium-high heat. Add the onion and cook, stirring frequently, until translucent and turning golden, about 8 minutes. Add all the remaining ingredients in the order given and without stirring. Lock the lid in place. Bring to 15psi over high heat and immediately reduce the heat to the lowest possible setting to stabilize and maintain that pressure. Cook for 6 minutes. Remove from the heat and use the natural release method before opening the lid. Use a handheld blender to puree the mixture to a smooth texture, or puree the soup in batches in a blender. Taste and adjust seasonings as needed. Serve hot.

Variation:
CREAM OF TOMATO SOUP

After the soup is pureed, stir in 1 cup heavy cream and heat through.

Variation:
TOMATO SOUP WITH GARDEN VEGETABLES

Add 1 cup each of small cubes of potatoes and frozen whole kernel corn. Substitute 2 (14-ounce) cans chicken broth for the beef broth. Do not puree.

Variation:

TOMATO SOUP WITH CHICKEN CHUNKS AND SUCCOTASH

Add 1 (10-ounce) package frozen succotash. Add 2 cups bite-size chicken chunks. Substitute 2 (14-ounce) cans chicken broth for the beef broth. Do not puree.

Variation:

TOMATO AND RICE SOUP

Add ½ cup long-grain white rice. Do not puree.

creamy potato soup with radish greens

It's a pity that in this land of plenty we waste a lot good food. Perhaps in part it's because in this era of fast food and packaged meals, we simply don't know how to wring every penny from our hard-earned food dollar. I've mentioned how frugal the cooks of generations past were, whether by economic necessity or perhaps because of traits instilled by our thrifty American heritage. In any event, they wasted nothing. This simple, rustic soup is an excellent example of how to use radish greens—something that most of us just throw away—and turn them into a lovely, fresh-tasting soup that can be served either piping hot or chilled. Radish leaves look like rough customers, all prickly-coarse, but they have a very mild and delicate flavor that doesn't taste anything like a radish. Fresh radish greens mix nicely in salads, they cook just like any other leafy greens, and they blend nicely with potatoes, too. • **SERVES 4**

- 2 strips bacon
- ½ cup finely chopped onion
- 2 cups peeled and cubed russet potatoes
- ⅓ cup peeled and finely chopped radishes, plus 3 large radishes, sliced, for garnish
- 1 teaspoon chicken bouillon granules
- 3 cloves garlic, roasted (see page 252) and mashed with a fork
- ¼ teaspoon ground nutmeg
- 1 teaspoon salt
- ¼ teaspoon coarsely ground black pepper
- 1 teaspoon snipped fresh thyme or ½ teaspoon dried thyme
- 3 cups radish greens (from about 2 large bunches of radishes)
- 1 cup half-and-half

Heat the pressure cooker over medium-high heat and fry the bacon to render out the fat. Transfer the bacon to paper towels to drain, and then crumble to use as a garnish. Cook the onion in the bacon fat until tender, about 3 minutes. Add the potatoes and chopped radishes. Add the bouillon, garlic, nutmeg, salt, pepper, and thyme. Add 2 cups water and the radish greens, stirring well. Lock the lid in place. Bring to 15psi over high heat and immediately reduce the heat to the lowest possible setting to stabilize and maintain that pressure. Cook for 4 minutes. Remove from the heat and use the natural release method before opening the lid. Add the half-and-half. Use a handheld blender to puree the soup to a smooth consistency. Taste, adjusting the seasonings as desired. Ladle into soup bowls and garnish with crumbled bacon bits and the radish slices.

fresh spinach and tortellini soup

Fresh green spinach is complemented by a light chicken stock and flavorful tortellini. This is an easy-to-prepare soup that makes for a simple, rustic meal with a crusty loaf of Italian bread. Three minutes to cook, so don't blink! • **SERVES 4**

2 tablespoons olive oil
½ cup diced sweet onion
½ teaspoon dried thyme
1 teaspoon dried basil
½ cup diced carrots
2 cloves garlic, minced
2 (15-ounce) cans chicken broth
8 ounces fresh tortellini (not frozen), any flavor
Salt and freshly ground black pepper, to taste
1 large bunch fresh spinach, stems removed and leaves coarsely chopped
1 (8-ounce) can tomato sauce
½ cup grated Parmigiano-Reggiano cheese, for garnish (optional)

Heat the oil in the pressure cooker over medium-high heat and cook the onion until soft and translucent, about 4 minutes. Add the thyme, basil, carrots, garlic, broth, tortellini, and salt and pepper, stirring to mix. Add the spinach and tomato sauce, but do not stir. Lock the lid in place. Bring to 15psi over high heat and immediately reduce the heat to the lowest possible setting to stabilize and maintain that pressure. Cook for 3 minutes. Remove from the heat and use the quick release method before opening the lid. Gently stir to mix all the ingredients. Taste and adjust seasonings as desired. Ladle into soup bowls and serve with a sprinkling of the cheese, if desired.

Variation:
FRESH SPINACH AND TORTELLINI SOUP WITH ITALIAN SAUSAGE

Add 1 pound Italian sausage, casings discarded. Brown the meat in the oil in the pressure cooker until crumbly, and then proceed as directed.

fresh tomato soup with grilled cheese croutons

Whether you grow your own or scour the supermarket ads for good prices, tomatoes are a universal favorite because they are so versatile and delicious—and of course, they are necessary for this fresh tomato soup. It's classic comfort food, and it must be hardwired into our genetic code that cold weather brings on the craving for a bowl of hot tomato soup and its companion, a grilled cheese sandwich. This recipe had every intention of being that classic American lunch menu, a mug of hot soup and a sandwich, right up until the moment when I discovered I didn't have enough bread for sandwiches for everyone, and my plan began to fall apart. Scrambling around for a substitute to feed a hungry family on the fly, the "grilled cheese crouton" was born. It's a miraculous invention, my dears, because you get a spoonful of soup with a bite of grilled cheese sandwich included. I should patent it! • **SERVES 4**

Step One: THE SOUP

1 tablespoon butter
1 medium onion, diced
4 cloves garlic, minced
2 stalks celery, diced
2 pounds Roma tomatoes, cut into wedges
2 (15-ounce) cans chicken broth or Richer Chicken Stock (page 63)
2 tablespoons tomato paste
½ teaspoon Louisiana-style hot sauce, or to taste
2 bay leaves
3 sprigs fresh thyme, each about 3 inches long
½ cup chopped fresh basil
Salt and coarsely ground black pepper to taste

Heat the butter in the pressure cooker over medium heat and cook the onion until soft and translucent but not brown, about 4 minutes. Add the garlic and cook until fragrant. Add the celery, tomatoes, broth, tomato paste, hot sauce, bay leaves, thyme, and basil. Stir until well mixed. Season with salt and pepper. Lock the lid in place. Bring to 15psi over high heat and immediately reduce the heat to the lowest possible setting to stabilize and maintain that pressure. Cook for 10 minutes. Remove from the heat and use the natural release method before opening the lid.

Step Two: THE CROUTONS

3 tablespoons butter, softened
½ teaspoon dried basil, finely crushed
4 slices seeded rye bread
2 slices sharp cheddar cheese

Mix the butter and basil until smoothly blended. Preheat a small skillet over medium heat. Generously butter one side of a slice of bread. Place the bread butter side down on the hot skillet and add 1 slice of cheese. Butter a second slice of bread on one side and place it on top, butter side up. Cook until lightly browned and then flip over; continue grilling until the cheese is melted and the bread is lightly browned. Repeat with the remaining slices of bread, butter, and cheese. Let the sandwiches cool slightly, and then cut them into 1-inch squares.

Step Three: THE FINALE

½ cup heavy cream
3 tablespoons fresh basil leaves, thinly sliced, for garnish

Remove the lid from the pressure cooker. Discard the bay leaves and thyme sprigs. Use a handheld blender to puree the soup until smooth. Alternatively, use a blender to puree the soup in batches until it is a smooth consistency. Stir in the cream and heat the pureed soup over medium heat. Taste and adjust seasonings as needed. Ladle into soup bowls and serve with a scattering of the basil leaves and grilled cheese croutons. Pass a plate with the extra croutons so they can be added to the soup as you eat.

creamy roasted garlic soup with savory herbed cheese flans

Everyone loves soups. They range from simple, warming, comfort food that's easy on your purse and made from ordinary pantry fare to elegant, gourmet recipes with pricey ingredients that send you out on a mad shopping expedition. This soup with its sweet flavor of roasted garlic makes a sophisticated meal, but the little savory cheese flans are the real prize. As the cheese begins to melt into the hot, creamy soup, it adds a new layer of nutty deliciousness. Spoon a bit of the savory flan on a chunk of plain crusty bread as you mop up the last drop of this wonderful soup. • **SERVES 4**

Step One: THE SOUP

30 cloves garlic, roasted (see page 252)
2 tablespoons butter
2 tablespoons olive oil
3 cups chopped onions
3 tablespoons chopped fresh thyme or 1 teaspoon dried thyme
2 cups diced peeled Yukon gold or similar yellow-fleshed potatoes
6 cups Richer Chicken Stock (page 63) or canned chicken broth
1 cup heavy cream
½ cup grated Parmesan or similar hard grating cheese
Salt and freshly ground black pepper to taste

Squeeze the roasted garlic cloves between your fingertips to pop the insides out into a small bowl, and mash with a fork to a smooth consistency. Melt the butter and oil in the pressure cooker over medium-high heat. Add onions and thyme and cook until the onions are translucent. Stir in the mashed garlic. Add the potatoes and stock, stirring to blend. Lock the lid in place. Bring to 15psi over high heat and immediately reduce the heat to the lowest possible setting to stabilize and maintain that pressure. Cook for 8 minutes. Remove from the heat and use the natural release method before opening the lid. Use a handheld immersion blender to puree the soup, or puree the soup in batches in a blender, until it is smooth. Add the cream and cheese and bring to a simmer, uncovered, cooking over low heat until heated through. Season with salt and pepper.

Step Two: THE FLANS

2 tablespoons butter
1 shallot, diced
½ cup heavy cream
1 large egg
½ teaspoon salt
¼ teaspoon cayenne pepper
2 tablespoons minced fresh thyme
½ cup packed shredded Jarlsberg or Swiss cheese

Melt the butter in the pressure cooker over medium heat and cook the shallot until soft. Add the shallot, but do not let it brown. Transfer to a food processor and let the mixture cool slightly. Add the cream, egg, salt, cayenne pepper, and thyme, and blend until smooth. Stir in the cheese. Spray 4 (4- to 6-ounce) ramekins with nonstick cooking spray. Divide the cheese mixture among the ramekins. Cover each ramekin tightly with aluminum foil. Place the cooking rack in the bottom of the pressure cooker and add ½ cup water. Place the ramekins on the rack, or put them in a steamer tray for easier removal. Lock the lid in place. Bring to 15psi over high heat and immediately reduce the heat to the lowest possible setting to stabilize and maintain that pressure. Cook for 4 minutes. Remove from the heat and use the natural release method before opening the lid.

Step Three: TO SERVE

Ladle the hot soup into individual bowls. Cut around the flans with a thin-bladed knife to loosen the sides, and then turn them out, placing each one in the center of a bowl of soup.

rustic mushroom bisque with savory homemade herbed croutons

Baby, it's cold outside! When the weather turns frosty, that means we all want a generous mug of hot soup to wrap our freezing fingers around and something tasty to take the chill off our insides. I like this mushroom soup, I mean, *bisque*. What's the difference, you ask? Well, my dears, there is no black-and-white division between the two words. The culinary boundaries are more flexible than ever, and everyone is naming their dishes whatever they like. Traditionally, a bisque—as the name suggests—describes a type of rich, thick, creamy-smooth soup. Foodie types are still debating the origins of the word, and some food historians believe that name refers to the fact that the soup is cooked twice. All you really need to know is that this is rich and delicious stuff. Serve this bisque as a stand-alone meal with a chunk of fresh bakery bread or as an elegant first course at a posh dinner party, or just add a big sandwich and have at it. • **SERVES 4**

Step One: THE BACON

6 strips bacon

Fry the bacon in the pressure cooker or a small skillet until crisp. Transfer to paper towels to drain. Reserve the bacon fat.

Step Two: THE CROUTONS

4 slices stale sourdough bread or any good rustic bread of your choice
2 to 3 tablespoons hot bacon fat
⅛ teaspoon freshly ground black pepper
1 tablespoon mixed dried herbs, such as basil, oregano, and/or Italian parsley

Preheat the oven to 325°F. Stack the bread slices and cut them into 1-inch cubes. Mix the hot bacon fat in a bowl with the pepper and dried herbs. Add the bread cubes, tossing lightly until coated with the fat and herbs. Spread the cubes on a baking sheet and bake for 15 to 20 minutes or until the cubes start to brown and turn crisp all the way through. Watch closely, as the baking time will vary depending on how moist the bread is. Set aside until ready to serve.

Step Three: THE MUSHROOMS

4 tablespoons (½ stick) butter
1 cup diced onions
3 cups mixed fresh mushrooms, such as portobello, shiitake, and/or cremini, washed and coarsely chopped
Salt and coarsely ground black pepper to taste
1 (14-ounce) can beef broth
¼ cup all-purpose flour
3 cups milk
⅓ cup good-quality dry sherry
1 cup heavy cream
Freshly cracked black pepper to taste

Melt half the butter in the pressure cooker over medium heat. Add the onions and cook until soft and translucent, about 4 minutes. Add the mushrooms, salt and coarsely ground pepper, and broth, stirring well. Lock the lid in place. Bring to 15psi over high heat and immediately reduce the heat to the lowest possible setting to stabilize and maintain that pressure. Cook for 4 minutes. Remove from the heat and use the quick release method before opening the lid.

Meanwhile, to thicken the broth, make a slurry of the flour and ½ cup of the milk and set aside. Remove the lid and use an immersion blender to puree the contents to a smooth consistency or puree the soup in batches in a blender. Simmer the broth mixture over medium heat. Add the remaining butter, stirring until it is melted and incorporated into the broth. Whisk the remaining milk into the simmering broth and add the sherry, stirring until the mixture begins to simmer. Whisk in the cream, and then slowly add the slurry. Turn up the heat a bit and keep stirring until the bisque is hot and it's the desired consistency. Taste and adjust seasonings as desired—a liberal amount of some beautiful, freshly cracked pepper would be appreciated. Ladle into soup bowls, add a few croutons, and sprinkle some of the crumbled bacon on top.

fresh spinach soup

The pressure cooker enhances the taste of fresh ingredients and lets the delicate flavors shine through. Spinach stars in this soup, and it's cooked just until the leaves are wilted, to preserve their vivid color and taste. Yes, my dears, you can do this in the pressure cooker by using the "zero-minute" cooking technique. This is one of those old tricks of pressure cookery that everyone who used one knew about, but times changed and you seldom see it used these days. However, it's really a very useful technique when cooking delicate fresh vegetables, like spinach, that can easily be overcooked. All it means is that we lock the lid in place and then bring the pressure cooker to 15psi as usual. As soon as the pressure cooker is fully pressurized, we remove it from the heat and then use the quick release to depressurize it. You'll want to remove the lid as soon as it's safe to do so, in order to stop the cooking and keep the baby spinach leaves looking fresh. Serve this soup with your favorite sandwich, a quiche, or a frittata. • **SERVES 4**

2 tablespoons olive oil
1 medium red onion, coarsely chopped
1 carrot, peeled and coarsely chopped
1 cup chopped celery
2 large cloves garlic, finely minced
6 cups chicken or vegetable broth
1 teaspoon sea salt
½ teaspoon coarsely ground black pepper
2 teaspoons mild curry powder
2 teaspoons chicken bouillon granules
2 cups chopped seeded tomatoes
½ cup long-grain white rice
5 cups fresh baby spinach leaves
Ground nutmeg, for garnish

Heat the oil in the pressure cooker over medium heat and cook the onion until soft and translucent, about 4 minutes. Add the carrots, celery, garlic, broth, and 2 cups water. Add the salt, pepper, curry powder, bouillon, tomatoes, and rice, stirring to mix. Lock the lid in place. Bring to 15psi over high heat and immediately reduce the heat to the lowest possible setting to stabilize and maintain that pressure. Cook for 4 minutes. Remove from the heat and use the natural release method before opening the lid. Add the spinach leaves on top without stirring. Lock the lid in place. Bring to 15psi over high heat and immediately reduce the heat to the lowest possible setting to stabilize and maintain that pressure. Cook for 0 (zero) minutes. Remove from the heat and use the quick release method before opening the lid. Stir the wilted spinach leaves into the soup. Taste and adjust seasoning as desired. Ladle into soup bowls and add a dash of nutmeg.

pot-o-gold soup

Have you ever noticed how often the phrase *comfort food* accompanies soup recipes? It's certainly true that a good soup does as much for the spirit as it does for the stomach, and I can't think of anyone who doesn't have a favorite soup. There's probably no other food that gives as much comfort to people of all cultures around the world. This delectable squash soup looks and feels like fall with its golden color and rich flavor. Serve it with crusty bread or your favorite sandwich for a satisfying meal. • **SERVES 5**

- 2 tablespoons butter
- 1 Vidalia onion, finely chopped
- 2 medium apples, peeled and grated
- 3 cloves garlic, minced
- 1 butternut squash (about 2 pounds), peeled, seeded, and cut into 1½-inch cubes
- 1 cup apple juice
- 2 (15-ounce) cans chicken broth
- 1 teaspoon ground turmeric
- Salt and freshly ground black pepper to taste
- 2 tablespoons dark brown sugar
- 1 teaspoon pumpkin pie spice, plus more for garnish
- Zest and juice of 1 lemon
- ⅓ cup sour cream, for garnish

Melt the butter in the pressure cooker over medium heat. Add the onion and cook until soft and translucent, about 4 minutes. Add the apples, garlic, squash, apple juice, broth, turmeric, and salt and pepper. Lock the lid in place. Bring to 15psi over high heat and immediately reduce the heat to the lowest possible setting to stabilize and maintain that pressure. Cook for 5 minutes. Remove from the heat and use the natural release method before opening the lid. Add the sugar, pumpkin pie spice, and the lemon juice and zest. Use a handheld blender, or blend the soup in batches in a blender, to puree the soup to a smooth, creamy consistency. Ladle into soup bowls and spoon a dollop of sour cream on top. Finish with a sprinkling of pumpkin pie spice.

red lentil soup

Lentils come in colors that range from yellow, orange, and red to green, brown, and black, and they are sold all over the world and in many forms from whole to split, with or without the skins. Like most dried peas and beans, lentils are usually mild in taste, so they need to be paired with bold ingredients and plenty of seasonings to add flavor. Lentils don't need to be soaked before cooking, so they cook very quickly in the pressure cooker, disintegrating into a rich and creamy texture for delicious, full-bodied, and very satisfying soups. That makes this Indian-inspired recipe a good choice for a quick and nutritious weekday dinner. I like to serve this soup with a hot Indian flatbread like chapati or naan—very quick and easy to make at home—brushed with melted butter. Substitute warmed tortillas or pita bread and a soft, spreadable herbed cheese if you prefer. • **SERVES 4**

1 cup split red lentils
1 tablespoon sesame oil
1 medium onion, chopped
One 1-inch piece fresh ginger, peeled and minced
2 large cloves garlic, minced
1 teaspoon ground cumin
½ teaspoon ground turmeric
Pinch of red pepper flakes, or more to taste
3 cups broth of your choice
2 tablespoons tomato paste
Salt and freshly ground black pepper to taste
½ cup plain regular or Greek-style yogurt (see page 246), for garnish
2 tablespoons finely chopped fresh cilantro leaves, for garnish

Spread the lentils out and pick out any that look blemished or any other odd bits, and then rinse them in cold water and drain. Heat the oil in the pressure cooker over medium-high heat and cook the onion until golden brown. Stir in the ginger, garlic, cumin, and turmeric and cook until fragrant, about 2 minutes. Add the red pepper flakes, lentils, and broth, and stir. Finally add the tomato paste on top; do not stir. Lock the lid in place. Bring to 15psi over high heat and immediately reduce the heat to the lowest possible setting to stabilize and maintain that pressure. Cook for 6 minutes. Remove from the heat and use the natural release method before opening the lid. Stir in the tomato paste until well combined and at the desired consistency, adding a bit of water to the soup if needed. Adjust seasonings with salt and black pepper. Serve hot with a dollop of the yogurt and a sprinkling of the cilantro.

soup of black-eyed peas and collards in ham broth

Soup is comfort food, and every household has a favorite soup recipe. In the southern part of the United States, some of the best soups are steeped in local tradition and history, and they are also very economical to make, with ingredients like black-eyed peas and collard greens. This soup demands hot, buttered cornbread, so pop the pan in the oven when the meaty broth is finished cooking and it will be ready when your soup is. Try my Sweet Buttermilk Cornbread with this (page 33).

Back in my grandparents' day, cooks were frugal people who scrimped in good times as well as hard times. In those bygone days, there was very little kitchen waste because what we so casually toss in the garbage today was routinely repurposed, with every sort of vegetable paring and meat scrap used to make the best-tasting stocks for those wonderful soups we all remember. Of course, a big side benefit to Grandma's penny-pinching ways was getting a big pot of soup that was practically free. So, my dears, if you want to cut your food budget, start saving and freezing those bits and scraps for your next pot of "free" soup. • **SERVES 4**

Step One: THE MEATY BROTH

Make this ahead of time if you prefer, or it's easy enough to make when needed. Either way will turn out the most delicious base for the finished soup.

1 meaty ham bone
1 medium onion, coarsely chopped
½ cup packed chopped fresh cilantro leaves and stems
1 tablespoon minced garlic
2 bay leaves
Pinch of red pepper flakes, or to taste
1 teaspoon dried rosemary, crushed
1 teaspoon dried thyme

Put all the ingredients into the pressure cooker and add 8 cups water or as needed to cover the ham bone. Lock the lid in place. Bring to 15psi over high heat and immediately reduce the heat to the lowest possible setting to stabilize and maintain that pressure. Cook for 15 minutes. Remove from the heat and use the natural release method before opening the lid. Take out the bone and pick off all the meaty bits, cutting them into small shreds; discard the bone. Strain the broth and discard the nonmeat solids. Pour the broth back into the pressure cooker and reserve the meat.

(continued)

Step Two: THE BLACK-EYED PEAS

2 cups dried black-eyed peas
1 bunch collard greens

While the broth is cooking, sort through the dried peas to remove any unwanted debris like teeny pebbles, and any broken or blemished peas, then rinse—no need to soak. Add the clean peas to the broth and give it a stir. Wash the collard greens in a sink filled with cold water. Submerge them and swish them around to loosen and remove any dirt. Remove and inspect the leaves one at a time, tearing off any bruised or discolored edges before laying them side on a towel to drain. Cut out the thick center ribs, and freeze those pieces for later use in another stock or soup recipe. Stack the leaves and cut lengthwise through the middle of the stack to divide them into two sections. Roll up each pile of stacked leaves from the long edge so it looks like a long cigar. Cut the leaves into 1-inch sections. Loosely pile the cut collard leaves on top of the peas and broth. Do not stir.

Lock the lid in place. Bring to 15psi over high heat and immediately reduce the heat to the lowest possible setting to stabilize and maintain that pressure. Cook for 10 minutes. Remove from the heat and use the natural release method before opening the lid. Return the bits of meat to the soup, and stir to blend. Taste the broth and adjust seasonings as needed. Ladle into soup mugs and serve.

COOK'S NOTE: If you don't have a nice ham bone handy, choose any other variety of smoked meats, such as ham hocks, pork neck bones, or turkey legs or thighs, but check the cooking time, as these will all need additional minutes to cook. Another option is bacon ends. These odd bits and pieces of smoky bacon are thicker and meatier than sliced bacon, and there is often a nice bit of the smoked rind attached, which adds wonderful flavor and aroma to the soup. Skim off any excess fat from the surface of the broth before adding the peas.

COOK'S NOTE: To serve this as a meat-free soup, omit the meat and add 3 cups Roasted Garlic Broth (page 66) to replace part of the water and add flavor.

---

rustic fava bean soup with roasted tomatoes and guajillo chiles

The guajillo (gwah-HEE-yoh) chile pepper is one of the most popular dried chiles, and it is prominently featured in traditional dishes from South America, Spain, the Middle East, Asia, and even the U.S. These dark reddish brown dried peppers can vary from mild to moderate in their heat, and like most dried chiles, unless you want a lot more heat in your recipe you'll want to cut them open and remove the stem, seeds, and veins before use. It's a good idea to wear food-preparation gloves when working with chiles, as the oils can irritate your skin. With their distinctive earthy taste, guajillo chiles add a hint of fruitiness and a berry aftertaste that adds a very nice depth of spicy flavor to this Spanish-inspired tomato soup. Serve with warm, buttered tortillas or a loaf of crusty bread. • **SERVES 4**

Step One: THE PRESOAK

2 cups dried fava beans, picked over and rinsed

Soak the beans in water to cover overnight.

Step Two: THE SOUP

2 or 3 dried guajillo chiles, seeded
1 pound Roma tomatoes, seeded and roasted (see page 299)
8 cloves garlic, roasted (see page 252)
10 to 12 sprigs fresh cilantro
2 tablespoons olive oil
1 large onion, coarsely chopped
1½ teaspoons ground cumin
1 cup dry red wine
Salt and freshly ground black pepper to taste

Coarsely chop the chiles and add the pieces to a blender or food processor; pulse until the pepper pieces are pulverized and very small, no bigger than the size of a lentil. Transfer to a bowl. Place the roasted tomatoes and any accumulated juice, the garlic pulp, and the cilantro in a food processor and pulse until the mixture has a smooth consistency. Heat the oil in the pressure cooker and cook the onion until soft and golden brown, about 5 minutes. Stir in the cumin and the pulverized chiles, letting them sizzle until the aroma becomes noticeably fragrant. Deglaze the cooker with the wine, scraping up all the browned bits from the bottom. Drain and rinse the beans, and add them to the pressure cooker. Add enough water to completely cover the beans

(continued)

by 2 inches and stir well. Add the tomato mixture on top and do not stir. Lock the lid in place. Bring to 15psi over high heat and immediately reduce the heat to the lowest possible setting to stabilize and maintain that pressure. Cook for 18 minutes. Remove from the heat and use the natural method before opening the lid. Stir the soup until well blended. Taste and adjust seasoning, adding salt and pepper as desired.

penny pincher's navy bean soup

To make a frugal soup from leftovers, start by making a flavorful stock as the base. Smoked pork neck bones are often used to add a robust flavor to beans, and they are very cheap, too. Unlike ham hocks, another popular choice, this meat doesn't have a great deal of waste, and there's much less fat and no inedible rind. Smoked pork neck bones have loads more meat and plenty of bone and connective tissue, the key elements to making a rich-tasting soup.

Inexpensive ingredients add body to the soup, plus a wonderfully fragrant aroma. Dried beans will go a long way to stretch your food budget, my dears—did your mama tell you that? It's quite true, and the yield is incredible, so I'm only using 1 cup for my cheap soup. Another penny-pinching trick that I learned from my grandma is to chop most of the meat into very small bits and shreds, but you'll also want to leave a few large pieces so it fools the eye into seeing just the bigger chunks. Serve your soup with a hunk of bakery bread or a pan of cornbread, and add some chopped hot pickled peppers if you like a little heat. • **SERVES 4**

Step One: THE PRESOAK

1 cup dried navy beans, picked over and rinsed

Soak the beans in water to cover for at least 4 hours.

Step Two: THE MEAT BROTH

½ pound smoked pork neck bones
1 large onion, chopped
2 carrots, peeled and diced
4 cloves garlic, smashed
½ bunch fresh cilantro, stems and leaves chopped
1 teaspoon dried thyme
1 teaspoon dried rosemary, crushed
2 bay leaves

Place all the ingredients in the pressure cooker. Add just enough water to almost cover the ingredients. Lock the lid in place. Bring to 15psi over high heat and immediately reduce the heat to the lowest possible setting to stabilize and maintain that pressure. Cook for 35 minutes. Remove from the heat and use the natural release method before opening the lid. The meat should be tender and easy pull away from the bone. If needed, return to pressure for an additional 5 minutes, and then use the natural release method before opening the lid. Discard the bay leaves. Transfer the meat to a cutting board and, when cool enough to handle, pick off all the meat and chop it into

(continued)

small shreds. Set aside. Use a handheld blender to puree the vegetables and broth to a smooth consistency or puree in batches in a blender.

Step Three: THE SOUP

Rinse the beans and discard the soaking water. Add the beans to the broth in the pressure cooker. If necessary, add more water so that the beans are covered by 1 inch. Lock the lid in place. Bring to 15psi over high heat and immediately reduce the heat to the lowest possible setting to stabilize and maintain that pressure. Cook for 12 minutes. Remove from the heat and use the natural release method before opening the lid. Check for doneness; a bean should be soft enough to mash between your thumb and forefinger. If needed, return to pressure for an additional 2 minutes, and again use the natural release method before opening the lid. For a creamier broth, use a handheld blender to partially puree the beans and broth, taking care to leave some beans whole. Return the meat to the beans and broth and heat through. Season to taste and serve.

navy bean soup with chicken, squash, and swiss chard

Most navy bean soups are strongly flavored with the addition of hearty smoked meats, but here's a different twist that features the more delicate taste of chicken. This allows the subtler flavors of the vegetables to shine through, and you can actually taste the pieces of squash and chard. If you haven't yet introduced chard to your family, this is a good way of sneaking it in. • **SERVES 6**

Step One: THE PRESOAK

1 pound dried navy beans, picked over and rinsed

Soak the beans in water to cover for at least 4 hours.

Step Two: THE CHICKEN AND BEANS

3 tablespoons olive oil
3 chicken breasts, skin removed
1 large onion, chopped
Two 3-inch sprigs fresh rosemary or 1 teaspoon dried rosemary
Four 3-inch sprigs fresh thyme or 1 teaspoon dried thyme
8 cloves garlic, roasted (see page 252) and mashed to a smooth pulp
½ teaspoon red pepper flakes
10 sprigs fresh cilantro, chopped
6 cups Richer Chicken Stock (page 63) or 4 (15-ounce) cans chicken broth
1 bunch Swiss chard, stalks cut into 1-inch slices and leaves coarsely torn and reserved

Heat the oil in the pressure cooker over medium-high heat, brown the chicken on both sides, and then set aside. Cook the onion until soft and caramel colored, stirring often to prevent burning, about 5 minutes. Stir in the rosemary and thyme, and cook until they begin to wilt and become fragrant. Stir in the garlic, red pepper flakes, cilantro, and the stock. Drain and rinse the soaked beans and add them to the pressure cooker. Add the sliced chard stalks. Place the chicken breasts on top. Lock the lid in place. Bring to 15psi over high heat and immediately reduce the heat to the lowest possible setting to stabilize and maintain that pressure. Cook for 8 minutes. Remove from the heat and use the quick release method before opening the lid.

(continued)

Step Three: THE VEGETABLES

2 carrots, peeled and diced
1 small butternut squash (about 1½ pounds), peeled and seeded, cut into 1-inch chunks
Salt and coarsely ground black pepper to taste
½ cup sour cream, for garnish

Lift out the chicken breasts to a cutting board and, when cool enough to handle, chop and pull the meat off the bones. Shred the meat into small pieces and return it, along with any accumulated juices, to the pressure cooker. Discard the bones. Stir in the carrots and squash. Lay the torn chard leaves on top and do not stir. Lock the lid in place. Bring to 15psi over high heat and immediately reduce the heat to the lowest possible setting to stabilize and maintain that pressure. Cook for 4 minutes. Remove from the heat and use the natural release method before opening the lid. Test to make sure beans are completely soft. Pull out the stems of rosemary and thyme. Stir the contents, mixing thoroughly. Taste the broth and correct the seasonings with salt and pepper. Ladle the soup into individual serving bowls and top each with a dollop of the sour cream.

COOK'S NOTE: For those of you who do not eat meat, simply omit the chicken and replace the chicken broth with a good, rich vegetable broth.

Banana-Nut Upside-Down Cake (see page 321)

Above: *Bacon, Potato, and Tomato Frittata* (see page 17)

Opposite: *Barbecued Pork Spareribs* (see page 201)

Opposite: *Blueberry Scones with Lemon-Vanilla Glaze* (see page 35)

Above: *Beef Stew with Roasted Tomatoes and Chipotles* (see page 110)

Above: *California Chicken Salad* (see page 56)

Right: *Zinfandel-Braised Pot Roast with Carrots and Parsnips* (see page 215)

Opposite: *Chicken Meatballs with Five-Spice Plum Sauce* (see page 176)

Chipotle Hot Wings with Creamy Cilantro Dipping Sauce (see page 47)

garbanzo bean and sausage soup with squash and collards

Sometimes a humble bowl of soup is just the perfect recipe. It can be complex or rustically simple, but that is what makes soup so beautiful. The flavors are always deliciously inviting, and whether it's a hearty meal by itself or it's teamed up with your favorite sandwich, a good soup is meant to show off nature's bounty. So start your soups with good-quality ingredients and you'll reap the benefits in flavor and great taste for everything you put in them. The foundation of this simple, rustic soup is garbanzo beans, one of the hardest dried beans on the market, but they are a protein powerhouse with a distinctive, slightly nutty flavor, and that makes them a valuable addition to your meal planning. With the pressure cooker, the fantastic properties of garbanzo beans really shine through and complement all the other delectable ingredients floating around in this dense soup, helping to fill up all those empty bellies. • **SERVES 4**

Step One: THE PRESOAK

2 cups dried garbanzo beans, picked over and rinsed

Soak the beans in water to cover for 8 hours or overnight.

Step Two: THE SOUP

1 to 1½ pounds collard greens, tough ribs removed (you may substitute mustard or other bitter greens)
2 tablespoons olive oil
1 large onion, chopped
1 pound kielbasa or andouille sausage, diced
4 cloves garlic, minced
2 stalks celery, chopped
2 carrots, peeled and sliced about ¼ inch thick
½ cup chopped fresh cilantro leaves
1 teaspoon dried thyme
1 teaspoon dried oregano
¼ teaspoon red pepper flakes
4 cups chicken or vegetable broth
3 cups cubed butternut squash or any variety winter squash
Salt and freshly ground black pepper to taste
Grated Parmesan cheese, for garnish

Stack the collard leaves. Roll them up and cut into 1-inch sections. Set aside. Heat the oil in the pressure cooker and cook the onion until soft and translucent, about 4 minutes. Add the sausage, in batches if necessary, and lightly brown the meat. Stir in the garlic, celery, carrots, cilantro, thyme, oregano, red pepper flakes, and broth. Drain and rinse the beans, and add them to the pressure cooker. Add enough water to cover

(continued)

the ingredients by 2 inches. Lock the lid in place. Bring to 15psi over high heat and immediately reduce the heat to the lowest possible setting to stabilize and maintain that pressure. Cook for 26 minutes. Remove from the heat and use the quick release method before opening the lid. Add the collard greens, pushing them into the liquid. Add the squash on top and do not stir. Lock the lid in place. Return to 15psi over high heat and immediately reduce the heat to the lowest possible setting to stabilize and maintain that pressure. Cook for 4 minutes. Remove from the heat and use the natural release method before opening the lid. Taste and adjust seasonings as desired. Ladle into soup bowls and add a sprinkling of Parmesan cheese.

azuki bean and vegetable soup with smoked turkey

Often referred to as the Mercedes of beans, the azuki has been cultivated in Asia for over three thousand years. *Azuki* means "little bean" in Japanese, and they are indeed small, being only about one-third the size of a pinto bean. Highly prized for use in making traditional bean paste, they are also used in Asian desserts. In the United States, azuki beans have found a new growing base of customers who enjoy these beans as a side dish or in soups. These beautifully colored beans are a rich, dark red with a contrasting bold white stripe, but it's their creamy texture and slightly sweet flavor that have made them very popular. Look for them with other packaged dried beans or in the ethnic foods aisle in the Asian section. With their delicate sweetness, these beans pair up with carrots, parsnips, and chard to balance the bits of smoked turkey in the broth. Serve this soup with Sweet Buttermilk Cornbread (page 33) if desired. • **SERVES 4**

Step One: THE PRESOAK

1 cup dried azuki beans, picked over and rinsed

Put the beans in a bowl and cover with 2 inches of water. Soak the beans for only 4 hours; they are a softer bean, and oversoaking will make them fall apart during cooking.

Step Two: THE MEAT AND BROTH

1 to 1½ pounds smoked turkey wings or turkey legs
1 medium sweet onion, diced
2 cloves garlic, minced
1 teaspoon dried basil
1 teaspoon dried thyme
1 teaspoon dried marjoram
1 teaspoon dried rosemary
¼ teaspoon freshly ground black pepper
2 bay leaves

Put the turkey in the pressure cooker. Add the onion, garlic, basil, thyme, marjoram, rosemary, pepper, and bay leaves. Pour in enough water to cover the ingredients. Lock the lid in place. Bring to 15psi over high heat and immediately reduce the heat to the lowest possible setting to stabilize and maintain that pressure. Cook for 30 minutes. Remove from the heat and use the natural release method before opening the lid. Transfer the meat to a cutting board and, when cool enough to handle, remove all the

(continued)

edible meat from the bones. Discard the bones and chop the meat into small pieces. Skim off any excess fat from the surface of broth. Discard the bay leaves.

Step Three: THE VEGETABLES AND BEANS

3 carrots, peeled and thinly sliced
3 parsnips, peeled and diced
6 to 8 stalks kale
Salt to taste

Drain and rinse the soaked beans and add them to the broth in the pressure cooker. Add the carrots and parsnips to the pressure cooker, and stir to mix. Trim the kale, cutting away one slice from the end of the stalks and removing any discolored spots on the leaves. Slice the kale stalks into 1-inch pieces and stir them into the broth. Roll up the leaves cigar-fashion and then cut them into 1-inch slices and place them on top of the other ingredients in the pressure cooker without stirring. If necessary, add enough additional water to cover all the ingredients by 1 inch. Lock the lid in place. Bring to 15psi over high heat and immediately reduce the heat to the lowest possible setting to stabilize and maintain that pressure. Cook for 7 minutes. Remove from the heat and use the natural release method before opening the lid. Return the chopped meat to the pressure cooker, stirring to mix. Taste and add salt as needed. Ladle into soup bowls and serve.

COOK'S NOTE: To serve this as a meat-free soup, omit the smoked turkey and add 3 cups Roasted Garlic Broth (page 66) to replace part of the water and add flavor.

---

navy bean soup with butternut squash and chard

Nutritious, inexpensive, and loaded with fiber, dried beans are a good addition to any menu, and they cook in just a few minutes using the pressure cooker. I like to begin by presoaking my beans so they stay plump and don't split, and then cooking them in a rich, well-seasoned broth, but occasionally you just don't have the time. If you find yourself short on time, don't give up on making a lovely bean soup for dinner, because I have just the solution you need. Let's skip the soaking process and bypass the broth making and still deliver a wholesome and deliciously tasty soup made with loads of colorful, fresh ingredients—sounds pretty good, right? Serve this soup with a fresh baguette, or add your favorite sandwich for heartier appetites. • **SERVES 4**

Step One: THE BROTH AND BEANS

- 2 tablespoons olive oil
- 2 large onions, coarsely chopped
- 4 cloves garlic, minced
- 2 sprigs fresh rosemary, each about 4 inches long
- 4 sprigs fresh thyme, finely chopped
- 1 teaspoon ground turmeric
- 1 cup dry white wine
- 1 pound dried navy beans, picked over and rinsed
- 4 cups chicken or vegetable broth

Heat the oil in the pressure cooker over medium-high heat, cooking and stirring the onions until they begin to turn a light golden brown. Add the garlic, rosemary, thyme, and turmeric, letting them sizzle until they become fragrant. Deglaze the pot with the wine, scraping up any crusty brown bits from the bottom. Add the dried beans and stock, stirring to mix. Lock the lid in place. Bring to 15psi over high heat and immediately reduce the heat to the lowest possible setting to stabilize and maintain that pressure. Cook for 30 minutes. Remove from the heat and use the natural release method before opening the lid.

Step Two: THE VEGETABLES

- 1 bunch Swiss chard
- 3 carrots, peeled and sliced
- 3 stalks celery, sliced
- 4 cups diced butternut squash
- 1½ teaspoons salt
- ½ teaspoon coarsely ground black pepper
- 1 (14-ounce) can diced tomatoes with juice
- 1 (14-ounce) can tomato sauce
- Fresh thyme leaves, for garnish

(continued)

Prepare the vegetables while the beans are cooking. Cut the chard leaves from the stalks and set aside. Trim the bottom ends off the stalks, then cut them into 1-inch slices. Trim the Swiss chard leaves, removing any bruised or blemished parts. Stack 3 or 4 leaves together and roll them lengthwise, making a long cigarlike cylinder. Cut the roll into 1-inch lengths. Repeat with the remaining leaves. When it's safe to open the pressure cooker, add 2 cups water, the carrots, celery, squash, the sliced chard stalks, salt, and pepper, stirring to mix. In the following order, add the diced tomatoes, the tomato sauce, and then spread the Swiss chard leaves on top. Lock the lid in place. Bring to 15psi over high heat and immediately reduce the heat to the lowest possible setting to stabilize and maintain that pressure. Cook for 4 minutes. Remove from the heat and use the quick release method before opening the lid. Stir the soup to distribute the ingredients. Pick out the rosemary stems if they are still whole. Taste and adjust seasonings. Ladle the soup into individual bowls and top with a few thyme leaves.

mayocoba beans in smoky meat broth with swiss chard

Mayocoba beans originated in Mexico and may be packaged under several different names, such as peruano, canary, Mexican yellow, or Peruvian beans. Whatever name is on the label, these beans have a subtle sweetness and creamy texture that have made them very popular in the western United States. These big pale yellow beans stay firm and the skins don't split, so they are excellent in soups, salads, and other bean dishes. I used dried chipotle peppers to add a subtle touch of heat, but do add a hotter variety if your palate is up to it. Serve this with a loaf of hot crusty bread and butter. • **SERVES 4**

Step One: THE PRESOAK

2 cups mayocoba beans, picked over and rinsed

Soak the beans in water to cover for at least 4 hours.

Step Two: THE MEAT BROTH

½ pound smoked pork neck bones
1 large onion, chopped
2 carrots, peeled and diced
4 cloves garlic, smashed
½ bunch fresh cilantro, stems and leaves chopped
3 stalks celery with leaves, chopped
1 dried ancho chile, seeded and finely chopped
1 dried pasilla chile, seeded and finely chopped
1 dried mulato chile, seeded and finely chopped
2 bay leaves

Place all the ingredients in the pressure cooker. Add just enough water to cover the ingredients. Lock the lid in place. Bring to 15psi over high heat and immediately reduce the heat to the lowest possible setting to stabilize and maintain that pressure. Cook for 35 minutes. Remove from the heat and use the natural release method before opening the lid. The meat should be tender and easy to pull away from the bone. If needed, return to pressure for an additional 5 minutes, and use the natural release method before opening the lid. Discard the bay leaves. Transfer the meat to a cutting board and, when cool enough to handle, pick off all the meat and chop it into small shreds. Set aside. Strain the broth, discarding all the solid matter. Return the broth to the pressure cooker.

(continued)

Step Three: COOK THE BEANS

Rinse the beans and discard the soaking water. Add the beans to the broth in the pressure cooker. Lock the lid in place. Bring to 15psi over high heat and immediately reduce the heat to the lowest possible setting to stabilize and maintain that pressure. Cook for 12 minutes. Remove from the heat and use the quick release method before opening the lid.

Step Four: FINISH THE SOUP

4 leafy stalks Swiss chard
Salt and coarsely ground black pepper to taste
2 jalapeño chiles, seeded and minced, for garnish (optional)

Cut the chard stalks into 1-inch slices and roughly chop the leaves, adding all the pieces to the pressure cooker. Press the chard into the broth. Lock the lid in place. Bring to 15psi over high heat and immediately reduce the heat to the lowest possible setting to stabilize and maintain that pressure. Cook for 4 minutes. Remove from the heat and use the natural release method before opening the lid. Add the reserved shredded meat to the pressure cooker and stir to blend all the ingredients. Taste and adjust seasonings with salt and pepper. Ladle into soup mugs and add the jalapeños if desired.

chicken and corn chowder

This is a substantial soup that is very flavorful with just a hint of Southwestern herbs and spices to kick it up a notch, and it looks as good as it tastes. The secret ingredient is lentils, which need no soaking and cook much more quickly than other dried legumes. These split lentils will completely break down as they cook, making the soup thicker and more substantial. The recipe uses the interrupted cooking method to first make a better-tasting broth for the soup base, and then the actual soup ingredients are added in the second phase. • **SERVES 4**

Step One: THE BROTH

4 strips bacon
2 chicken breasts or 5 chicken thighs
1 medium onion, diced
4 cloves garlic, minced
10 sprigs fresh cilantro, minced
2 jalapeño chiles, seeded and minced
1 poblano chile, seeded and diced
1 teaspoon ground cumin
1 teaspoon dried thyme
1 teaspoon salt
½ teaspoon freshly ground black pepper
½ cup split red or yellow lentils, picked over and rinsed
4 cups chicken broth

Heat the pressure cooker over medium-high heat and cook the bacon until crisp, then set aside to drain on paper towels. Crumble when cool. Wash the chicken and pat dry with paper towels. Remove the skin if preferred. Add the chicken to the hot bacon fat and brown the meat on both sides. Add the onion and cook until soft. Stir in the garlic, cilantro, jalapeños, poblano, cumin, thyme, salt, pepper, lentils, and broth. Add 2 cups water. Lock the lid in place. Bring to 15psi over high heat and immediately reduce the heat to the lowest possible setting to stabilize and maintain that pressure. Cook for 8 minutes. Remove from the heat and use the quick release method before opening the lid. Transfer the chicken to a cutting board, remove the skin if present, and take the meat off the bones. Dice or shred the meat into small pieces and return it to the broth. Skim off any excess fat from the surface of the broth.

Step Two: THE CHOWDER

1 small red bell pepper, seeded and diced
2 parsnips, peeled and diced
2 yellow-fleshed potatoes such as Yukon Gold, peeled and diced
4 cups fresh or thawed frozen corn kernels, drained
1 cup sour cream

(continued)

Add the bell pepper, parsnips, potatoes, and corn to the broth in the pressure cooker, stirring well. Lock the lid in place. Bring to 15psi over high heat and immediately reduce the heat to the lowest possible setting to stabilize and maintain that pressure. Cook for 4 minutes. Remove from the heat and use the natural release method before opening the lid. Stir in the sour cream, and simmer over low heat until the chowder is heated through. Taste and adjust the seasonings as desired. Ladle the chowder into soup mugs and garnish with a sprinkle of the crumbled bacon.

COOK'S NOTE: If you prefer a creamier consistency, use a handheld blender to quickly puree the chowder a little, or a lot, to suit your preference.

Variation:

CHEESY CHICKEN AND CORN CHOWDER

Cook as directed. When the chowder is finished, stir in 2 cups shredded cheddar cheese, simmering over low heat until it is melted.

portuguese chicken and potato soup with watercress

Mother learned to make this soup the year we lived in Lisbon, Portugal, in the late 1950s. I had forgotten all about it until I rediscovered her recipe while researching for this cookbook. The key ingredient is watercress, and if you are fond of cilantro, you will probably like watercress too. Watercress was very popular in my mother's day, and it was a requirement at any proper social gathering, where guests could expect to be served a watercress soup at a swanky luncheon or nibble tiny tea sandwiches with a filling spiked with the unique, peppery taste of watercress. As things do, watercress went out of vogue—supplanted by bean dip in a can, as I recall—and for many years cress was only seen occasionally at farmer's markets, but now it's back and popular again as cooks explore a wider variety of fresh ingredients. Look for little bunches of brilliant green watercress stocked with the other herbs or greens in your supermarket produce aisle. Most vintage recipes call for pureeing the ingredients of watercress soup, but my mom's Portuguese version was more of a hearty, rustic soup that used bits of chicken, sausage, or ham. The watercress leaves are added at the end of cooking so that they are just wilted to the point where they are soft but you can still enjoy their vivid color and taste their peppery flavor in every delicious spoonful. • **SERVES 4**

Step One: THE CHICKEN

1 tablespoon olive oil
1 skinless, boneless chicken breast
2 tablespoons butter
1 large onion, finely chopped
3 cloves garlic, finely minced
4 cups chicken or vegetable broth or Roasted Garlic Broth (page 66)
1 teaspoon salt

Heat the oil in the pressure cooker, brown the chicken on all sides, and transfer to a plate.

Heat the butter in the pressure cooker and cook the onion until soft and translucent, about 4 minutes. Add the garlic and cook until soft. Add the chicken, broth, 1 cup water, and the salt. Lock the lid in place. Bring to 15psi over high heat and immediately reduce the heat to the lowest possible setting to stabilize and maintain that pressure. Cook for 4 minutes. Remove from the heat and use the quick release method before opening the lid. Transfer the chicken to a cutting board and dice it into small pieces. Return it to the pressure cooker.

(continued)

Step Two: THE VEGETABLES

- 4 medium red or white potatoes, peeled and diced
- 1 stalk celery, diced
- 1 carrot, peeled and diced
- 1 bunch watercress

Add the potatoes, celery, and carrot to the broth, stirring to mix. Lock the lid in place. Bring to 15psi over high heat and immediately reduce the heat to the lowest possible setting to stabilize and maintain that pressure. Cook for 3 minutes. Remove from the heat and use the quick release method before opening the lid. Cut the bottom stems off the bunch of watercress and then coarsely chop the leaves. Simmer the soup over medium heat and stir in the watercress leaves, cooking just until they begin to soften and wilt. Taste and adjust seasoning as desired. Ladle into soup mugs and serve.

beef, wild mushroom, rice, and barley soup

This is an absolutely delicious and hearty soup that's warming and filling, perfect for those chilly days that are made for family-pleasing recipes like this. If you have leftovers, they are even better the next day! Serve this soup with a nice chunk of crusty bread and it's a fantastic meal.

• **SERVES 4**

1½ pounds round steak, cut into bite-size pieces
Salt and freshly ground black pepper to taste
2 tablespoons olive oil
2 medium onions, chopped
2 large cloves garlic, finely minced
1 teaspoon dried sage
1 teaspoon dried thyme
1 cup dry red wine
1 cup pearled barley
⅓ cup wild rice
2 teaspoons beef bouillon granules
2 stalks celery with leaves, chopped
1 cup dried wild mushrooms of your choice, chopped

Season the steak with salt and pepper. Heat the oil in the pressure cooker over medium-high heat and sear the meat in small batches, browning all sides. Set aside on a plate. Cook the onions and garlic in the pressure cooker until soft, about 3 minutes. Add the sage and thyme, stirring until they become fragrant. Deglaze the pressure cooker with the wine, scraping up all those crusty brown bits from the bottom. Add 8 cups water, the barley, rice, bouillon, celery, and mushrooms, stirring to mix. Lock the lid in place. Bring to 15psi over high heat and immediately reduce the heat to the lowest possible setting to stabilize and maintain that pressure. Cook for 15 minutes. Remove from the heat and use the natural release method before opening the lid. Stir the soup and taste before adjusting the seasonings as needed. Ladle into soup bowls.

pisto manchego: a spanish ratatouille

My mother collected recipes when we lived in Spain, no doubt inspired by the local cuisine and the huge selection of foods available in the open-air market where we shopped almost every day. With an abundance of fresh produce on hand, she made a delicious thick and spicy vegetable stew—pisto manchego. This popular dish might be served either hot or chilled, depending on the season. Sometimes we ate it as a main dish, sometimes as a side dish with meats or fish, and sometimes even over pasta with grated hard cheese, but always with crusty fresh bread and maybe a plate of brined local olives. The leftovers made a very tasty tapas-style spread with a squeeze of lemon. Leftover pisto manchego was also turned into a breakfast casserole with some fried eggs and melted cheese on top, served on thick slabs of garlic toast with fat, spicy Spanish sausages. Ahh, life was grand!

I had completely forgotten about this recipe until I was watching *Ratatouille*, the wonderful Pixar movie, and it dawned on me that my mom's pisto manchego was like a spicy ratatouille. The recipe my mom used was not exact because she used seasonal vegetables and the proportions varied according to what was in our pantry at the moment. Still, our homey vegetable stew was tomato based and usually included eggplants and squash, which are the main attraction of any ratatouille recipe. My mom was never shy about the quantities of onions, garlic, and spices she used to flavor that mix of fresh vegetables, and it was always tasty. So no matter what name you want to give it, this is still a luscious and fresh vegetable stew with a wide variety of uses, and it goes without saying that the flavors will only improve if allowed to mingle overnight. • **SERVES 4**

Step One: THE SOFRITO

The small-diced aromatic vegetables will cook down into the tomatoes to thicken and flavor the sauce.

- 1 large onion, quartered
- 1 large green bell pepper, seeded and quartered
- 10 sprigs fresh cilantro
- 6 large cloves garlic, peeled
- 6 leaves fresh basil
- 2 to 3 tablespoons olive oil
- 1 teaspoon ground cumin
- 1 tablespoon dried oregano
- 1 tablespoon hot smoked Spanish paprika (pimentón de la Vera picante)
- ½ cup dry white wine

Use a food processor to chop the onion, bell pepper, cilantro, garlic, and basil into pieces about the size of a pea. Heat the oil in the pressure cooker over medium-high heat and cook the mixture until the onions look translucent and soft, about 4 minutes. Add the cumin, oregano, and paprika, frying until they become fragrant. Deglaze the cooker with the wine, scraping up any crusty bits from the bottom.

Step Two: THE VEGETABLES

- 2 tablespoons balsamic vinegar
- 3 cups cubed butternut squash
- 1 large onion, chopped
- 1 cup thickly sliced fresh mushrooms
- 4 cups cubed eggplant
- 1 large red bell pepper, seeded and chopped
- 2 cups sliced zucchini
- 2 cups cut green beans (2-inch lengths)
- 1½ teaspoons sea salt, or to taste
- ½ teaspoon coarsely ground black pepper, or to taste
- ½ teaspoon red pepper flakes
- 10 large Roma tomatoes, roasted (see page 299) and coarsely chopped
- 1 (14-ounce) can tomato sauce
- 2 tablespoons tomato paste
- 1 teaspoon sugar (optional)

Add the vinegar to the sofrito mix in the pressure cooker. Add the squash, onion, mushrooms, eggplant, bell pepper, zucchini, and green beans. Stir in the salt, black pepper, and red pepper flakes, mixing well. Add the tomatoes, tomato sauce, and tomato paste, in that order, and do not stir. Lock the lid in place. Bring to 15psi over high heat and immediately reduce the heat to the lowest possible setting to stabilize and maintain that pressure. Cook for 4 minutes. Remove from the heat and use the natural release method before opening the lid. Taste and adjust seasoning as needed, adding sugar if the tomatoes are bitter. Serve hot or cold as desired.

chicken stew with potatoes, parsnips, and corn

When I was growing up, one of my first kitchen jobs was peeling potatoes and other vegetables my mother needed for our dinner. Along the way I learned many other cooking skills, and as I watched my mom cook all the good food that graced our kitchen table, I slowly absorbed her recipes as well. Of course, I did not appreciate all that acquired knowledge until I was much older and had moved out on my own. I didn't really begin cooking for myself until I was a starving student with an almost nonexistent food budget, and necessity then proved to be the mother of all inventions. I quickly discovered that creating something delicious from practically nothing was hugely satisfying. Over the ensuing years, as circumstance allowed for a more sumptuously stocked pantry, I have reworked many of my favorite frugal recipes, revising them to accommodate suggestions from family and friends along the way. This stew is especially good when fresh corn is abundant, but it's also versatile enough to easily adapt to the ingredients on hand throughout the rest of the year. • **SERVES 4**

2 tablespoons vegetable oil
1 large onion, diced
2 skinless, boneless chicken breasts
4 medium potatoes, peeled and diced
2 parsnips, peeled and diced
3 cups fresh or frozen corn kernels (about 2 large ears, save those cobs!) or 2 (15-ounce) cans whole kernel corn, drained
3 cups Sweet Corn Stock (page 67) or 2 (15-ounce) cans chicken broth
2 teaspoons chicken bouillon granules
1½ teaspoons dried thyme
2 teaspoons ground turmeric
Salt and coarsely ground black pepper to taste
1 (15-ounce) can cream-style corn
2 tablespoons cornstarch
1½ cups heavy cream
Paprika, for garnish (optional)

Heat the oil in the pressure cooker over medium-high heat and cook the onion until soft and translucent, about 4 minutes. Add the chicken, potatoes, parsnips, corn kernels, and stock. Stir in the bouillon, thyme, turmeric, and salt and pepper. Add the cream-style corn on top and do not stir. Lock the lid in place. Bring to 15psi over high heat and immediately reduce the heat to the lowest possible setting to stabilize and maintain that pressure. Cook for 6 minutes. Remove from the heat and use the natural release method before opening the lid. Transfer the chicken to a cutting board and dice the meat.

To thicken the soup, make a slurry by mixing the cornstarch into ½ cup of the heavy cream. Slowly stir the slurry into the soup, simmering gently over medium heat as it begins to thicken. Add the diced chicken and the remaining cream, cooking until heated through and at the desired consistency. Taste and adjust seasonings to your liking. Ladle into soup mugs and dust with a bit of paprika if desired.

Variation:

CREAMY STEW OF HAM WITH POTATOES, PARSNIPS, AND CORN

Substitute 2 cups cooked or leftover ham for the chicken. Add it at the same time.

creamy chicken stew

This hearty stew is chock-full of potatoes and carrots, green beans and corn, and lots of tender white meat chicken simmering in a creamy base with a hint of bacon. There's a minimal amount of prep work, so your family can still sit down to a hot, home-cooked in just minutes. Garnished with crispy bacon, this flavorful stew is a cold weather feast. Add a pan of hot biscuits or dinner rolls and a plate of crunchy celery sticks to round out your meal. • **SERVES 4**

2 strips bacon, diced
1½ pounds skinless, boneless chicken breasts
1 medium onion, sliced
1 teaspoon dried basil, crushed
1 teaspoon dried marjoram, crushed
¼ teaspoon freshly ground black pepper
3 cups Sweet Corn Stock (page 67) or 2 (15-ounce) cans chicken broth
1 (10-ounce) can cream of chicken soup
2 teaspoons chicken bouillon granules
3 thin-skinned potatoes, peeled and cut into 1-inch cubes
2 carrots, peeled and diced
2 cups frozen cut green beans
1 cup frozen corn kernels
2 teaspoons dried Italian parsley
Salt to taste

Cook the bacon in the pressure cooker over medium-high heat, stirring often, until crisp. Remove the bacon and drain on paper towels. Add the chicken and brown both sides in the bacon fat. Transfer the chicken to a plate. Add the onion to the pressure cooker and cook until soft, stirring occasionally, about 4 minutes. Stir in the basil, marjoram, pepper, stock, cream of chicken soup, and bouillon. Add the potatoes, carrots, green beans, corn, and 1 cup water, stirring the contents to mix. Lock the lid in place. Bring to 15psi over high heat and immediately reduce the heat to the lowest possible setting to stabilize and maintain that pressure. Cook for 5 minutes. Remove from the heat and use the natural release method before opening the lid. Move the chicken to a cutting board and chop into small pieces. Return the chicken to the pressure cooker and stir in the parsley. Taste and adjust seasonings, adding salt if needed. Ladle into soup bowls and garnish with a scattering of crispy bacon pieces on top.

mexican pork stew with tomatillos

Mexican recipes often combine robustly flavored herbs and piquant spices with fresh meats and vegetables. This is a good opportunity to try the interesting flavor of tomatillos, a relative of the tomato that provides a uniquely tart flavor that distinguishes Mexican green sauces. Adding mild Mexican chile peppers will give this dish lots of flavor but only a touch of heat. Use your food processor to cut the prep time and serve this popular Mexican dish quickly to the hungry crowd at your house. Serve by itself with a handful of crushed corn chips and a dollop of crema agria, a thicker and richer version of sour cream. For more variety, this is a very versatile dish that works well when served over cooked pinto beans, Old-Fashioned Creamy Mashed Potatoes 101 (page 258), hot egg noodles, or fluffy white rice . . . good suggestions for most any leftovers.

• **SERVES 4 OR 5**

2 tablespoons olive oil
2½ pounds boneless pork, cut into 2-inch cubes
1 large onion, chopped
1 tablespoon chili powder
1 teaspoon ground cumin
1 (12-ounce) bottle of beer
6 tomatillos, roasted (see page 299) and chopped
2 mild chiles, such as Anaheim, poblano, or pasilla, roasted (see page 299) and chopped
½ cup chopped fresh cilantro leaves and stems
2 cloves garlic, minced
1 (12-ounce) can whole kernel corn, drained
2 cups fresh or prepared hot or mild tomato salsa, plus more for serving (optional)
Sour cream, for garnish (optional)

Heat the oil in the pressure cooker over medium-high heat, and brown the pork on all sides in small batches. Once each batch is browned, set aside in a bowl to reserve the drippings. Cook the onion, stirring often, until soft and golden brown. Stir in the chili powder and cumin. Add the beer to the cooker to deglaze the pot, scraping the browned bits from the bottom of the pot. Add the tomatillos, chiles, cilantro, garlic, corn, and salsa. Return the meat to the pressure cooker and stir. Lock the lid in place. Bring to 15 psi over high heat and immediately reduce the heat to the lowest possible setting to stabilize and maintain that pressure. Cook for 15 minutes. Remove from the heat and use the natural release method before opening the lid. For a garnish, I like some extra salsa and a spoonful of sour cream.

smoky beef stew

Paprika is the Hungarian word for "dried and ground red peppers." There are six classes of paprika, ranging from delicately sweet to "Man, that's hot!" The latter is the one you'll want to use for this dish, my dears. The combination of the smoked bacon, dried chipotle peppers, fire-roasted tomatoes, and pungent flavors of good smoked paprika and cumin give this beefy stew a deep, complex flavor that's even better the next day—if you still have some leftovers to taste. Serve over buttered noodles, smashed potatoes (page 256), or baked potatoes, and add a plate of cucumber and tomato slices marinated in a minimalist vinaigrette. • **SERVES 5 OR 6**

½ cup all-purpose flour
1 teaspoon salt
½ teaspoon freshly ground black pepper
2 pounds boneless beef chuck, fat trimmed and cut into 1-inch chunks
3 strips thick-cut bacon, cut into ½-inch pieces
1 large onion, finely chopped
1½ tablespoons smoked paprika
Pinch of cayenne pepper, or more to taste
½ cup dry red wine
8 Roma tomatoes, roasted (see page 299) and coarsely chopped
1 (8-ounce) can tomato sauce
2 tablespoons tomato paste
1½ cups sour cream
3 sliced scallion tops, for garnish

Put the flour, salt, and black pepper in a large sealable plastic bag and add the beef. Close the bag and shake until all the cubes are coated in flour, and then shake off the excess flour. Heat the pressure cooker over medium-high heat and fry the bacon to render the fat; transfer the pieces to paper towels to drain. Add the beef to the hot fat in small batches, browning all sides. Set aside on a plate. Add the onion and cook, stirring often, until soft and caramel colored, about 5 minutes. Stir in the paprika and cayenne, cooking just until the spices start to sizzle and become fragrant. Deglaze the pot with the wine, scraping up all those crusty brown bits from the bottom. Return the bacon, the beef, and any accumulated meat juices from the plate to the pressure cooker. Stir in the tomatoes and tomato sauce. Add the tomato paste on top and do not stir. Lock the lid in place. Bring to 15psi over high heat and immediately reduce the heat to the lowest possible setting to stabilize and maintain that pressure. Cook for 15 minutes. Remove from the heat and use the natural release method before opening the lid. Stir in the sour cream and add salt to taste. Garnish with a sprinkle of scallions.

COOK'S NOTE: This stew has a lively heat that is somewhat mellowed by the added sour cream. If you prefer a milder version, omit the cayenne and reduce the amount of smoked paprika to 1 or 2 teaspoons.

---

essential beef stew

This is a simple, rustic dish, a traditional beef stew. Don't be fooled by the short ingredient list, because this stew is packed with flavor. There are lots of tender beef chunks with onions, little potatoes, and carrots in a full-flavored tomato-based sauce. Like most stews, this will mellow if you can make it ahead of time to allow the flavors to marry. • **SERVED 5 OR 6**

½ cup all-purpose flour
1 teaspoon salt
½ teaspoon freshly ground black pepper
2 pounds boneless beef chuck, fat trimmed and cut into 1½-inch chunks
2 tablespoons olive oil
2 medium yellow onions, coarsely chopped
1 cup dry red wine
2 cloves garlic, minced
2 stalks celery, thinly sliced
1 teaspoon dried basil
1 teaspoon dried oregano
1 (28-ounce) can stewed tomatoes with juice
12 baby potatoes (less than 2 inches in diameter)
12 baby carrots

Combine the flour, salt, and pepper in a sealable plastic bag and add the beef. Shake until the pieces are coated on all sides. Heat the oil in the pressure cooker over medium-high heat and brown the beef on all sides. Set aside on a plate. Lower the heat and add the onions and continue cooking, stirring often, until they are soft and lightly browned, about 5 minutes. Deglaze the pot with wine, scraping up all those crusty brown bits from the bottom. Return the beef to the pressure cooker along with any juices that may have accumulated. Add the garlic, celery, basil, and oregano and stir to mix. Add the tomatoes with juice on top and do not stir. Lock the lid in place. Bring to 15psi over high heat and immediately reduce the heat to the lowest possible setting to stabilize and maintain that pressure. Cook for 12 minutes. Remove from the heat and use the quick release method before opening the lid. Add the potatoes and carrots. Return to pressure, locking the lid in place and bringing to 15psi over high heat. Immediately reduce the heat to the lowest possible setting to stabilize and maintain that pressure. Cook for 4 more minutes. Remove from the heat and use the natural release method before opening the lid.

Thicken the broth if desired, with a slurry using 2 tablespoons of the flour mixture and ½ cup water. Stir the slurry into the broth, simmering gently over medium heat until it reaches the desired consistency. Taste and adjust seasoning as desired. Serve hot.

beef stew with roasted tomatoes and chipotles

There is nothing more comforting and delicious than a big bowl of beefy stew on a cold day. This is not your ordinary meat-potatoes-carrots version; there must be a hundred minor variations on that boring old ho-hum recipe. This is a meat dish for meat lovers. It's got huge, fork-tender chunks of beef in a very spicy and aromatic sauce that will make your kitchen smell scrumptious when you take the lid off the pressure cooker! If you want potatoes, serve this over my Old-Fashioned Creamy Mashed Potatoes 101 (page 258), or try it with the Soft and Creamy Polenta (page 278). And a plate of hot, buttery biscuits would not go amiss, my dears.

• **SERVES 5 OR 6**

½ cup all-purpose flour
1 teaspoon salt
½ teaspoon freshly ground black pepper
2 pounds boneless beef chuck, fat trimmed and cut into 2-inch chunks
2 tablespoons olive oil
3 medium onions, chopped
1 cup dry red wine
5 cloves garlic, roasted (see page 252) and mashed to a pulp
2 dried chipotle chiles, seeded and finely chopped
2 chipotle chiles in adobo sauce, seeded and minced
2 tablespoons adobo sauce from the canned chipotles
2 bay leaves
10 large Roma tomatoes, roasted (see page 299) and coarsely chopped
1 cup sour cream, for garnish (optional)

Put the flour, salt, and pepper in a large sealable plastic bag and add the beef. Close the bag and shake until all the cubes are coated, and then shake off the excess flour. Heat the oil in the pressure cooker over medium-high heat and brown the beef in small batches, searing all sides. Transfer the pieces of meat to a plate as they finish browning. Add the onions and cook, stirring often, until they are soft and caramel colored. Deglaze the cooker with the wine, scraping up any crusty brown bits from the bottom. Add the garlic pulp, the dried and canned chipotle peppers and adobo sauce, and bay leaves. Stir in the roasted tomatoes and any juices. Add the meat and any accumulated juices. Lock the lid in place. Bring to 15psi over high heat and immediately reduce the heat to the lowest possible setting to stabilize and maintain that pressure. Cook for 18 minutes. Remove from the heat and use the natural release method before opening the lid. Discard the bay leaves.

To thicken the broth, make a slurry using 2 tablespoons of the flour mixture and ½ cup water. Stir the slurry into the broth, simmering gently over medium heat until it's the desired consistency. Taste and adjust seasoning as desired. Ladle into bowls and serve topped with a spoonful of the sour cream if desired.

hearty beef and cabbage stew

When I was growing up all of us kids had regular kitchen chores that included peeling, chopping, and slicing, as well as all the washing and drying—"manual" dishwashers being the standard model in those days. This soup was one of our favorites, not only because it's very flavorful, but also because it meant that we didn't have a pile of dirty pots and pans to clean after dinner. With six in the family, we had enough dishes to wash after each meal! Teach your children how to cook and they will thank you for it later, but teach them to use a pressure cooker and they will never go hungry. Serve this soup with lots of crusty bread to soak up the delicious juice. • **SERVES 5 OR 6**

½ pound stew beef
1 teaspoon salt
½ teaspoon freshly ground black pepper
3 tablespoons olive oil
2 medium onions, diced
4 cloves garlic, minced
½ teaspoon red pepper flakes
1 tablespoon dried dill weed
2 tablespoons smoked paprika
2 (14-ounce) cans chicken broth
1 (26-ounce) can diced tomatoes with juice
2 tablespoons tomato paste
2 medium potatoes, peeled and diced
2 medium carrots, peeled and diced
1 medium head cabbage, coarsely chopped
1 cup sour cream, for garnish

Season the beef with the salt and black pepper. Heat the oil in the pressure cooker over medium-high heat and brown the meat on all sides. Add the onions, garlic, red pepper flakes, dill weed, paprika, broth, tomatoes with juice, and 2 cups water, stirring to mix. Add the tomato paste, but do not stir. Lock the lid in place. Bring to 15psi over high heat and immediately reduce the heat to the lowest possible setting to stabilize and maintain that pressure. Cook for 20 minutes. Remove from the heat and use the quick release method before opening the lid. In the following order, add the potatoes and carrots, and then the cabbage, without stirring. Return to pressure and cook for an additional 3 minutes. Remove from the heat and use the natural release method before opening the lid. Stir to blend the ingredients. Taste and adjust seasonings as desired. Ladle into soup bowls and top with a dollop of the sour cream.

the famous meat and potato stew

My father, a meat-and-potatoes guy, taught me to make this recipe. Tongue in cheek, he said it had been handed down for generations. The famous recipe story grew larger over the years, becoming the favorite recipe of this or that famous person . . . whose name and relationship to our family changed with each retelling of Dad's fanciful tale. In one version, he said that the recipe had come over on the *Mayflower*, but in another telling he had Pocahontas secretly passing it on to Captain John Smith, who then built the Smithsonian just to archive it. Mind you, my father told these tales about the famous recipe in all seriousness, and it was no surprise that my younger siblings likewise fell for Dad's charming famous recipe stories. Thus, over the span of time, this simple but delicious stew did in fact become famous, at least in our family. I hope it does in yours, too. • **SERVES 5 OR 6**

½ cup all-purpose flour
1 teaspoon salt
½ teaspoon freshly ground black pepper
2 pounds round steak, cut into 1-inch cubes
3 tablespoons olive oil
1 medium onion, diced
1 cup dry red wine
4 cups beef broth
1 tablespoon dried oregano
2 teaspoons dried basil
1 (6-ounce) can tomato paste
8 medium white potatoes, scrubbed and cut into quarters

In a sealable plastic bag, mix together the flour, salt, and pepper. Add the beef to the bag and shake gently until each piece is lightly coated. Heat the oil in a large pressure cooker over medium heat. Add the beef and cook in small batches until well browned on all sides. Set aside on a plate until finished. Add the onion and cook until soft, about 4 minutes. Deglaze the pot with the wine, scraping up all those crusty brown bits from the bottom. Return the meat and any accumulated juices to the pressure cooker and add the broth, oregano, and basil, stirring to mix. Dot the tomato paste on top without stirring. Lock the lid in place. Bring to 15psi over high heat and immediately reduce the heat to the lowest possible setting to stabilize and maintain that pressure. Cook for 15 minutes. Remove from the heat and use the quick release method before opening the lid. Add the potatoes on top and do not stir. Return to pressure and cook for 4 minutes. Remove from the heat and use the natural release method before opening the lid. Stir gently to blend the ingredients. Taste and adjust seasonings.

To thicken the broth, make a slurry using 2 tablespoons of the flour mixture mixed with ⅓ cup cold water. Stir the slurry into the broth, simmering gently over medium heat until it's the desired consistency. Ladle into individual bowls and serve.

pomegranate lamb tagine

The traditional Middle Eastern tagine is a large cooking pan with a conical lid that traps steam and circulates it through the food as it slowly cooks. Not unlike a pressure cooker, it doesn't require a lot of liquid, so the meats and spices cook down to make a rich and fragrant sauce. This recipe begins with lamb and layers on the flavors with caramelized onions, fresh ginger, cinnamon sticks, and dried apricots that balance the tartness of the pomegranate juice. Serve this over couscous or white rice. • **SERVES 4 TO 6**

1½ pounds boneless lamb, trimmed of fat and cut into 2-inch chunks
1 teaspoon salt
Freshly ground black pepper to taste
2 tablespoons olive oil
2 large onions, thinly sliced
1 tablespoon minced fresh ginger
4 cloves garlic, minced
½ cup chicken stock
⅓ cup 100% pomegranate juice
Zest and juice of 1 lemon
2 cinnamon sticks
1 teaspoon ground coriander
4 carrots, peeled and sliced
2 stalks celery, sliced
1 large green bell pepper, seeded and chopped
⅓ cup chopped dried apricots
⅓ cup chopped dried dates
¼ cup slivered almonds, for garnish

Generously season the lamb with the salt and black pepper. Heat the oil over medium-high heat in the pressure cooker, and brown the meat on all sides. Transfer to a plate. Reduce the heat to medium-low and add the onions to the pressure cooker. Cook for about 15 minutes or until the onions begin to caramelize and turn golden brown. Add the minced ginger and garlic, cooking until soft, stirring frequently. Deglaze the cooker with the stock, scraping up all those crusty brown bits from the bottom. Return the meat and any accumulated juices to the pressure cooker. Add the pomegranate juice, lemon juice and zest, cinnamon sticks, and coriander, stirring to blend. Add the carrots, celery, bell pepper, apricots, and dates and do not stir. Lock the lid in place. Bring to 15psi over high heat and immediately reduce the heat to the lowest possible setting to stabilize and maintain that pressure. Cook for 12 minutes. Remove from the heat and use the natural release method before opening the lid. Discard the cinnamon sticks. Stir well to blend. Taste and adjust seasonings as desired. Garnish with a sprinkling of the slivered almonds.

black bean ancho chili

Mexican food features fresh herbs, chiles, and bold spices. Black beans, a Mexican staple, are very popular these days with their deep earthy flavor, and they make a great-tasting chili. You might serve this chili with a full complement of assorted toppings in small bowls and let everyone help themselves. Or serve it plain with a pan of hot cornbread (page 33) as a delicious accompaniment. If you have the time, this chili benefits from some extra time to let the flavors merge and mellow in the refrigerator, so it's perfect for a make-ahead meal. • **SERVES 4 TO 6**

Step One: THE PRESOAK

1 pound dried black beans, picked over and rinsed

Soak the beans in water to cover for 4 hours.

Step Two: THE MEAT BROTH

1 pound smoked pork neck bones or ham hocks or a meaty ham bone
1 large onion, chopped
2 large pasilla, poblano, or Anaheim chiles, seeded and chopped
4 dried ancho chiles, seeded and chopped
1 small bunch fresh cilantro (about 20 sprigs), leaves and stems finely chopped
4 cloves garlic, mashed
Zest and juice of 1 large lime
1 cup dry red wine
1 (28-ounce) can tomato puree
1 (28-ounce) can diced tomatoes with juice
Salt and freshly ground coarse black pepper to taste
2 bay leaves
1 teaspoon dried oregano
1 tablespoon sweet paprika
½ teaspoon hot smoked Spanish paprika (pimentón de la Vera picante), or more to taste
1 tablespoon ground cumin
½ teaspoon ground cinnamon
¼ teaspoon ground cloves

Add all the ingredients to a large pressure cooker along with enough cold water to cover. Lock the lid in place. Bring to 15psi over high heat and immediately reduce the heat to the lowest possible setting to stabilize and maintain that pressure. Cook for 40 minutes. Remove from the heat and use the natural release method before opening the lid. Transfer the meat to a cutting board and, when cool enough to handle, remove all the edible meat from the bones. Discard the bones and chop the meat into small pieces. Skim off any excess fat from the surface of the broth. Discard the bay leaves.

Step Three: THE BEANS

Drain and rinse the soaked beans and add them to the broth in the pressure cooker. If necessary, add enough additional water to cover all the ingredients by 1 inch. Lock the lid in place. Bring to 15psi over high heat and immediately reduce the heat to the lowest possible setting to stabilize and maintain that pressure. Cook for 12 minutes. Remove from the heat and use the natural release method before opening the lid. Check the beans for doneness by smashing one between your thumb and forefinger and looking for a soft center. If the beans aren't tender, return to pressure for an additional 2 minutes, again using the natural release method before opening the lid.

Step Four: TO THICKEN (OPTIONAL)

2 tablespoons masa harina

This recipe has plenty of vegetable pulp, but to add additional thickness mix the masa harina with ⅓ cup cold water and stir into the chili. Simmer over medium heat, uncovered, as the mixture thickens.

Step Five: THE CONDIMENTS

1 cup crema agria (Mexican-style sour cream)
8 ounces Monterey Jack or sharp cheddar cheese, shredded
1 avocado, pitted, peeled, and chopped
1 small red onion, diced
2 limes, cut into wedges
1 (6-ounce) can sliced pitted black olives
2 cups crushed corn chips of your choice

Serve this chili in large bowls to allow plenty of room for condiments. Put a spoonful of crema agria on top of each bowl of chili and sprinkle with cheese and any other toppings as desired.

smoky beef-and-bacon pinto bean chili

Smoky bacon, chipotle and ancho peppers, roasted tomatoes and peppers, and spicy smoked paprika give this chili recipe a deep, complex flavor, and a nice pleasant kick too. Now, I know some of you will look at this recipe and run away screaming to pull out a can of chili instead, but hold on to your apron strings, my dears. Sit down here . . . That's it. . . And breathe into this paper bag . . . It's really not all that bad. It's just measuring, and you can do that. And that food processor that's holding down the back corner of your unused kitchen gadget cupboard? Drag it out and let it do most of the work for you. Okay, so you have to do a little roasting in advance, but do a big batch a day or two ahead and then freeze the extra. There's some frying, too, but we're talking bacon here, so this really doesn't count, and if you make enough to treat yourself to a BLT on the side, it's all good!

Now c'mon . . . I even broke everything up into easy-to-do steps that you can do at your leisure—like during commercial breaks when you aren't busy washing, scrubbing, diapering, or cleaning up after the puppy. So add the ingredients to your shopping list and make this chili. While it's great right straight out of the pot, it thickens overnight and the flavors will round out and deepen, so it's even better the next day. • **SERVES 4 TO 6**

Step One: THE PRESOAK

2 cups dried pinto beans, picked over and rinsed

Soak the beans in water to cover for at least 4 hours.

Step Two: THE TOASTED SPICES

1 dried ancho chile, seeded and pulverized
1 dried pasilla chile, seeded and pulverized
1 dried mulato chile, seeded and pulverized
2 tablespoons chili powder
1 tablespoon ground cumin
½ teaspoon cayenne pepper
1 tablespoon sweet smoked Spanish paprika (pimentón de la Vera)

Toast all the ingredients in a small cast-iron skillet over medium heat until they begin to darken and become fragrant. Stir constantly to prevent scorching. This takes only about 2 minutes, so watch closely. Scrape the toasted spices onto a plate and spread them out to cool.

Step Three: THE MEATS

6 strips thick-cut smoky bacon, diced
1½ pounds lean ground beef
½ pound hot sausage

Heat the pressure cooker over medium-high heat and fry the bacon until crisp. Transfer to paper towels. Add the ground beef and sausage and lightly brown the meat until crumbly. Set aside on a plate.

Step Four: THE SOFRITO

2 large sweet onions, diced
1 large poblano chile, seeded and quartered
1 small bunch fresh cilantro (about 20 sprigs)
8 cloves garlic, roasted (see page 252) and mashed to a pulp
1 (12-ounce) bottle dark Mexican beer

Use a food processor to chop the onions, chile, cilantro, and garlic into pieces about the size of a pea. Add the sofrito mix to the hot bacon fat in the pressure cooker, and cook until the onions are translucent and soft, about 4 minutes. Add the toasted spices, frying until they become fragrant. Add the beer to the cooker to deglaze the pot, scraping up all the browned bits from the bottom.

Step Five: THE VEGETABLES

6 large Roma tomatoes, roasted (see page 299) and chopped
2 large pasilla, poblano, or Anaheim chiles, roasted (see page 299), seeded, and chopped
1 or 2 chipotle chiles in adobo sauce, seeded and minced
2 teaspoons adobo sauce from the canned chipotles
1 (8-ounce) can tomato sauce
Salt and freshly ground black pepper to taste
2 limes, each cut into 6 wedges, for garnish

Drain and rinse the soaked beans and add them to the pressure cooker. Add enough water to cover the beans by 1 inch. Stir in the tomatoes, roasted chiles, chipotle chile, adobo sauce, and the tomato sauce. Return the fried bacon pieces, the ground beef, and sausage to the pressure cooker. Stir well. Lock the lid in place. Bring to 15psi over high heat and immediately reduce the heat to the lowest possible setting to stabilize and maintain that pressure. Cook for 8 minutes. Remove from the heat and use the natural release method before opening the lid. Taste and adjust seasonings with salt and pepper. Ladle the chili into bowls and serve with the lime wedges on the side.

spicy taco chili

I created this recipe on a cool, gray, wet, and windy fall day when the mister and I had been battling the symptoms of oncoming colds. I felt that something hot and spicy would help our sniffles, and even if there isn't any scientific evidence that says eating your way through a big pot of spicy food will cure a cold, good food sure does seem to make you feel better. I love the piquant flavors and complex tastes of Mexican foods, and the thick and spicy chili turned out to be just what we needed. My original version was made with a mix of precooked black beans and pintos that were waiting their turn in the freezer and one lonesome can of red kidney beans that was hiding out in the back of the pantry. Use any variety of beans, or combinations of your favorites, in this chili, but if you have the time, precook your own dried beans. It's a big time-saver—and much more cost efficient than buying cans. Because I am genetically predisposed to being a frugal cook, I like to stock up on a variety of plain, cooked beans in the freezer to use in recipes like this. And yes, you can use them frozen in this recipe. • **SERVES 4**

1 tablespoon olive oil
1 pound ground beef
½ pound chorizo sausage
1 tablespoon chili powder
2 teaspoons ground cumin
1 medium onion, chopped
2 small jalapeño chiles, seeded and chopped
2 chiles, such as Anaheim, poblano, or pasilla, seeded and chopped
2 chipotle chiles in adobo sauce, seeded and minced
10 sprigs fresh cilantro, minced
4 cloves garlic, minced
2 tablespoons adobo sauce from the canned chipotles
3 (14-ounce) cans pinto, kidney, or black beans, rinsed and drained, or 4 cups cooked dried beans of your choice, picked over and rinsed
1 teaspoon salt
1 cup Roasted Garlic Broth (page 66) or chicken broth
1 (20-ounce) can crushed tomatoes with juice
3 tablespoons tomato paste
2 tablespoons fresh lime juice
Tortilla chips of your choice
Toppings: chopped fresh cilantro, shredded cheese of your choice, sour cream or crema agria, salsa, and/or guacamole

Heat the oil in the pressure cooker over medium-high heat and brown the beef and sausage until crumbly and no longer pink. Pour off any excess grease. Add the chili powder and cumin and fry the spices, stirring until they start to sizzle and become fragrant. Add the onion, all the chiles, the cilantro, garlic, adobo sauce, beans, salt, and broth. Stir to mix. Add the tomatoes on top and do not stir. Dot the tomato paste over the top. Lock the lid in place. Bring to 15psi over high heat and immediately reduce the heat to the lowest possible setting to stabilize and maintain that pressure. Cook for 8 minutes. Remove from the heat and use the natural release method before opening the lid. Stir in the lime juice. Taste and adjust seasonings as preferred. To serve, crush some tortilla chips into each individual bowl and ladle a generous portion of the chili on top. Let each person add their toppings of choice.

one-pot meals

risotto with tomatoes and sausage

I think many people have the idea that risotto is really hard and tricky to make, but nothing could be easier than risotto in the pressure cooker. It's a quick one-pot meal that's easily customizable for a different kind of risotto for dinner every night. I swear I never get tired of eating this. Serve it to impress people who think that risotto is hard to cook, and be sure to try and look suitably exhausted after your 7 minutes of "hard work." • **SERVES 4**

- 2 tablespoons olive oil
- 1 pound Italian sausage, casings removed
- 1 small onion, diced
- 3 cloves garlic, finely minced
- 1 cup Arborio or similar short-grain white rice
- ½ cup dry white wine
- 1 (14-ounce) can chicken broth
- 1 (14-ounce) can diced tomatoes with juice
- Salt and coarsely ground black pepper to taste
- 1 teaspoon crushed fennel seeds
- ½ cup grated Parmesan cheese, plus more for garnish (optional)
- 2 tablespoons butter
- 1 small bunch fresh spinach, tough stems removed and chopped into bite-size pieces

Heat the oil in the pressure cooker over medium-high heat and cook the sausage until crumbly. Cook the onion until soft and translucent but not brown, about 4 minutes. Add the garlic and rice, stirring until the rice is coated and opaque. Pour in the wine, broth, and tomatoes, and season with salt and pepper and the fennel seeds. Lock the lid in place. Bring to 15psi over high heat and immediately reduce the heat to the lowest possible setting to stabilize and maintain that pressure. Cook for 7 minutes. Remove from the heat and use the quick release method before opening the lid. Stir the butter and Parmesan cheese into the rice mixture; it will thicken as it cools. Adjust seasonings as needed. Stir in the spinach and serve immediately with a sprinkle of additional Parmesan on top, if desired.

rotini in tomato sauce

In a pressure cooker, pasta absorbs the flavors of the other recipe ingredients during cooking. This absorption cooking method has recently been discovered by celebrity chefs and become very popular on TV cooking shows, but pressure cooker enthusiasts have been using this as a standard cooking technique since the earliest days of pressure cookery. Absorption cooking results in pasta that has a more robust taste than pasta that is cooked in boiling water. Make this meatless recipe as a stand-alone meal, or serve it as an accompaniment to a meat entree. See the variations that follow for meatier versions. Any way you make it, there is plenty of delicious, tangy tomato flavor in this most pleasant meal. Serve with a green salad and garlic toast. • **SERVES 4**

2 tablespoons vegetable oil
1 medium onion, chopped
2 cloves garlic, smashed
1 teaspoon dried Italian herb blend
1 medium green bell pepper, seeded and chopped
2½ cups rotini
1 (15-ounce) can chicken broth
1 (15-ounce) can diced tomatoes with juice
Salt and coarsely ground black pepper to taste
1 (15-ounce) can tomato sauce
2 tablespoons tomato paste
1½ cups shredded mozzarella cheese
Grated Parmesan cheese, for garnish (optional)

Heat the oil in the pressure cooker over medium-high heat and cook the onion until translucent. Add the garlic and the herb blend, cooking until fragrant. Add the bell pepper, pasta, broth, tomatoes with juice, and salt and black pepper, stirring to mix. Add water if necessary to just barely cover the pasta. In a small bowl, blend the tomato sauce with the tomato paste, and then use a rubber spatula to add it to the top of the other ingredients in the pressure cooker, but do not stir. Lock the lid in place. Bring to 15psi over high heat and immediately reduce the heat to the lowest possible setting to stabilize and maintain that pressure. Cook for 6 minutes. Remove from the heat and use the natural release method before opening the lid. Stir in the mozzarella cheese and cover with a regular lid. Wait about 5 minutes to allow the cheese to melt and any remaining sauce to be absorbed. Serve immediately with grated Parmesan if desired.

Variation:

ROTINI IN MEATY TOMATO SAUCE

Add 1 pound lean ground beef or Italian-style bulk sausage, browned until crumbly, to the ingredients and cook as directed.

Variation:

ROTINI AND SAUSAGE IN TOMATO SAUCE

Add 8 ounces smoked sausage, such as kielbasa, sliced and browned, to the ingredients and cook as directed.

pasta with sausage and roasted vegetables in tomato-cheese sauce

Everyone loves pasta! Better yet, how about cute little wagon wheel pasta? Let's add some smoky roasted peppers and tomatoes, too . . . sounding good? Okay, are you in for some mildly spicy sausage and some Italian cheese? All righty, then, this is your kinda dish, and mine, too! Now, here's my trick; I roast the vegetables well in advance—even a couple of days ahead is fine—so that I'm not rushing around trying to do everything at once when everyone is hungry and pounding the table for food. You know how it is, right? Once the roasting is out of the way, it takes only a few minutes to cook this recipe, and it's soooo delicious that you'll enjoy a quiet interlude with nothing but the sound of happy munching. • **SERVES 4**

3 strips bacon, diced
1 pound smoked kielbasa sausage (any variety), sliced
1 large onion, diced
½ cup dry white wine
2 teaspoons smoked paprika
1 teaspoon dried oregano
1 teaspoon dried basil
2 cloves garlic, minced
1 red bell pepper, roasted (see page 299), seeded, and chopped
1 green bell pepper, roasted (see page 299), seeded, and chopped
6 Roma tomatoes, roasted (see page 299) and chopped
1 (14-ounce) can chicken broth
3 cups rotelle (wagon wheel pasta)
1 (14-ounce) can tomato sauce
1½ cups grated Pecorino Romano or similar hard grating cheese
Salt and coarsely ground black pepper to taste

Fry the bacon in the pressure cooker over medium heat until crisp. Set aside on paper towels. Add the kielbasa to the hot bacon fat in the pressure cooker and brown the meat on both sides. Add the onion and cook until soft, about 4 minutes. Deglaze the cooker with the wine, scraping up all those crusty brown bits from the bottom. Add the paprika, oregano, basil, garlic, peppers, tomatoes, broth, and pasta. Return the bacon to the pressure cooker and add only enough water to barely cover the ingredients; stir to mix. Add the tomato sauce, but do not stir. Lock the lid in place. Bring to 15psi over high heat and immediately reduce the heat to the lowest possible setting to stabilize and maintain that pressure. Cook for 5 minutes. Remove from the heat and use the natural release method before opening the lid. Add the cheese and stir gently to mix. Cover the pressure cooker with a regular lid and wait about 5 more minutes or until the cheese melts. Taste and adjust seasoning as desired.

pasta with chicken and artichokes in tomato-alfredo sauce

Tender chunks of chicken with delicious bites of artichoke hearts, all nestled in pasta with a creamy tomato sauce, makes for such an easy, throw-together dinner that just takes a few minutes to get on the table. Serve with a crisp green salad and garlic toast. • **SERVES 4**

2 tablespoons vegetable oil
1 small onion, diced
3 cloves garlic, minced
1 teaspoon dried oregano
1 (14-ounce) can diced tomatoes with juice
2 skinless, boneless chicken breasts
3 cups fusilli
1 (10-ounce) container refrigerated Alfredo sauce
1 (14-ounce) can artichoke hearts, drained and quartered
1 cup sliced pitted black olives
⅓ cup herbed crumbled feta cheese, for garnish

Heat the oil in the pressure cooker over medium-high heat and cook the onion until soft, about 4 minutes. Stir in the garlic, oregano, and tomatoes. Add the chicken and then the pasta, in that order. Add only enough water to barely cover the pasta. Lock the lid in place. Bring to 15psi over high heat and immediately reduce the heat to the lowest possible setting to stabilize and maintain that pressure. Cook for 6 minutes. Remove from the heat and use the natural release method before opening the lid. Transfer the chicken to a cutting board and chop into bite-size pieces. Gently stir the Alfredo sauce, chicken pieces, artichoke hearts, and olives into the pressure cooker, simmering over low heat until heated through. Spoon into a serving bowl and sprinkle the cheese on top.

fusilli with chicken and mushrooms in creamy pesto sauce

This recipe is elaborate enough for an elegant dinner. With bite-size pieces of chicken and mushrooms, and pasta in a creamy pesto sauce, it's the perfect marriage of the fresh taste and aroma of the basil leaves slipping through the luscious creamy sauce; it's scrumptious stuff, my dears. Serve this with crunchy Italian bread sticks and a crisp romaine salad with a simple vinaigrette dressing . . . and a really good dry white wine . . . maybe a couple of candles, Andrea Bocelli on the stereo . . . you get the idea, yes? • **SERVES 4**

Step One: THE PESTO

2 cups fresh basil leaves
3 cloves garlic
⅓ cup pine nuts
½ cup extra-virgin olive oil
½ cup grated Parmigiano-Reggiano or Pecorino Romano cheese
Salt and freshly ground black pepper to taste

Combine the basil, garlic, and pine nuts in a food processor and pulse a few times. Slowly add the oil in a constant stream while the food processor is running. Scrape down the sides of the bowl with a rubber spatula. Add the cheese and pulse again until blended. Add salt and pepper to taste. Set aside.

Step Two: THE SAUCE

2 tablespoons butter
2 tablespoons all-purpose flour
1 cup milk

Heat a small saucepan over medium-high heat and melt the butter. Sprinkle in the flour and cook, stirring, for 2 minutes. Stir in the milk and cook for another 5 minutes or until slightly thickened. Remove from the heat and set aside.

Step Three: THE CHICKEN AND PASTA

- 2 tablespoons olive oil
- 3 skinless, boneless chicken breasts
- 1 shallot, diced
- 1 cup dry white wine
- 2 cups sliced fresh white or cremini mushrooms
- 3 cups fusilli
- 1 (15-ounce) can chicken broth
- 1 cup grated Parmesan cheese

Heat the oil in the pressure cooker over medium-high heat and brown the chicken on both sides. Transfer to a plate. Cook the shallot until soft. Deglaze the pot with the wine, scraping up all those crusty brown bits from the bottom. Add the mushrooms, pasta, and broth, stirring well. Add the chicken back to the pressure cooker, and add enough water to be sure that the ingredients are just barely covered. Lock the lid in place. Bring to 15psi over high heat and immediately reduce the heat to the lowest possible setting to stabilize and maintain that pressure. Cook for 5 minutes. Remove from the heat and use the natural release method before opening the lid. Transfer the chicken to a cutting board and chop the meat into bite-size pieces. Return the chicken to the pressure cooker, but do not stir yet. Mix the pesto into the cream sauce and stir in the cheese. Pour the creamy pesto sauce over the pasta and chicken, and gently fold the ingredients to mix. Cook over low heat without a lid until the mixture is heated through. Cover and wait about 5 minutes for the cheese to melt and the sauce to thicken.

penne and mushrooms in tomato sauce

Make this as a simple and tasty main dish and serve with a salad and some crusty Italian bread, or use it as a side dish to accompany a meat-based main dish. Either way, this is a fast weekday recipe that will get your dinner on the table in just minutes. • **SERVES 4**

- 1 tablespoon olive oil
- 1 onion, diced
- 4 to 6 cloves garlic, minced
- ¼ cup chopped fresh oregano
- ½ cup chopped fresh basil
- 8 ounces fresh white or cremini mushrooms, washed and halved
- 3 cups penne or ziti
- 1 (16-ounce) jar tomato pasta sauce
- ½ cup grated Parmesan cheese
- Salt and coarsely ground black pepper to taste

Heat the oil in the pressure cooker over medium-high heat and cook the onion until soft, about 4 minutes. Add the garlic, oregano, and half the basil, stirring until fragrant. Add the mushrooms and pasta, stirring to mix. Add just enough water to barely cover the ingredients. Add the pasta sauce on top but do not stir. Lock the lid in place. Bring to 15psi over high heat and immediately reduce the heat to the lowest possible setting to stabilize and maintain that pressure. Cook for 6 minutes. Remove from the heat and use the natural release method before opening the lid. Add the cheese and the remaining basil, stirring gently to blend. Taste and adjust seasonings with salt and pepper as desired.

Variation:

PENNE AND MUSHROOMS IN TOMATO SAUCE WITH PORK CHOPS

Season 4 bone-in pork chops (½ inch thick) with salt and pepper. Heat the oil in the pressure cooker over medium-high heat and brown the meat on both sides. Set aside while you cook the onions, and then return the chops to the pressure cooker, arranging them on the bottom. Add all the remaining ingredients on top of the chops and proceed with the recipe.

Variation:

PENNE AND MUSHROOMS IN TOMATO SAUCE WITH CHICKEN

Season 4 skinless chicken thighs with salt and pepper. Heat the oil in the pressure cooker over medium-high heat and brown the chicken on both sides. Set aside while you cook the onions, and then return the chicken to the pressure cooker, arranging the pieces on the bottom. Add all the remaining ingredients on top of the chicken and proceed with the recipe.

pasta with chicken in creamy mushroom sauce

This is a great weekday recipe that uses lots of fresh ingredients. With a little chopping and slicing, you'll get a big payoff with the flavorful, two-course meal of chicken and pasta with a creamy mushroom sauce. Instead of boiling the pasta in plain water and having it turn out tasteless, we use the infusion cooking method so that the pasta absorbs all the flavors of the other ingredients. • **SERVES 6**

2 tablespoons olive oil
6 chicken thighs or legs
2 cups chicken broth
¼ cup dry sherry
2 stalks celery, sliced
1 small onion, diced
2 leeks, white parts only, sliced
4 large cloves garlic, finely chopped
8 ounces fresh cremini mushrooms, washed and sliced
1 teaspoon salt
¼ teaspoon freshly ground black pepper
1 teaspoon dried thyme
3 cups radiatore or fusilli
1 cup sour cream
1 cup grated Pecorino Romano or any hard Italian grating cheese

Heat the oil in the pressure cooker over medium-high heat and brown the chicken on all sides. Transfer to a plate. Deglaze the cooker with the broth, scraping up any crusty brown bits from the bottom. Stir in the sherry, celery, onion, leeks, garlic, mushrooms, salt, pepper, and thyme. Add the pasta and add just enough water to barely cover. Add the chicken on top but do not stir. Lock the lid in place. Bring to 15psi over high heat and immediately reduce the heat to the lowest possible setting to stabilize and maintain that pressure. Cook for 5 minutes. Remove from the heat and use the natural release method before opening the lid. Transfer the chicken to a serving dish. Add the sour cream and cheese to the pasta mixture and simmer gently over low heat until the cheese is melted and the sauce is creamy and heated through. Taste and adjust the seasonings. Spoon the pasta and sauce into a serving bowl.

ravioli with onions and zucchini in tomato sauce

My dear friend the Cast Iron King wondered whether it was possible to cook ravioli in the pressure cooker. I thought, sure, and let's make it a nice Italian-inspired ravioli dish with some veggies in a seasoned tomato sauce. Of course, it had to be super simple, but also flavorful, and fast cooking for an uncomplicated weeknight dinner. I also wanted it to be a one-pot meal for easy cleanup. So this is the combination of ravioli with zucchini, Italian herbs, and tomatoes that I used. Serve with a crisp romaine salad and zesty Italian dressing, and some crunchy Italian bread sticks. • **SERVES 4**

- 2 tablespoons vegetable oil
- 1 large onion, diced
- 4 cloves garlic, minced
- 2 medium zucchini, cut into ¼-inch-thick slices
- 4 ounces fresh cremini mushrooms, washed, stems trimmed, and sliced
- 1 pound frozen large ravioli of your choice
- 1 (14-ounce) can diced tomatoes with juice
- 1 cup dry red wine
- 2 teaspoons dried Italian herb blend
- ½ teaspoon red pepper flakes
- 1 (14-ounce) can tomato sauce
- 2 tablespoons tomato paste
- ½ cup grated Parmesan cheese
- Salt and coarsely ground black pepper to taste

Heat the oil in the pressure cooker over medium-high heat and cook the onion until translucent and soft, about 4 minutes. Stir in the garlic, zucchini, mushrooms, ravioli, tomatoes, wine, herb blend, and red pepper flakes. In a separate bowl, mix the tomato sauce and the tomato paste to combine. Spread the tomato mixture over the ingredients in the pressure cooker, but do not stir. Lock the lid in place. Bring to 15psi over high heat and immediately reduce the heat to the lowest possible setting to stabilize and maintain that pressure. Cook for 4 minutes. Remove from the heat and use the natural release method before opening the lid. Add the Parmesan cheese and stir gently to combine. Taste and add salt and black pepper as needed. Serve hot.

Variation:

RAVIOLI WITH SAUSAGE, ONIONS, AND ZUCCHINI IN TOMATO SAUCE

Heat the oil in the pressure cooker over medium-high heat and brown 1 pound hot or sweet Italian sausage, casings removed, until crumbly and no longer pink. Add the onion and continue with the recipe as directed.

creamy chicken succotash

The bright, fun colors make this dish look very festive on your table. This is a versatile recipe that can be served as a stand-alone main dish, or spoon it over cooked egg noodles, fluffy white rice, or hot split biscuits. • **SERVES 4 OR 5**

2 tablespoons butter
1 pound skinless, boneless chicken breasts or thighs
1 small onion, chopped
1 (16-ounce) bag frozen succotash (baby lima beans and corn) or similar mixed vegetables
1 (14-ounce) can chicken broth
½ teaspoon dried thyme
Salt and freshly ground black pepper to taste
1 (4-ounce) jar pimientos, drained and chopped
1 cup heavy cream
1 to 2 tablespoons instant potato flakes

Melt the butter over medium heat in the pressure cooker and lightly brown the chicken pieces. Cut the chicken into 1½-inch chunks and place them on the bottom of the pressure cooker. Add the onion, succotash, broth, thyme, and salt and pepper. Lock the lid in place. Bring to 15psi over high heat and immediately reduce the heat to the lowest possible setting to stabilize and maintain that pressure. Cook for 4 minutes. Remove from the heat and use the natural release method before opening the lid. Stir in the pimientos and add the cream. Heat over medium-low heat, and stir in the potato flakes to thicken the sauce to the desired consistency.

Variation:
CREAMY TURKEY SUCCOTASH

Substitute 1 pound skinless, boneless white turkey meat, cut into 1-inch chunks, for the chicken.

Variation:
CREAMY HAM SUCCOTASH

Substitute 1 pound cooked ham, trimmed of fat and cut into ½-inch chunks, for the chicken. Skip the browning step.

Variation:
CREAMY TUNA SUCCOTASH

Substitute 2 (6-ounce) cans water-packed tuna for the chicken (do not drain). Flake the tuna with a fork before adding to the pressure cooker. Skip the browning step.

ravioli in a cheesy tomato-alfredo sauce

I love pasta in the pressure cooker because it makes a quick and easy one-pot meal. The almost limitless variety of choices among pasta shapes and all the accompanying ingredients make for some tasty and flavorful dishes. From a simply delicious weekday meal for the family to something fabulous that will impress your dinner guests, there are endless possibilities for combinations of pasta shapes and flavorsome ingredients to suit any occasion and tempt even the pickiest palates. This is the perfect combo of tomatoes and cheese with ravioli, and it is very satisfying as a stand-alone main dish with a crisp romaine salad and some crunchy bread sticks. For heartier appetites, I've even included lots of meaty variations. • **SERVES 4**

2 tablespoons olive oil
1 large onion, coarsely chopped
½ cup minced fresh oregano
2 cups sliced fresh white mushrooms
6 cloves garlic, minced
½ teaspoon red pepper flakes
1 green bell pepper, seeded and chopped
1 (14-ounce) can pitted black olives, sliced
3 cups frozen ravioli of your choice
1 (14-ounce) can diced tomatoes with juice
1 (24-ounce) jar tomato pasta sauce or 3 cups homemade tomato sauce (see pages 281–283)
½ cup heavy cream
1½ cups shredded mozzarella cheese
½ cup grated Parmesan cheese
Salt and coarsely ground black pepper to taste

Heat the oil in the pressure cooker over medium-high heat and cook the onion until soft, stirring often, about 4 minutes. Add the fresh oregano and stir until fragrant. Add the mushrooms, garlic, red pepper flakes, bell pepper, olives, ravioli, and tomatoes, stirring to mix. Add just enough water to barely cover the ingredients. Add the pasta sauce on top but do not stir. Lock the lid in place. Bring to 15psi over high heat and immediately reduce the heat to the lowest possible setting to stabilize and maintain that pressure. Cook for 5 minutes. Remove from the heat and use the natural release method before opening the lid. Add the cream and mozzarella and Parmesan cheeses, stirring gently to blend. Taste and adjust seasonings as desired. Cover the pressure cooker with a lid and allow about 5 minutes for the cheese to melt. Serve hot.

Variation:

BEEF AND RAVIOLI IN A CHEESY TOMATO-ALFREDO SAUCE

Heat the oil in the pressure cooker over medium-high heat and brown ½ pound lean ground beef on all sides. Add the onion and proceed with the recipe.

Variation:

ITALIAN SAUSAGE AND RAVIOLI IN A CHEESY TOMATO-ALFREDO SAUCE

Cut ½ pound hot or sweet Italian sausage links into ½-inch slices. Heat the oil in the pressure cooker over medium-high heat and brown the sausage slices on both sides. Add the onion and proceed with the recipe.

Variation:

CHICKEN AND RAVIOLI IN A CHEESY TOMATO-ALFREDO SAUCE

Cut 1 pound skinless, boneless chicken pieces (whatever you prefer) into bite-size pieces. Heat the oil in the pressure cooker over medium-high heat and brown the chicken on both sides. Add the onion and proceed with the recipe.

Variation:

PORK CHOPS AND RAVIOLI IN A CHEESY TOMATO-ALFREDO SAUCE

Season 4 to 6 bone-in pork chops (½ inch thick) with salt and pepper. Heat the oil in the pressure cooker over medium-high heat and brown the meat on both sides. Transfer to a plate and cook the onions, and then return the chops to the pressure cooker, arranging them on the bottom. Add all the remaining ingredients on top of the chops and proceed with the recipe.

swiss chicken with tarragon wine sauce and mashed potatoes

This two-course meal will need a 6-quart or larger pressure cooker to accommodate the two stacked insert pans. My PIP cooking method is combined with the tiered cooking method to cook the well-seasoned chicken and sauce and the creamy mashed potatoes at the same time. Alternatively, each dish may be cooked separately. If you're looking for a great alternative to the same old chicken recipes, give this one a try. This is a pantry-friendly dish that uses simple ingredients that don't need a lot of prep work, so you'll have a full meal on the table in only a few minutes from start to finish. • **SERVES 4 GENEROUSLY**

Step One: THE CHICKEN

6 skinless chicken thighs
Salt and freshly ground black pepper to taste
2 teaspoons Hungarian paprika
2 tablespoons olive oil
1 cup dry white wine or chicken broth
2 teaspoons dried tarragon
1 teaspoon Dijon mustard

Season the chicken with salt and pepper to taste, and dust with the paprika. Heat the oil in a large pressure cooker, brown the meat on both sides, and transfer to a plate. Deglaze the pot with the wine, scraping up all those crusty brown bits from the bottom. Add the tarragon and mustard, stirring to blend. Return the chicken to the pressure cooker.

Step Two: THE MASHED POTATOES

2 pounds russet potatoes, peeled and cut into 2-inch cubes
½ cup (1 stick) butter, softened
Salt and freshly ground black pepper to taste
⅓ cup milk, or as needed

Place the cut potatoes in a perforated steamer tray that will fit inside the pressure cooker. Place the pan of potatoes on top of the chicken. Lock the lid in place. Bring to 15psi over high heat and immediately reduce the heat to the lowest possible setting to stabilize and maintain that pressure. Cook for 6 minutes. Remove from the heat and use the natural release method before opening the lid. Transfer the potatoes to a mixing bowl and smash them with a potato masher or use your own preferred method. To use a stand mixer with the paddle attachment, just pulse the power, taking care not to overwork the potatoes or they will become a glob of glue. Add the butter and salt and pepper to the potatoes. Use only enough milk to get the desired consistency and mix gently. Spoon the mashed potatoes into a serving bowl, and arrange the chicken on a platter. Place in a warm oven while preparing the sauce.

Step Three: THE SAUCE

1 tablespoon cornstarch
1½ cups shredded Swiss cheese

Simmer the broth in the pressure cooker over medium heat. To thicken, mix the cornstarch with ⅓ cup cold water and stir it into the broth. Turn down the heat and stir occasionally as the sauce thickens. Add the cheese, stirring until it is melted and blended into the sauce. Adjust seasonings to taste. Pour the sauce into gravy boat or bowl to pass at the table, spooning it over the chicken and potatoes.

creamy chicken and vegetables over mashed potatoes

This recipe uses a rich, blond roux to thicken the sauce. Now don't start hyperventilating, because *roux* is just a fancy French term for some melted butter and flour . . . easy stuff! This is a hearty two-course meal that's cooked all at the same time in the pressure cooker using the tiered cooking method. • **SERVES 4 OR 5**

Step One: THE BLOND ROUX

2 tablespoons butter
2 tablespoons all-purpose flour

Makes this in advance if you like. In a small skillet, melt the butter over low heat, taking care not to let it burn. Add the flour and stir until all the flour is smoothly incorporated into the butter. Stir regularly while cooking for a minimum of 2 minutes or until the thick, pastelike mixture turns a light golden blond color. The roux will get darker the longer it cooks, so don't overcook it beyond the pale blond color. Place the roux in a covered bowl and refrigerate if not using immediately.

Step Two: THE CHICKEN, POTATOES, AND VEGETABLES

2 pounds russet potatoes, peeled and cut into 2-inch cubes
1 pound skinless, boneless chicken breasts, thighs, or legs, cut into 1-inch chunks
1 medium onion, diced
1 (10-ounce) package frozen mixed peas and carrots or frozen vegetables of your choice
1 (14-ounce) can chicken broth
1 teaspoon chicken bouillon granules
½ teaspoon dried thyme
1 teaspoon garlic powder
Salt and coarsely ground black pepper to taste

Place the potatoes in a flat-bottomed stainless steel pan that will fit inside your pressure cooker. Add the chicken, onion, vegetables, broth, bouillon, thyme, garlic powder, and salt and pepper to the pressure cooker. Stir to mix. Place the pan of potatoes on top of the chicken and vegetable mixture. Lock the lid in place. Bring to 15psi over high heat and immediately reduce the heat to the lowest possible setting to stabilize and maintain that pressure. Cook for 5 minutes. Remove from the heat and use the natural release method before opening the lid.

Step Three: THE MASHED POTATOES

⅓ cup butter, softened
⅓ cup half-and-half, warmed
Salt and coarsely ground black pepper to taste

Unlike waterlogged boiled potatoes, these steamed potatoes will be dry, which means they will mash up very light and fluffy. Mash the potatoes by whatever method you prefer. To use a stand mixer with the paddle attachment, place the potatoes in the mixing bowl and add the butter. Briefly pulse the mixer on and off in short bursts to break up the potatoes. Add the warm half-and-half and pulse again to get a creamy consistency, taking care not to overdo it. Taste the potatoes and add salt and pepper as needed. Transfer the mashed potatoes to a serving bowl and keep warm.

Step Four: THE GRAVY

If you've refrigerated the roux, scoop it into a skillet and warm it over medium heat. Slowly whisk a little of the hot broth from the pressure cooker into the roux. This will temper the roux and prevent lumps. Continue stirring until the roux until it is smoothly blended. Pour the roux into the broth mixture in the pressure cooker and stir over medium heat until the gravy thickens. Remove from the heat. Taste the sauce and adjust salt and pepper as needed. Pour the chicken mixture into a serving bowl. Serve over the mashed potatoes.

COOK'S NOTE: The sauce will thicken as it cools, and any refrigerated leftovers may be thinned by adding a little more broth, milk, or cream to reach the desired consistency.

---

lemon-thyme chicken and rice

This is my go-to dish for a quick, family-friendly one-pot meal. It's simple and easy to prepare, and with only a few ingredients you'll have a delicious dinner on the table in just minutes. Serve this with a green salad or sliced tomatoes. • **SERVES 4 TO 6**

2 pounds skinless, boneless chicken breasts, thighs, or legs
½ cup dry white wine
2 (15-ounce) cans chicken broth
½ cup diced onion
Juice of 1 lemon
½ teaspoon garlic powder
1 teaspoon dried thyme
1 teaspoon chicken bouillon granules
1½ cups long-grain white rice
½ teaspoon lemon pepper, or to taste

Add all the ingredients to the pressure cooker and stir to mix. Lock the lid in place. Bring to 15psi over high heat and immediately reduce the heat to the lowest possible setting to stabilize and maintain that pressure. Cook for 4 minutes. Remove from the heat and use the natural release method before opening the lid. Transfer the chicken to a cutting board and cut into bite-size pieces. Stir the chicken back into the rice. Taste and adjust seasonings. Spoon the mixture into a serving bowl.

Variation:
LEMON-THYME SALMON AND RICE

Substitute 1½ pounds salmon fillets for the chicken. Cook as directed.

Variation:
LEMON-THYME HAM AND RICE

Substitute 1 pound cubed ham for the chicken. Cook as directed.

hungarian chicken paprikash with rice

My mother used to make the best chicken paprikash when we were growing up! The delicious aroma of pungent spices that flavored the rice and the smoky paprika taste of the chicken was enough to make us kids clean our plates. This is an easy enough meal to serve during the week, as there isn't a lot of heavy prep work needed and it only takes a few minutes to cook. Include a simple side dish of sliced tomatoes and cucumbers marinated in a well-seasoned vinaigrette, and a loaf of crusty bread, and dinner is done! • **SERVES 8**

- 8 chicken thighs and legs
- 1 teaspoon salt
- ½ teaspoon freshly ground black pepper
- 2 tablespoons hot Hungarian paprika
- 1 tablespoon smoked paprika
- 2 tablespoons olive oil
- 1 large onion, chopped
- 2 large cloves garlic, minced
- 3 tablespoons minced fresh dill weed or 1 tablespoon dried dill weed
- 2 (14-ounce) cans chicken broth
- 1 cup sliced fresh white mushrooms
- 1 large bell pepper, seeded and chopped
- Zest and juice of 1 lemon
- 2 cups long-grain white rice
- 1 (28-ounce) can diced tomatoes with juice
- 3 tablespoons tomato paste
- 1 cup sour cream
- 2 tablespoons minced fresh Italian parsley, for garnish

Wash the chicken and pat dry with paper towels. Combine the salt, black pepper, and both paprikas in a small bowl, and season the chicken, pressing the spices evenly into the meat with your fingers. Shake off any excess and reserve the remaining paprika mixture. Heat the oil in the pressure cooker over medium-high heat and brown the chicken in batches without crowding, searing all sides. Transfer to a plate. Add the onion, cooking until soft, about 4 minutes. Stir in the garlic, dill, and the remaining paprika mixture, cooking and stirring until the spices sizzle and become fragrant. Deglaze the pot with the broth, scraping up all those crusty brown bits from the bottom. Add the mushrooms, bell pepper, the lemon zest and juice, and the rice, stirring to mix. Return the chicken pieces to the pressure cooker. Add the tomatoes with juice and dot the tomato paste over the top; do not stir. Lock the lid in place. Bring to 15psi over high heat and immediately reduce the heat to the lowest possible setting to stabilize and maintain that pressure. Cook for 6 minutes. Remove from the heat and use the natural release method before opening the lid. Remove the chicken pieces from the pressure cooker. Stir in the sour cream and heat through over low heat. Taste and adjust seasonings. Spoon the rice mixture onto a deep serving platter and arrange the chicken pieces on top. Garnish with the parsley.

quick and cheesy chicken divan

This fast and no-fuss one-pot meal has been a family favorite ever since the kids were tykes. The prep work takes more time than the actual cooking, making this a good choice for busy cooks who need to get dinner on the table. Chicken, broccoli, and rice make it a colorful meal-in-one, and by cooking the broccoli in a foil packet it will retain its color and still be tender-crisp when mixed in with the rice. Pop a pan of refrigerated biscuits in the oven before pressurizing the cooker so they will be ready at the same time, and serve everything with sliced tomatoes. • **SERVES 4**

2 tablespoons butter
3 skinless, boneless chicken breasts or 4 or 5 skinless, boneless chicken thighs
½ cup diced onion
1½ cups long-grain white rice
1 teaspoon chicken bouillon granules
2 tablespoons Dijon mustard
1 teaspoon dried thyme
¼ teaspoon freshly ground black pepper
3 cups chicken broth or stock
1 (10-ounce) package frozen chopped broccoli
1½ cups shredded sharp cheddar cheese
Salt to taste

Heat the butter in the pressure cooker, brown the chicken on both sides, and transfer to a plate. Add the onion and cook until soft and translucent, about 4 minutes. Return the chicken pieces to the pressure cooker. Stir in the rice, bouillon, mustard, thyme, pepper, and broth. Break apart the frozen broccoli if necessary to separate the pieces and then spread them out on a sheet of aluminum foil. Loosely fold the aluminum foil over the broccoli to make a packet and crimp the edges tightly to seal. Place the broccoli packet on top of all the other ingredients in the pressure cooker. Lock the lid in place. Bring to 15psi over high heat and immediately reduce the heat to the lowest possible setting to stabilize and maintain that pressure. Cook for 4 minutes. Remove from the heat and use the natural release method before opening the lid. Carefully lift out the broccoli packet and cut it open in a colander to drain off any accumulated water. Transfer the chicken pieces to a cutting board and chop them into small pieces. Stir the chicken pieces, broccoli, and cheese back into the pressure cooker and cover with a regular lid for a few minutes, until the cheese has melted. Taste and add salt as desired. Spoon the rice mixture into a serving bowl.

spinach-stuffed chicken pinwheels with sherry cream sauce and basmati rice timbales

This two-course meal is as beautiful to look at as it is to eat. Plan on using a 6-quart or larger pressure cooker to accommodate the two stacked insert pans needed to cook this pressure cooker recipe that uses my PIP cooking method in combination with the tiered cooking method. Alternatively, each dish may be cooked separately.

You'll need a meat mallet or something similar to get started making this visually impressive dish. Don't worry if you don't (yet) have one; a small heavy skillet will work in a pinch. When I was growing up, a meat mallet was a commonplace kitchen tool, and while not as popular in today's home kitchen, it's still a very handy gadget. In the days before the food processor, mallets weren't just used for tenderizing meat; they pulverized everything from spices to bread crumbs to nuts to ice blocks, and maybe even pounded an occasional nail or two. In my grandma's day, every cook had several mallets to choose from. I remember one gigantic mallet that hung in a place of honor above the stove, and it was a device so huge that it might have been used in medieval warfare. As I remember the tale told by Grandpa, that great wooden mallet actually belonged to old John Henry, the mythical railroad man of American folklore. Being a railroad man himself, my grandpa would soon have everyone singing the chorus of the folk song while we trembled in awe as my sturdy little old grandma wielded that mighty meat mallet with practiced ease, flattening whole chickens with just a couple of well-placed whacks. Back when young brides-to-be dutifully included a shiny new meat mallet on their wish list, I was delighted to open a beautifully wrapped wedding present from a distant relation to find my very own hand-carved, wooden meat mallet. • **SERVES 4**

Step One: THE STUFFING

- 1½ to 2 cups finely chopped fresh spinach leaves
- 10 sprigs fresh cilantro, finely chopped
- ½ cup minced onion
- ⅔ cup seasoned dry bread crumbs
- ½ cup ricotta cheese
- 2 tablespoons butter, softened

Place all the ingredients in a glass bowl and stir to blend.

(continued)

Step Two: THE CHICKEN

4 skinless, boneless chicken breasts
Salt and coarsely ground black pepper to taste
2 teaspoons paprika
1 tablespoon butter, softened

Place the chicken breasts between two pieces of plastic wrap and use the flat side of a meat mallet to gently pound the chicken to a ¼-inch thickness. Take care not to pound too hard or the meat may get too thin and tear. Turn the breasts smooth side down and season with salt and pepper. Divide the stuffing mixture into four equal parts. Spread each breast with a layer of the stuffing mixture. Starting at the largest end, roll each breast up tightly, rolling toward the smaller end. Secure each roll with toothpicks as needed. Dust the paprika over each roll. Brush the butter on the bottom of a metal insert pan that will fit inside your pressure cooker and place the chicken rolls in the pan, seam side down. Place the cooking rack in the pressure cooker and pour in 1 cup water. Place the insert pan with the chicken rolls on the rack.

Step Three: THE RICE

1 cup long-grain white basmati or Texmati rice, rinsed until the water runs clear
2 tablespoons butter
1 teaspoon chicken bouillon granules
1½ teaspoons ground turmeric

Select a 1½-quart stainless steel insert pan that will stack on top of the insert pan with the chicken rolls, and add the rice, 2 cups water, the butter, bouillon, and turmeric. Place the insert pan with the rice mixture on top of the chicken in the pressure cooker. Lock the lid in place. Bring to 15psi over high heat and immediately reduce the heat to the lowest possible setting to stabilize and maintain that pressure. Cook for 5 minutes. Meanwhile, prepare the sauce.

Step Four: THE SAUCE

2 tablespoons butter
⅓ cup chicken broth
⅓ cup dry sherry
1 teaspoon herbes de Provence
½ cup half-and-half
Salt and freshly ground black pepper to taste

While the courses are cooking in the pressure cooker, there's just enough time to prepare the sauce. Melt the butter in a heavy saucepan over medium-low heat. Add the broth, sherry, and herbes de Provence and cook until reduced by half. Add half-and-half and reduce the heat; continue to cook and stir for a few minutes more or until the mixture is thickened. Season with salt and pepper.

To serve, remove the rice from the pressure cooker and gently pack a portion of rice into a 1-cup measuring cup, a suitably sized ramekin, or a custard cup. Unmold the rice timbale in the center of each individual serving plate. Transfer the chicken rolls to a cutting board and remove the toothpicks. Use a sharp knife to cut each breast into equal slices about 1½ inches thick. Divide the pinwheel slices into portions and arrange them in a circle around each of the rice timbales. Drizzle some of the sauce over the top of the rice and the pinwheel slices. Pass the remainder at the table.

Variation:

CHICKEN PINWHEELS STUFFED WITH BABY ASPARAGUS

Instead of the spinach stuffing mixture, substitute 12 ounces thin, baby asparagus tips. Depending on the size, use 3 or 4 asparagus tips per chicken breast. Proceed as directed.

Variation:

CHICKEN PINWHEELS STUFFED WITH GREEN BEANS AND PROSCIUTTO

Instead of the spinach stuffing mixture, use 8 ounces fresh green beans, ends trimmed, and 4 pieces of prosciutto. Place a slice of prosciutto on each pounded chicken breast. Depending on the size, use 4 or 5 green beans per chicken breast. Proceed as directed.

Variation:

CHICKEN PINWHEELS STUFFED WITH RED PEPPERS AND MOZZARELLA CHEESE

Instead of the spinach stuffing mixture, use 1 red bell pepper, seeded and cut into thin strips, divided into 4 portions, and 4 pieces of string cheese. Place a piece of string cheese and a portion of the red bell pepper strips on top of each pounded chicken breast. Proceed as directed.

turkey fillets with pasta in onion-pepper sauce

Turkey is low in fat and high in protein, which makes it a great meal option, and although fairly inexpensive compared to other meats, it's often neglected as we plan out everyday menus. Maybe our brains are hardwired to only think of turkey as the star attraction at the big family Thanksgiving feast, but have you seen all the different cuts that are available now? I really try to set out a variety of different main dishes, and so I have come up with some new pressure cooker recipes to bring more turkey dishes to the table. This dish doesn't need much in the way of intense preparation, and if you use a food processor, it's almost no work at all. For a side dish, I would suggest freshly cooked spinach or chard. • **SERVES 4**

1 to 1½ pounds turkey breast fillets or cutlets
1 tablespoon poultry seasoning
2 tablespoons olive oil
2 cups diced onion
1 cup apple juice
1 teaspoon garlic powder
½ teaspoon salt
½ teaspoon freshly ground black pepper
1 red bell pepper, seeded and chopped
1 green bell pepper, seeded and chopped
2 cups chicken broth
3 cups bowtie pasta or small pasta shells
1 teaspoon dried Italian parsley, for garnish
1 cup sour cream

Season both sides of the turkey with the poultry seasoning; reserve any extra seasoning. Heat the oil in the pressure cooker over medium-high heat and brown the turkey on all sides. If the fillets do not all fit, brown them in batches. Set aside on a plate. Add the onion and stir in the remaining poultry seasoning. Cook the onion until soft. Deglaze the cooker with the apple juice, scraping up all those brown bits from the bottom. Add the garlic powder, salt, black pepper, the red and green bell peppers, and the broth, stirring to mix. Add the pasta, pushing it down under the liquid. Add additional water only if necessary to just barely cover the pasta. Add the turkey on top; do not stir. Lock the lid in place. Bring to 15psi over high heat and immediately reduce the heat to the lowest possible setting to stabilize and maintain that pressure. Cook for 5 minutes. Remove from the heat and use the natural release method before opening the lid. Transfer the turkey to a serving plate and garnish with half the parsley. Add the sour cream to the pasta mixture and simmer gently over low heat until the sauce is creamy and heated through. Taste and adjust the seasonings. Spoon the pasta and sauce into a serving bowl and sprinkle the remaining parsley on top.

pork chops, sauerkraut, and potatoes

These days, most shoppers prefer the convenience of boneless pork chops. The old fashioned bone-in chops are almost a forgotten heirloom, but put them on your shopping list for this recipe. This cut of pork chop is usually cheaper, and the bone provides a lot of added flavor. When I found this old recipe in Grandma's recipe box, it reminded me of all those big old crocks of her homemade sauerkraut that lived under the stairs down in the root cellar. I like cabbage, but not sauerkraut so much . . . or that dark old scary cellar. Grandma's kraut was strong enough to strip paint off a tractor, and Grandpa was only too eager to point out the spot of bare metal on the old John Deere to prove it! He didn't much care for kraut, either.

Years later, I learned the secret of taming sauerkraut by rinsing it well and adding just the tiniest little bit of brown sugar. Now I can honestly say that I really like sauerkraut, and I hope you will try this and discover how to tame sauerkraut so that even the kids will like it. • **SERVES 4**

Salt and coarsely ground black pepper to taste
½ teaspoon dried thyme
4 center-cut loin pork chops, about ½ inch thick
2 tablespoons vegetable oil
1 tablespoon dark brown sugar
½ cup apple juice
6 medium russet potatoes, scrubbed and each cut into 4 wedges
28 ounces refrigerated or canned sauerkraut, rinsed in cold water and well drained

Rub the salt, a generous amount of pepper, and the thyme into both sides of the chops. Heat the oil in the pressure cooker over medium-high heat and brown the chops on all sides. Dissolve the sugar into the apple juice and deglaze the pot with the mixture, scraping up all those crusty brown bits from the bottom. Arrange the potato wedges on top of the chops. Add the sauerkraut over the potatoes. Lock the lid in place. Bring to 15psi over high heat and immediately reduce the heat to the lowest possible setting to stabilize and maintain that pressure. Cook for 4 minutes. Remove from the heat and use the natural release method before opening the lid. Use a slotted spoon to divide the chops, potatoes, and kraut between serving plates. Spoon a little of the pan sauce on top of the potatoes, or pass it at the table if desired.

cheesy sausage and potato casserole

This super-quick shortcut meal is a kid-friendly, man-pleasin', meat-and-potatoes dinner that is fast and easy enough for a weeknight meal. Serve with sliced cucumbers and tomatoes in a tangy vinaigrette, and you're done! • **SERVES 4**

1 tablespoon olive oil
2 tablespoons butter
1 large onion, chopped
2 cloves garlic, minced
½ teaspoon ground sage
1 teaspoon salt, or to taste
½ teaspoon freshly ground black pepper
1 to 1½ pounds kielbasa, cut into ½-inch-thick slices
½ cup beef broth
4 medium potatoes, peeled and cut into 1-inch cubes
1 (16-ounce) container chunky salsa of your choice
1½ cups cubed American cheese

Heat the oil and butter in the pressure cooker over medium-high heat and cook the onion until translucent and soft, about 4 minutes. Stir in the garlic, sage, salt, pepper, and kielbasa, cooking until the sausage is lightly browned. Deglaze the pot with the broth, scraping up all those crusty brown bits from the bottom. In the following order, add the potatoes and then 1½ cups salsa, without stirring. Lock the lid in place. Bring to 15psi over high heat and immediately reduce the heat to the lowest possible setting to stabilize and maintain that pressure. Cook for 4 minutes. Remove from the heat and use the quick release method before opening the lid. Stir in the cheese and cover the pressure cooker with a regular lid for about 4 minutes while the cheese melts. Taste and adjust seasonings as needed. Spoon the mixture into a serving bowl. Pour the remaining salsa into a small bowl to be passed at the table.

sausage, potatoes, and green beans

This simple recipe combines potatoes with spicy Italian sausages and fresh green beans, all tossed with butter and herbs. Serve this with garlic bread, or try it with my Soft and Creamy Polenta (page 278). • **SERVES 4**

2 tablespoons olive oil
1 pound Italian sausage, casings removed and cut into 2-inch pieces
1 medium onion, halved and sliced
4 small red potatoes, scrubbed and quartered
2 carrots, peeled and sliced
1 pound green beans, ends trimmed and cut into 2-inch pieces
2 tablespoons butter
1 teaspoon dried Italian herb blend
Salt and coarsely ground black pepper to taste
½ cup grated Parmigiano-Reggiano cheese

Heat the oil in the pressure cooker over medium-high heat and brown the sausage on all sides. Transfer to a plate. Place the cooking rack in the bottom of the pressure cooker and add ½ cup water. Spread the sausage and onion over the rack. Layer the potatoes, carrots, and green beans in a steamer tray and place it on top of the meat. Lock the lid in place. Bring to 15psi over high heat and immediately reduce the heat to the lowest possible setting to stabilize and maintain that pressure. Cook for 4 minutes. Remove from the heat and use the quick release method before opening the lid. Melt the butter and stir in the herb blend. Transfer the vegetables and sausages to a serving bowl. Pour the butter and herbs over the mixture, and add salt and pepper to taste, and toss gently to mix. Sprinkle the cheese on top and serve hot.

creole beef and rice

Reminiscent of Louisiana Creole cuisine, this recipe has a nice spicy flavor, but it's still tame enough for the timid. Very filling and pocketbook friendly, it's a simple meal to prepare, and if you use a food processor for most of the chopping, it's even faster. • **SERVES 5**

Step One: THE BEEF

1 to 1½ pounds boneless beef rump or chuck steak (any cut that is about 1 inch thick)
Salt and freshly ground black pepper to taste
2 tablespoons olive oil
1 medium onion, chopped
1 small moderately hot fresh chile, such as jalapeño, cayenne, or wax, seeded and minced, or to taste
4 cloves garlic, crushed
1 (15-ounce) can diced tomatoes with juice
1 cup dry red wine
1 teaspoon dried basil
1 tablespoon dried oregano
1 bay leaf

Season the beef with salt and pepper. Heat the oil in the pressure cooker over medium-high heat and brown the meat on all sides. Transfer to a plate. Add the onion to the pressure cooker and cook until soft. Add the chile, garlic, tomatoes with juice, wine, basil, oregano, and bay leaf, stirring to mix. Return the meat and any accumulated juices to the pressure cooker. Lock the lid in place. Bring to 15psi over high heat and immediately reduce the heat to the lowest possible setting to stabilize and maintain that pressure. Cook for 16 minutes. Remove from the heat and use the quick release method before opening the lid.

Step Two: THE RICE

1 cup long-grain white rice
1 (6-ounce) can tomato sauce
1 green bell pepper, seeded and chopped
2 carrots, peeled and diced
1 cup frozen corn kernels
½ cup packed chopped fresh cilantro
1 heaping tablespoon tomato paste
Tabasco or similar Louisiana-style hot sauce to taste (optional)

Add the rice and tomato sauce to the broth in the pressure cooker, stirring to blend. Add the bell pepper, carrots, corn, and cilantro on top with the tomato paste, but do not stir. Lock the lid in place. Bring to 15psi over high heat and immediately reduce the heat to the lowest possible setting to stabilize and maintain that pressure. Cook for 4 minutes. Remove from the heat and use the natural release method before opening the lid.

Remove the beef and slice against grain into ½-inch slices. Put the slices back into the pressure cooker and stir. Taste and adjust seasonings, adding hot sauce as desired. Remove the bay leaf. Spoon into a serving bowl.

beef tips and rice

This is a very easy meal with almost no prep work. The beef flavors the rice, and the colorful peas and carrots add a nice complexity. • **SERVES 5**

1½ to 2 pounds boneless beef chuck, flatiron, or shoulder steaks, less than ½ inch thick, trimmed of fat
Salt and freshly ground black pepper to taste
½ teaspoon garlic powder
2 tablespoons vegetable oil
1 small onion, chopped
1 cup dry wine
2 cloves garlic, minced
1 (14-ounce) can beef broth
1½ cups long-grain white rice
1 (10-ounce) package frozen peas and carrots

Season the meat with salt and pepper and the garlic powder. Heat the oil in the pressure cooker over medium-high heat and brown the meat on all sides. Cook the onion until translucent. Deglaze the pot with the wine, scraping up all those crusty brown bits from the bottom. Add the garlic, broth, and rice and stir to combine. Place the frozen peas and carrots on top, and do not stir. Lock the lid in place. Bring to 15psi over high heat and immediately reduce the heat to the lowest possible setting to stabilize and maintain that pressure. Cook for 4 minutes. Remove from the heat and use the natural release method before opening the lid. Transfer the beef to a serving plate. Fluff up the rice and vegetables and spoon them into a bowl.

zesty beef and rice casserole

Get your kids in the kitchen and teach them how to cook, and they'll thank you for it later; trust me on this. Even small children—boys and girls alike, please—can be given small tasks appropriate for their ages, from washing vegetables to measuring ingredients to learning how to read a recipe. Simple recipes with several different tasks like this one are good for training. The bigger kids can be started with peeling and then progress to chopping as they gain kitchen skills, and they'll be so proud of what they accomplish when the meal is served and they actually get to see—and eat—the fruits of their labor. Brings back great memories, my dears, and I hope you'll have the same. • **SERVES 4**

1 tablespoon olive oil
1 large onion, diced
2 cloves garlic, minced
1 tablespoon chili powder
1 pound lean ground beef
1 carrot, peeled and diced
1 green bell pepper, seeded and chopped
1 cup frozen corn kernels
2 (14-ounce) cans stewed tomatoes with juice
1 cup long-grain white rice
1 (14-ounce) can chicken broth
1 teaspoon salt, or to taste
½ teaspoon freshly ground black pepper
1½ cups shredded cheddar cheese

Heat the oil in the pressure cooker over medium-high heat and cook the onion until translucent. Stir in the garlic and chili powder and add the beef, cooking until brown and crumbly. Add the carrot, bell pepper, corn, tomatoes with juice, rice, broth, salt and black pepper, stirring well. Lock the lid in place. Bring to 15psi over high heat and immediately reduce the heat to the lowest possible setting to stabilize and maintain that pressure. Cook for 4 minutes. Remove from the heat and use the natural release method before opening the lid. Stir in the cheese and cover the pressure cooker with a regular lid for about 4 minutes while the cheese melts. Taste and adjust seasonings as needed. Spoon the mixture into a serving bowl.

hungarian goulash over mashed potatoes

Everyone has a favorite version of goulash; some recipes have tomatoes or green bell peppers, and most are served over noodles, but not this one. This recipe was passed along by my grandma, who got it from the "Austrian lady" who bought eggs at the farm every week. I've updated it slightly—no more lard and less wine—and I've learned that you can never use too much paprika in Hungarian goulash. Be sure to use real Hungarian paprika. Nothing else will make the rich, deliciously spicy sauce. • **SERVES 6**

Step One: THE BEEF

4 tablespoons olive oil
2 medium onions, chopped
1 teaspoon salt
½ teaspoon freshly ground black pepper
2 pounds boneless beef chuck, trimmed of fat
½ cup all-purpose flour
2 tablespoons sweet Hungarian paprika
2 bay leaves
⅔ cup dry red wine
4 medium russet potatoes, peeled and cubed
1 cup sour cream, for garnish

Heat 2 tablespoons of the oil in the pressure cooker over medium-high heat and cook the onions until they are tender and caramel colored, about 5 minutes, and then transfer to a plate. Rub the salt and pepper into the meat, and then cut it into 2-inch cubes. Put the flour in a quart-size sealable plastic bag and add a few pieces of beef at a time, shaking to coat. Reserve the remaining flour. Heat the remaining 2 tablespoons oil in the pressure cooker and sear the meat in small batches, browning all sides. Add the paprika and fry until fragrant. Add the bay leaves. Deglaze the cooker with the wine, scraping up all those crusty brown bits from the bottom. Return the onions to the pressure cooker. Lock the lid in place. Bring to 15psi over high heat and immediately reduce the heat to the lowest possible setting to stabilize and maintain that pressure. Cook for 18 minutes. Use the quick release method to open the lid and add the potatoes.

Step Two: THE MASHED POTATOES

- 2 pounds russet potatoes, peeled and cut into 2-inch cubes
- ½ cup (1 stick) butter, softened
- Salt and freshly ground black pepper to taste
- ⅓ cup half-and-half or milk, warmed, or as needed
- 1 pat butter, for garnish

Place the cooking rack in the bottom of the pressure cooker and add ½ cup water. Place the potatoes in an insert pan that will fit inside the pressure cooker. Place the pan of potatoes on top of the cooking rack. Lock the lid in place. Bring to 15psi over high heat and immediately reduce the heat to the lowest possible setting to stabilize and maintain that pressure. Cook for 5 minutes. Remove from the heat and use the quick release method before opening the lid. Drain the water from the pressure cooker and use your own preferred method to mash the potatoes. To use a stand mixer with the paddle attachment, transfer the potatoes to the prewarmed mixing bowl and just pulse the power to break up the potatoes. Add the softened butter and salt and pepper to the potatoes. Pulse again, taking care not to overwork the potatoes or they will become a glob of glue. Use only enough half-and-half to get the desired consistency and mix gently. Spoon the mashed potatoes into a serving bowl, and keep warm in the oven while making the sauce. Garnish with an additional pat of butter just before serving if desired.

Step Three: THE SAUCE

To thicken the broth, make a slurry using 2 tablespoons of the reserved flour mixed with ⅓ cup cold water. Use a slotted spoon to transfer the meat to a dish. Discard the bay leaves. Stir the slurry into the broth, simmering gently over medium heat until it's the desired consistency. Return the meat and any accumulated juices to the broth. Taste and adjust seasonings. To serve, spoon a mound of mashed potatoes on each individual plate, and ladle on a portion of the meat and sauce. Top with a dollop of sour cream.

shortcut recipes

shortcut chicken noodle soup

Nothing beats a bowl of good-tasting soup on a cold night, and this quick and easy winter warmer is great for a fast meal. Loaded with lots of familiar and comforting ingredients, this soup is flavorful and filling. Serve with some garlic bread sprinkled with grated Italian cheese as the perfect accompaniment. • **SERVES 4**

- 2 tablespoons olive oil
- 1 small onion, diced
- 6 to 8 cups chicken stock or broth
- 2 skinless, boneless chicken breasts or thighs, cut into 1-inch pieces
- 1 (16-ounce) package frozen mixed vegetables, such as carrots, corn, and green beans
- 8 ounces spaghetti, broken into 2- to 3-inch pieces
- 1 (4-ounce) can sliced mushrooms, drained
- 1 teaspoon dried thyme
- 1 teaspoon garlic powder
- 1 teaspoon salt
- ½ teaspoon coarsely ground black pepper

Heat the oil in the pressure cooker over medium-high heat. Add the onion, and cook, stirring, until softened, about 4 minutes. Add the stock, chicken, frozen vegetables, spaghetti, mushrooms, thyme, garlic powder, salt, and pepper and stir to mix. Lock the lid in place. Bring to 15psi over high heat and immediately reduce the heat to the lowest possible setting to stabilize and maintain that pressure. Cook for 4 minutes. Remove from the heat and use the quick release method before opening the lid. Taste the broth and adjust seasonings as needed. Ladle into soup bowls and serve immediately.

shortcut chicken and vegetable soup

Of course, every recipe assumes that you already have all the ingredients on hand, but who does? I started my "shortcut recipes" by thinking of commonplace foods that are routinely stocked as staple items in almost every kitchen. I also wanted these recipes to be easy to prepare for tired and hungry families, so they also need to be quick cooking. I envisioned someone coming home after a busy day, with no meat defrosted, and this fast, great-tasting shortcut soup was the deliciously easy solution. Serve with some crusty bread or saltine crackers, or include a sandwich for a heartier meal. • **SERVES 4**

2 tablespoons butter
½ cup diced onion
2 skinless, boneless chicken thighs
2 (15-ounce) cans chicken broth
2 (15-ounce cans) mixed vegetables, such as corn, carrots, and green beans, drained
1 teaspoon dried thyme
1 teaspoon chicken bouillon granules
Salt and coarsely ground black pepper to taste

Heat the butter in the pressure cooker over medium-high heat, add the onion, and cook, stirring, until softened and translucent, about 4 minutes. Add 1 cup water, the chicken, broth, vegetables, thyme, and bouillon, mixing well. Lock the lid in place. Bring to 15psi over high heat and immediately reduce the heat to the lowest possible setting to stabilize and maintain that pressure. Cook for 4 minutes. Remove from the heat and use the quick release method before opening the lid. Transfer the chicken to a cutting board and chop the meat into small pieces. Stir the meat back into the soup. Taste and adjust the seasonings as desired. Ladle the soup into big mugs and serve piping hot.

shortcut green chile and corn chowder

Make this hearty soup, a quick meal using common ingredients found in most cupboards, and you'll be eating dinner in less than half an hour. Serve with a simple green salad and biscuits, or add your favorite sandwich for bigger appetites. • **SERVES 4**

- 2 tablespoons butter
- 1 small onion, diced
- 2 large potatoes, peeled and diced
- 2 cups frozen or drained canned whole kernel corn
- 1 (4-ounce) can diced green chiles with juice
- 2 cups diced cooked ham
- 1 (15-ounce) can chicken broth or 1½ cups Sweet Corn Stock (page 67)
- 1 (15-ounce) can cream-style corn
- 1 cup milk or half-and-half
- 1 cup shredded Monterey Jack cheese
- Salt and freshly ground black pepper to taste
- 2 tablespoons instant potato flakes (optional)

Heat the butter in the pressure cooker over medium-high heat, add the onion, and cook, stirring, until softened and translucent, about 4 minutes. Add the potatoes, corn kernels, chiles with juice, ham, broth, and cream-style corn, in that order. Do not stir. Lock the lid in place. Bring to 15psi over high heat and immediately reduce the heat to the lowest possible setting to stabilize and maintain that pressure. Cook for 6 minutes. Remove from the heat and use the quick release method before opening the lid. Add the milk and cheese. Simmer over medium heat until the cheese has melted and the soup is heated through. Taste and add salt and pepper as needed. If desired, thicken the soup by stirring in the potato flakes.

shortcut tuna and rice casserole

Everyone makes a favorite version of this popular dish that's even a favorite of young children. This is an easy one-pot meal and very quick to prepare with very little prep work. The ingredients are usually found in most pantries, and it's budget friendly, too. Serve with a plate of sliced tomatoes. • **SERVES 4**

1 (15-ounce) can chicken broth
1 (10-ounce) can cream of mushroom soup
2 (6-ounce) cans water-packed tuna with juice, flaked
1½ cups long-grain white rice
1 cup frozen peas or your family's favorite frozen vegetable
1 tablespoon butter
1 tablespoon fresh lemon juice
1 teaspoon dried thyme
Salt and freshly ground black pepper to taste

Add the broth, soup, tuna with juice, rice, peas, butter, lemon juice, and thyme to the pressure cooker. Stir in 2⅔ cups water. Lock the lid in place. Bring to 15psi over high heat and immediately reduce the heat to the lowest possible setting to stabilize and maintain that pressure. Cook for 4 minutes. Remove from the heat and use the natural release method before opening the lid. Season with salt and pepper as needed, and transfer the mixture to a serving bowl. Fluff with a fork and serve.

shortcut tuna and noodles with green peas

I can remember my mom making this easy and delicious shortcut recipe when I was a child. Let me tell you about a nifty little pressure cooker trick that lets you cook the peas along with the rest of the ingredients and still retain that beautiful, bright green color. Normally we would cook peas in just 3 minutes and use the cold water release method to keep them fresh looking, but this recipe needs twice as long and uses the natural release method, which would normally turn our delicate peas into mush. What to do? If you've read my advice about using inserts in pressure cookery, then you know I recommend stainless steel, but here's the exception. In this recipe, we will use a heatproof glass or ceramic insert because these materials heat up slower and that delays the cooking. We will also cover the bowl with a sheet of foil to protect the peas from direct exposure to the superheated steam. Again, the whole purpose is to delay the cooking time for the peas so that it fits in with the cooking time for the other recipe ingredients. How cool is that? • **SERVES 4**

2 tablespoons olive oil
1 small onion, diced
2 (6-ounce) cans water-packed tuna with juices, flaked
1 (4-ounce) can sliced mushrooms, drained
1 teaspoon dried thyme
1 teaspoon salt
½ teaspoon freshly ground black pepper
1 (15-ounce) can chicken broth
3 cups wide noodles (made from durum semolina wheat)
1 (10-ounce) can cream of mushroom soup
2 cups frozen green peas

Heat the oil in the pressure cooker over medium-high heat. Add the onion, and cook, stirring, until softened, about 4 minutes. Add the tuna with juices, stirring to break up any chunks into smaller flakes. Add the mushrooms, thyme, salt, and pepper, and then stir in the chicken broth to blend. Add the noodles. Add additional water only if necessary to just barely cover the pasta. Spread the mushroom soup over the surface. Put the frozen peas in a ceramic or glass bowl and cover securely with a sheet of aluminum foil. Center the bowl on top of the other ingredients in the pressure cooker. Lock the lid in place. Bring to 15psi over high heat and immediately reduce the heat to the lowest possible setting to stabilize and maintain that pressure. Cook for 5 minutes. Remove from the heat and use the natural release method before opening the lid. Carefully lift out the insert dish of peas and remove the foil cover. Pour off any water that may have accumulated and then add the peas to the tuna mixture in the pressure cooker. Stir gently to blend the ingredients. Taste and adjust the seasoning as desired, then transfer to a serving bowl. Serve hot.

shortcut barbecued chicken

This is so simple and easy to make on those days when you come home and realize that you forget to thaw anything for dinner. Serve with a prepackaged green salad or coleslaw, and your favorite side dish if desired. • **SERVES 4**

2 pounds chicken thighs and drumsticks
Salt and freshly ground black pepper to taste
2 cups barbecue sauce of your choice

Season the chicken with salt and pepper. Place the cooking rack in the bottom of the pressure cooker and pour in ½ cup water. Add the chicken pieces. Lock the lid in place. Bring to 15psi over high heat and immediately reduce the heat to the lowest possible setting to stabilize and maintain that pressure. Cook for 5 minutes. Remove from the heat and use the natural release method before opening the lid.

Preheat the broiler. Pour the barbecue sauce into a measuring cup, dip each piece of chicken in the sauce, and then arrange them on a baking sheet. Place the chicken under the broiler, watching closely as the surface begins to bubble and caramelize. Turn the chicken, basting on more barbecue sauce until they are nicely browned. Transfer to a serving platter and pass the remaining barbecue sauce at the table.

shortcut italian chicken and shells in tomato-mozzarella sauce

This cheesy Italian-style shortcut entree can be assembled in just minutes using simple ingredients that are commonly found in every cupboard. This is a great one-pot meal that is family friendly and easy on the budget, too. Round out the meal with a fresh green salad and warm garlic bread.

• **SERVES 5**

1 (15-ounce) can Italian-style stewed or sliced tomatoes
1 (1-ounce) packet Italian spaghetti sauce mix
1 teaspoon dried Italian herb blend
3 cups shell macaroni
2 skinless, boneless chicken breasts or thighs
1 (15-ounce) can tomato sauce
2 cups shredded mozzarella or Italian cheese blend
Grated Parmesan cheese, for garnish (optional)

Add the tomatoes, spaghetti sauce mix, and herb blend to the pressure cooker. Add the pasta and stir in just enough water to barely cover the ingredients. Add the chicken pieces, pushing them below the liquid. Add the tomato sauce on top, and do not stir. Lock the lid in place. Bring to 15psi over high heat and immediately reduce the heat to the lowest possible setting to stabilize and maintain that pressure. Cook for 6 minutes. Remove from the heat and use the natural release method before opening the lid.

Transfer the chicken to a cutting board and chop into bite-size pieces. Return the chicken to the pressure cooker and add the mozzarella. Stir gently to blend. Cover with a regular lid until the cheese has melted. Spoon into a serving bowl and sprinkle Parmesan cheese on top, if desired.

shortcut creamy pesto chicken with bowtie pasta

I'm always getting requests for new recipes that not only cook fast and don't need a lot of prep work, but that also use ingredients that don't take a big bite out of the food budget. This easy shortcut recipe makes a great midweek, one-pot dinner that goes to the top of the list. Serve with a tossed salad and warm dinner rolls or hot biscuits for a complete meal. • **SERVES 4**

- 2 tablespoons butter
- 2 skinless, boneless chicken breasts, cubed
- 1 small onion, diced
- 1 (14-ounce) can chicken broth
- 1 (10-ounce) can cream of chicken soup
- 1 teaspoon garlic powder
- 3 cups bowtie pasta
- ½ cup grated Parmesan cheese
- 1 cup fresh or refrigerated prepared pesto sauce
- Salt and freshly ground black pepper to taste

Heat the butter in the pressure cooker over medium-high heat, add the chicken in batches, and sear the chicken cubes, browning them on all sides. Remove the chicken from the cooker. Add the onion and cook, stirring, until softened, about 4 minutes. Stir in the broth, soup, garlic powder, and all the chicken. Add the pasta, pushing it down under the liquid. If necessary, add only enough additional water to barely cover the pasta.

Lock the lid in place. Bring to 15psi over high heat and immediately reduce the heat to the lowest possible setting to stabilize and maintain that pressure. Cook for 6 minutes. Remove from the heat and use the natural release method before opening the lid. Sprinkle the cheese on top and dot the pesto sauce over the surface. Gently stir to blend and simmer over low heat until heated through. Taste and adjust seasoning with salt and pepper as desired, then transfer to a serving bowl. Serve hot.

shortcut five-can chicken chili

It's always in the middle of the week when those blustery, rainy days hit, drilling the cold deep into your bones, and you want a hot meal but there's no way you have time to cook. People sometimes have the notion that they should only use a pressure cooker for long-cooking recipes from scratch, so I came up with the idea of shortcut recipe solutions requiring little prep work that let you use prepackaged foods for convenience. Now you can quickly prepare that warming bowl of chili that you've been a-hankerin' for. • **SERVES 4 TO 6**

- 2 tablespoons olive oil
- 4 skinless, boneless chicken breast halves, cut into bite-size pieces
- 1 (14-ounce) can chicken broth
- 1 medium onion, chopped
- 1 green bell pepper, seeded and chopped
- 1 (1½-ounce) packet chili seasoning mix
- 1 (28-ounce) can great Northern or cannellini beans, rinsed and drained
- 1 (14-ounce) can whole kernel corn, drained
- 2 (14-ounce) cans diced tomatoes and green chiles with juice
- Freshly ground black pepper to taste
- 1½ cups shredded pepper Jack cheese

Heat the oil in the pressure cooker over medium-high heat, add the chicken, and cook until browned on all sides. Add the broth, onion, bell pepper, and chili seasoning mix, stirring to blend well. In the following order, add the beans, corn, and tomatoes; do not stir. Lock the lid in place. Bring to 15psi over high heat and immediately reduce the heat to the lowest possible setting to stabilize and maintain that pressure. Cook for 8 minutes. Remove from the heat and use the natural release method before opening the lid. Stir to mix. Taste and add black pepper as desired. Ladle the chili into bowls and top with the cheese before serving.

shortcut chicken and pasta in tomato sauce

This simple and easy one-pot meal looks and smells terrific. It only takes 5 minutes in the pressure cooker, so this is a great midweek meal. Add a salad and garlic bread, and you're all set.

• **SERVES 4 OR 5**

3 skinless, boneless chicken breast halves, cut into bite-size pieces
1 small onion, chopped
1 green bell pepper, seeded and chopped
2 tablespoons minced garlic
1 teaspoon crushed dried rosemary
1 (14-ounce) can chicken broth
3 cups shell macaroni
1 (28-ounce) jar prepared tomato pasta sauce of your choice
1½ cups shredded mozzarella cheese
Salt and freshly ground black pepper to taste

Add the chicken, onion, and bell pepper to the pressure cooker. Stir in the garlic, rosemary, and broth. Add the pasta, pushing it under the liquid. Add only enough water to barely cover the pasta. Add the pasta sauce on top, and do not stir. Lock the lid in place. Bring to 15psi over high heat and immediately reduce the heat to the lowest possible setting to stabilize and maintain that pressure. Cook for 5 minutes. Remove from the heat and use the natural release method before opening the lid. Carefully stir in the cheese. Cover with a regular lid and let the cheese melt. Taste and season with salt and black pepper as needed.

shortcut creamy pork chops and rice

Take advantage of what's in your pantry for a super-quick one-pot meal using prepackaged convenience products. My shortcut recipes are designed for the hectic days when there's no time for lengthy prep work, or fussing and stirring and waiting to eat. This simple, easy dinner includes pork chops and rice in a creamy mushroom sauce. Serve with a side of green beans or a green salad. • **SERVES 4**

1 tablespoon vegetable oil
1⅓ cups long-grain white rice
1 (15-ounce) can chicken broth
1 (1-ounce) envelope ranch salad dressing mix
1 (10-ounce) can cream of mushroom soup
4 pork chops, cut ½ inch thick
Paprika, for garnish
½ cup milk (optional)

Heat the oil in the pressure cooker over medium-high heat. Add the rice, and cook, stirring, until it looks translucent. Add the broth, salad dressing mix, and soup, stirring until will blended. Add the pork chops, pushing them below the liquid. Lock the lid in place. Bring to 15psi over high heat and immediately reduce the heat to the lowest possible setting to stabilize and maintain that pressure. Cook for 4 minutes. Remove from the heat and use the natural release method before opening the lid. Transfer the pork chops to individual plates and add a sprinkle of paprika. For a creamier rice, stir in the milk. Spoon the rice mixture onto each plate and serve.

shortcut beef and bean burritos

Talk about fast food! When your schedule is frenzied and your kids are acting like starving orphans, admit it—you want to head for the nearest drive-through, right? Well, take a deep breath, and try this quickie DIY meal that uses your own pantry ingredients and fresh veggies to deliver a homemade version of a fast-food favorite. Nothing fancy here, just kid-friendly burritos that are fun to eat and easy on your wallet. • **SERVES 6**

1 tablespoon vegetable oil
1 small onion, chopped
1 pound ground beef
½ cup prepared salsa
1 (1-ounce) packet taco seasoning
1 (15-ounce) can refried beans
6 burrito-size (10- or 12-inch) flour tortillas
1 cup sour cream
3 cups shredded iceberg lettuce
4 Roma tomatoes, chopped
2 cups shredded Monterey Jack cheese

Heat the oil in the pressure cooker over medium-high heat. Add the onion, and cook, stirring, until softened, 3 to 4 minutes. Add the beef and cook, stirring and breaking it up, until it is crumbled and no longer pink. Add the salsa and taco seasoning, and stir in ¼ cup water. Scoop the refried beans out of the can and place the whole lump on top of the other ingredients in the pressure cooker, but do not stir. Lock the lid in place.

Bring to 15psi over high heat and immediately reduce the heat to the lowest possible setting to stabilize and maintain that pressure. Cook for 4 minutes. Remove from the heat and use the natural release method before opening the lid.

Meanwhile, heat the tortillas in a microwave until soft and pliable, about 30 seconds each. To assemble, lay the tortillas on a flat surface. Spread 2 tablespoons of sour cream on each tortilla. Spoon ⅔ cup of the meat mixture lengthwise down the center of each tortilla, leaving about 3 inches on the bottom of the tortillas clear. Layer the desired amount of lettuce, tomatoes, and cheese on top of the meat mixture. Fold the bottom end of the tortilla up over the filling so it doesn't fall out. Wrap one side of the tortilla over the top of the filling, and then fold the remaining side over. Place the burritos seam side down on a serving plate.

COOK'S NOTE: Alternatively, lightly toast each tortilla on the stove directly over a medium gas flame, turning two or three times with tongs until puffed and pliable, about 45 seconds. Or heat the tortillas in a hot cast-iron skillet, turning them until they are soft and pliable.

---

shortcut beef pot roast with mushroom gravy

This is a super-easy shortcut recipe. It uses a very inexpensive but very tough cut of beef that would usually take hours to cook without a pressure cooker. The steam-roasting method quickly transforms even the toughest meat into a delicious, fork-tender main dish in less than a third of the time of ordinary cooking methods. This recipe is perfect for both beginning pressure cooker users and novice cooks because it takes practically no prep work, uses common ingredients, and even makes its own gravy. What's not to love? Serve with mashed potatoes or buttered noodles, or simply slice for sandwiches and freeze the excellent broth for another day. • **SERVES 6**

2 tablespoons vegetable oil
3 pounds beef chuck roast, about 3 inches thick, trimmed of fat
1 cup beef or chicken broth
1 (10-ounce) can cream of mushroom soup
1 (1½-ounce) packet onion or onion-mushroom soup mix

Heat the oil in the pressure cooker over medium-high heat, add the meat, and cook until browned on all sides. Transfer to a plate. Deglaze the pot with the broth, scraping up all those crusty brown bits from the bottom. Stir in the mushroom soup and the soup mix until blended. Return the meat to the pressure cooker along with any accumulated juices. Lock the lid in place. Bring to 15psi over high heat and immediately reduce the heat to the lowest possible setting to stabilize and maintain that pressure. Cook for 40 minutes. Remove from the heat and use the natural release method before opening the lid. Transfer the meat to a cutting board and slice thinly, cutting across the grain. Arrange the slices on a serving plate. Pour the gravy into a bowl and pass at the table.

shortcut italian beef and brown rice

Brown rice is not only very nutritious, but it's also easy to make, and it has much more flavor than white rice. Because of the outer bran coating—that's where all the good stuff is—more water and a longer cooking time are needed, but that's where a pressure cooker makes quick work of brown rice. This beefy shortcut recipe is a nice way of bringing brown rice to your dinner table. • **SERVES 4 TO 6**

2 tablespoons vegetable oil
2 pounds round steak, cut into 1-inch cubes
1 large onion, chopped
2 cups beef broth
2 cups long-grain brown rice
2 green bell peppers, seeded and chopped
2 tablespoons dried Italian herb blend
1 teaspoon salt
½ teaspoon coarsely ground black pepper
½ teaspoon garlic powder

Heat the oil in the pressure cooker over medium-high heat and sear the steak in small batches, browning all sides. Add the onion and cook, stirring, until softened and translucent, about 4 minutes. Add 2 cups water, then stir in the broth, rice, bell peppers, herb blend, salt, black pepper, and garlic powder. Lock the lid in place. Bring to 15psi over high heat and immediately reduce the heat to the lowest possible setting to stabilize and maintain that pressure. Cook for 12 minutes. Remove from the heat and use the natural release method before opening the lid. Stir with a fork to fluff up the rice and adjust the seasonings to taste. Spoon the mixture onto a serving platter and serve immediately.

shortcut taco casserole

This shortcut recipe has lots of cheesy beefy goodness in a one-pot taco-style casserole that uses ingredients that are probably already in your pantry. It's quick and easy to prepare, so it's a good choice for a hurry-up weeknight dinner. Pasta cooks in the pressure cooker by the absorption method, requiring only an amount of liquid that allows the pasta to become infused with the flavorful sauce. • **SERVES 4 OR 5**

1 pound lean ground beef
2½ cups shell macaroni
2½ cups chicken stock
1 (10-ounce) can diced tomatoes and green chiles
1 (6-ounce) can large pitted ripe olives, drained and sliced
1 large onion, chopped
1 (1-ounce) packet taco seasoning
1 (15-ounce) can tomato sauce
2 cups shredded pepper Jack cheese

Brown the beef in the pressure cooker over medium-high heat. Add the pasta, stock, tomatoes, olives, onion, and taco seasoning. Add water only if necessary to just barely cover the pasta. Stir to mix. Add the tomato sauce on top, and do not stir. Lock the lid in place. Bring to 15psi over high heat and immediately reduce the heat to the lowest possible setting to stabilize and maintain that pressure. Cook for 6 minutes. Remove from the heat and use the natural release method before opening the lid. Stir in the cheese and cover with a regular lid. Allow about 5 minutes for the cheese to melt and the sauce to thicken before transferring the mixture to a serving dish.

shortcut steak 'n' stein stew

Here's a super-fast, super-easy, one-pot stew recipe takes advantage of prepackaged, shortcut ingredients, so almost no prep work is needed. Add a loaf of warm, crusty bread, and you can serve a hearty and home-style family meal in minutes. • **SERVES 5 OR 6**

- 1 tablespoon vegetable oil
- 1 pound thin-cut boneless beef tri-tip steak, cut into 1½-inch cubes
- 1 (24-ounce) package frozen mixed stew vegetables, such as potatoes, carrots, and celery
- 1 (12-ounce) bottle dark beer
- 1 medium onion, coarsely chopped
- 2 tablespoons Worcestershire sauce
- 1 (10-ounce) can tomato soup
- 1 (1-ounce) packet beef gravy mix
- Salt and freshly ground black pepper to taste

Heat the oil in the pressure cooker, add the steak cubes, and cook until browned on all sides. Add the vegetables, beer, onion, and Worcestershire sauce and stir to combine. In a separate bowl, mix the soup and the gravy mix with 1½ cups water. Pour the soup mixture over the ingredients in the pressure cooker, but do not stir. Lock the lid in place. Bring to 15psi over high heat and immediately reduce the heat to the lowest possible setting to stabilize and maintain that pressure. Cook for 6 minutes. Remove from the heat and use the quick release method before opening the lid. Stir the contents gently and taste, adjusting seasonings with salt and pepper. Ladle into individual bowls and serve immediately.

penny pincher's tips

1. Cut up your own fresh potatoes, carrots, and celery in place of a prepackaged mix.
2. Substitute 1 cup leftover brewed coffee and ½ cup water, or 2 cups beef broth, for the beer.
3. Substitute 1 pound browned and crumbled ground beef for the steak.

shortcut beefed-up macaroni and cheese

This is a really good, kid-friendly recipe that is made to order for those days when your schedule goes crazy and you get home late with everyone nagging about what's for dinner. Here, make this recipe and enjoy a few extra minutes of peace . . . well, it's a nice thought, anyway. These simple pressure cooker pasta dishes used to be all the rage when I was growing up, but we sure didn't have all the modern-day convenience foods that fill our neighborhood supermarkets now. Of course, we didn't really have too many fast-food joints either, so the pressure cooker was our fast-food machine. • **SERVES 4 OR 5**

2 tablespoons olive oil
1 pound lean ground beef
1 green bell pepper, seeded and chopped
1 (14-ounce) can whole kernel corn, drained
1 (14-ounce) can beef broth
1 (1-ounce) packet dried onion soup mix
3 cups elbow or shell macaroni
1 (26-ounce) jar pasta sauce of your choice
½ cups shredded cheddar cheese
⅔ cup sour cream, for garnish (optional)

Heat the oil in the pressure cooker over medium-high heat and brown the ground beef until crumbly. Pour off any excess fat. Add the bell pepper, corn, broth, and the soup mix, stirring to mix. Add the pasta and just enough water to barely cover the ingredients, stirring well. Add the pasta sauce on top, and do not stir. Lock the lid in place. Bring to 15psi over high heat and immediately reduce the heat to the lowest possible setting to stabilize and maintain that pressure. Cook for 6 minutes. Remove from the heat and use the natural release method before opening the lid. Gently stir in the cheese to blend. Taste and adjust seasonings. Ladle into individual serving bowls and top with sour cream, if desired.

Variation:

SHORTCUT MACARONI AND CHEESE WITH SAUSAGE

Substitute 1 pound spicy Italian Sausage (removed from casings) for the ground beef. Cook as directed.

shortcut chili in five minutes

My "shortcut" recipes use convenient ingredients that almost everyone already has on hand. A big and hearty chili with just enough spice to make it interesting, this one-pot recipe doesn't need too much prep work, so it's super-fast and makes a super-easy family meal. • **SERVES 4 TO 6**

- 1 pound ground beef
- 2 (14-ounce) cans pinto, kidney, or black beans, rinsed and drained
- 1 large onion, chopped
- 1 green bell pepper, seeded and chopped
- 1 cup tomato juice
- 1 (1-ounce) packet chili or taco seasoning mix
- Salt and freshly ground black pepper to taste
- 1 (28-ounce) can crushed tomatoes
- 1 (14-ounce) can tomato puree
- Optional garnishes: sour cream, shredded cheddar cheese, crushed tortilla chips

Heat the pressure cooker over medium heat, add the beef, and cook, stirring and breaking it up, until lightly brown and crumbly. Add the beans, onion, bell pepper, tomato juice, seasoning mix, salt and black pepper, and crushed tomatoes, and stir to mix. Add the tomato puree last, and do not stir. Lock the lid in place. Bring to 15psi over high heat and immediately reduce the heat to the lowest possible setting to stabilize and maintain that pressure. Cook for 5 minutes. Remove from the heat and use the natural release method before opening the lid. Taste and adjust seasonings. Ladle into individual serving bowls and top with the garnishes of your choice.

BONUS RECIPE

quick chili goulash

- 2½ cups elbow or shell macaroni
- 1 (14-ounce) can whole kernel corn, drained
- 1 (14-ounce) can diced tomatoes with juice
- 1 teaspoon smoked paprika
- Sour cream, for garnish (optional)

Stir the macaroni, corn, tomatoes, and smoked paprika into the chili mixture, just before you add the tomato puree. Add just enough water to barely cover the ingredients. Stir well. Cook as directed. Serve topped with a dollop of sour cream if desired.

SERVES 8

---

penny pincher's tips

1. Pressure cook your favorite variety of dried beans in advance instead of using canned beans.
2. Use leftover chili as a topping for pressure-cooked "baked" potatoes, and top with grated cheese.

shortcut hearty beef stew

Ground beef and vegetables in a rich gravy make this convenient, shortcut recipe a great weekday meal. There's almost no prep work: Just pop everything in the pressure cooker, give it a few minutes, and dinner is done. Serve with warm dinner rolls and you've got a nice hot meal on the table with a minimum of fuss. • **SERVES 4**

1 tablespoon vegetable oil
1 pound lean ground beef
2 (14-ounce) cans beef broth
1 (14-ounce) can diced tomatoes with juice
1 teaspoon ground sage
1 teaspoon garlic powder
1 (16-ounce) package frozen mixed stew vegetables, such as potatoes, carrots, and celery
1 (1-ounce) packet beef gravy mix

Heat the oil in the pressure cooker over medium-high heat and brown the beef until crumbled and no longer pink. Pour off any excess fat. Add the broth, tomatoes with juice, sage, garlic powder, frozen vegetables, and gravy mix, stirring to blend. Lock the lid in place. Bring to 15psi over high heat and immediately reduce the heat to the lowest possible setting to stabilize and maintain that pressure. Cook for 6 minutes. Remove from the heat and use the natural release method before opening the lid. Taste and adjust seasoning. Ladle into bowls and serve.

fish, poultry, and meat

salmon steaks poached with lemons in wine sauce

Poached salmon requires little effort, and with just a few herbs and a splash of white wine, it's so quick and easy to make that it's perfect for a midweek dinner. For a change of pace, select any other type of firm-fleshed fish, like sole, flounder, turbot, or halibut, in place of the salmon.

• **SERVES 4**

2 tablespoons butter
Juice of 2 lemons
½ cup dry white wine
1 tablespoon soy sauce
1 teaspoon ground turmeric
4 salmon steaks, about 1 inch thick
1 large lemon, sliced and seeds removed
¼ cup finely chopped fresh cilantro
Freshly ground black pepper to taste

Heat the butter in the pressure cooker and add the lemon juice, wine, soy sauce, and turmeric, stirring to mix. Place the salmon in the sauce and turn once to coat both sides. Arrange the lemon slices on the fish, sprinkle the cilantro on top, and sprinkle with pepper. Lock the lid in place. Bring to 15psi over high heat and immediately reduce the heat to the lowest possible setting to stabilize and maintain that pressure. Cook for 4 minutes. Remove from the heat and use the quick release method before opening the lid. Transfer the salmon with the lemon slices on top to a plate and keep warm. Heat the remaining sauce in the pressure cooker over medium-high heat, uncovered. Cook, stirring occasionally, until the sauce is reduced and begins to thicken, about 8 minutes. Drizzle the sauce over the top of the fish before serving.

chicken meatballs with five-spice plum sauce

For a change of pace, switch from ground beef to ground chicken for these meatballs. I've kicked up the flavor with the spicy, Asian-inspired, easy-to-make Five-Spice Plum Sauce. These meatballs make a great gourmet snack with the sauce for dipping, or serve the meatballs on a bed of hot steamed rice with the sauce spooned over the top and a side of Asian-style vegetables for an impressive meal. To develop the maximum flavor in the sauce, prepare it several hours before serving, or even a day ahead. • **SERVES 4**

Step One: THE FIVE-SPICE PLUM SAUCE

1 cup plum preserves
½ teaspoon Chinese five-spice powder
2 tablespoons rice wine vinegar
2 cloves roasted garlic (see page 252)
1 tablespoon dark brown sugar
¼ cup minced onion
1 teaspoon minced fresh ginger
Tabasco sauce to taste

Combine all the ingredients in a saucepan. Bring to a boil over medium heat, stirring as the preserves melt to incorporate all the ingredients. Taste and adjust seasonings as preferred. Let cool, and then refrigerate for several hours or overnight until well chilled and the flavors are blended. Reheat the sauce just before serving.

Step Two: THE MEATBALLS

1 large egg, beaten
1 pound ground chicken
½ cup fine dry bread crumbs
⅓ cup finely chopped fresh cilantro
½ medium onion, minced
1½ teaspoons smoked paprika
½ teaspoon ground cumin
1 tablespoon teriyaki sauce
3 scallion tops, finely chopped, for garnish

Combine all the ingredients, except for the scallions, in a large bowl and mix thoroughly until the seasonings are well blended and evenly distributed throughout. Shape the meat mixture into 1-inch balls and arrange them in a perforated steamer tray that will fit inside your pressure cooker. Pour ½ cup water into the pressure cooker and add a cooking rack. Place the steamer tray in the pressure cooker. Lock the lid in place.

Bring to 15psi over high heat and immediately reduce the heat to the lowest possible setting to stabilize and maintain that pressure. Cook for 4 minutes. Remove from the heat and use the quick release method before opening the lid. Transfer the meatballs to a serving dish and sprinkle the scallions on top. Pass the sauce at the table.

Variation:

TURKEY MEATBALLS

Substitute 1 pound ground turkey meat for the chicken and cook as directed.

chicken quarters in mushroom-herb sauce

Thyme adds a wonderful aromatic quality to this simple chicken dish. Meaty chicken leg quarters are usually economically priced and often available in bulk packaging, and they make a very impressive-looking main dish for a quick but elegant weekday dinner. The pan sauce is made with white wine, roasted garlic, and lemons for a fresh citrus flavor. Serve this dish with rice or mashed potatoes and steamed vegetables. • **SERVES 4 GENEROUSLY**

- 3 tablespoons olive oil
- 4 chicken leg quarters
- Salt and freshly ground black pepper to taste
- 1 small onion, finely chopped
- 8 ounces fresh mushrooms of your choice, washed and sliced
- 1 head garlic, roasted (see page 252) and mashed to a smooth pulp
- 1 teaspoon dried thyme
- Zest and juice of 1 lemon
- ½ cup dry white wine
- ¾ cup sour cream or crème fraîche
- ¼ cup all-purpose flour

Heat the oil in the pressure cooker over medium-high heat and brown each chicken piece to a deep golden color on both sides. Add salt and pepper, the onion, mushrooms, garlic, thyme, lemon juice, and wine, stirring to mix. Arrange the chicken on top. Lock the lid in place. Bring to 15psi over high heat and immediately reduce the heat to the lowest possible setting to stabilize and maintain that pressure. Cook for 6 minutes. Remove from the heat and use the natural release method before opening the lid. Transfer the chicken to a serving plate. Skim off any excess fat from the surface of the broth. Simmer the mushrooms and broth over medium-low heat. Combine the sour cream and flour in a bowl, then slowly whisk in the sour cream and flour mixture into the mushroom mixture, stirring until the sauce is well blended and heated through, but do not boil or the mixture may curdle. Stir in the lemon zest and pour the mushrooms and sauce into a small serving bowl to be spooned over the chicken at the table.

honey-lemon chicken with asian vegetables

This convenient meal is a snap to make on those "too tired to cook" days. Take advantage of frozen chicken and vegetables for a quick no-stir "stir-fry." There's almost no prep work, and I kept the sauce nice and simple with just some honey and lemon and a prepared spice blend. This dish should appeal to any persnickety eaters in your family, but to kick up the flavor, just add the fresh ginger. Serve this dish as is, or spoon it over a mound of steaming hot, fluffy rice to soak up all the extra sauce. • **SERVES 4**

½ cup chicken broth
1 tablespoon soy sauce
Zest and juice of 1 lemon
1 teaspoon Chinese five-spice powder
1 pound frozen chicken tenders
1 tablespoon grated fresh ginger (optional)
1 (16-ounce) package frozen stir-fry vegetables
⅓ cup honey
⅓ cup chopped cashews or peanuts, for garnish

Add the broth, soy sauce, lemon juice, and five-spice powder to the pressure cooker, stirring to mix. Arrange the chicken pieces in the sauce mixture. Add the ginger and frozen vegetables, breaking up any clumps and spreading the vegetables on top of the chicken pieces, but do not stir. Lock the lid in place. Bring to 15psi over high heat and immediately reduce the heat to the lowest possible setting to stabilize and maintain that pressure. Cook for 3 minutes. Remove from the heat and use the quick release method before opening the lid. Transfer the vegetables and chicken pieces to two separate dishes. Heat the sauce in the pressure cooker over medium-high heat and let it cook, uncovered, until it is reduced by half. Add half the lemon zest and the sauce to the vegetables, tossing gently to coat. Add the honey to the pressure cooker and heat until bubbly, and then quickly add the chicken pieces, stirring to coat. Spoon the chicken pieces and any extra honey sauce into a serving bowl and sprinkle the remaining lemon zest on top. Garnish the chicken with the chopped cashews, if desired.

chicken cordon bleu with mornay sauce

I know, everyone is skeptical: Chicken cordon bleu in the pressure cooker . . . impossible! Well, I wanted to find a faster way to make these because—I mean, dang!—what's not to like about chicken breasts stuffed with ham and melted cheese? Exactly, my dears, and this is a gorgeously good nosh! Traditionally, you're supposed to use prosciutto and Gruyère cheese for this gourmet recipe, but that can be expensive. If your purse is fat, then go that route. But less costly alternatives are available, and that's in keeping with my goal of making sure that all my recipes use common ingredients that are easy to find in most supermarkets, while not sacrificing any flavor. In my very tasty American version of this classic French dish, we'll use deli-style ham and provolone to stuff the chicken, and add a creamy, cheese-based Mornay sauce. What a fancy way to impress your main squeeze or dazzle your guests! Oh, and if you bought that new meat mallet like I've suggested, you'll need it for this recipe. Serve this with Old-Fashioned Creamy Mashed Potatoes 101 (page 258) or Risotto with Asparagus (page 273) and Garlicky Green Beans and Summer Squash (page 254). • **SERVES 4**

Step One: THE CHICKEN ROLLS

4 large skinless, boneless chicken breasts
Salt and freshly ground black pepper
16 slices provolone cheese
8 thin slices deli ham

Lay a chicken breast between 2 pieces of plastic wrap. Using the flat side of the meat mallet, gently pound each breast to an even ¼-inch thickness. Take care not to pound too hard or the meat may get too thin and tear. Season both sides of the meat with salt and pepper. With the smooth side down, position 2 slices of cheese on each breast, followed by 2 slices of ham, and 2 more of cheese; leaving a ¼-inch margin around the edges to help seal the roll. Tightly roll each breast lengthwise like a jellyroll, tucking in the ends to close each roll and securing the seams with however many toothpicks you need. Place the cooking rack in the bottom of the pressure cooker and add ½ cup water. Arrange the rolled chicken breasts in a lightly greased insert pan the will fit within the pressure cooker. Lock the lid in place. Bring to 15psi over high heat and immediately reduce the heat to the lowest possible setting to stabilize and maintain that pressure. Cook for 4 minutes. Remove from the heat and use the natural release method before opening the lid.

Step Two: THE CRISPINESS

¼ cup all-purpose flour
2 large eggs beaten with 2 teaspoons water
1 cup panko bread crumbs
⅓ cup vegetable oil

Meanwhile, set up your breading station by arranging the flour, egg mixture, and bread crumbs in three separate shallow bowls. Transfer the chicken rolls to a cutting board and pull out all the toothpicks. Start by dipping a roll in the flour for a light coating, and then brush on the egg wash. Press the chicken roll into the bread crumbs, making sure the entire surface is coated with an even layer. Repeat for all four breasts. Heat the oil in a medium heavy cast-iron skillet over medium-high heat; it should be very hot before adding the chicken. Quickly brown each chicken roll until the coating is crisp and golden. Transfer the rolls to paper towels, and then arrange them on a platter in a warm oven while preparing the sauce.

Step Three: THE MORNAY SAUCE

2 tablespoons butter
2 tablespoons all-purpose flour
2 cups milk
¼ cup shredded Swiss cheese
¼ cup grated Parmesan cheese
Salt and freshly ground black pepper to taste
Pinch of ground nutmeg

Melt the butter in a small saucepan over medium heat, and stir in the flour until smooth. Continue cooking for about 2 minutes, stirring often. Very slowly pour the milk into the flour mixture, whisking constantly to prevent lumps. Continue stirring as the sauce thickens. Remove from the heat and add the cheeses, stirring until they have melted and the sauce is smooth. Add salt and pepper to taste and a pinch of nutmeg. To serve, arrange the chicken on serving plates and spoon some of the Mornay sauce across the center of each. Pass the remaining sauce at the table.

chicken mole

A classic mole can take several hours to make, but a respectable version of this popular Mexican sauce can be made from my Red Mole Sauce (page 294). If you don't have time to make the mole sauce, you can take some easy shortcuts and still bring dinner to table quickly for a weekday meal. Prepared mole sauce is available in the ethnic foods aisle with other Mexican foods in most well-stocked supermarkets. I'll show you how to make this chicken dish with both versions. Serve with Cilantro and Lime Rice (page 277). • **SERVES 4 TO 6**

Version One

- 6 pieces chicken, such as breasts, legs, or thighs
- Salt and coarsely ground black pepper to taste
- 2 tablespoons vegetable oil
- ½ cup chicken broth
- 1½ cups Red Mole Sauce (page 294)
- 1 tablespoon toasted sesame seeds, for garnish

Wash the chicken pieces and pat dry. Season the chicken with salt and pepper. Heat the oil in the pressure cooker over medium-high heat and brown the meat on both sides. Deglaze the pot with the broth, scraping up all those crusty brown bits from the bottom. Lock the lid in place. Bring to 15psi over high heat and immediately reduce the heat to the lowest possible setting to stabilize and maintain that pressure. Cook for 6 minutes. Remove from the heat and use the natural release method before opening the lid. Transfer the chicken to a plate. Stir the mole sauce into the broth in the pressure cooker and simmer over medium heat until reduced be half. Taste and adjust seasonings as desired. Return the chicken pieces to the pressure cooker and turn several times until the pieces are well coated and heated through. Arrange the chicken on serving plates and sprinkle the sesame seeds over the top. Pour the mole sauce into a separate bowl to be passed at the table.

Version Two

- 6 pieces chicken, such as breasts, legs, or thighs
- Salt and coarsely ground black pepper to taste
- 2 tablespoons vegetable oil
- 2 cups chicken broth
- ½ of 1 (8-ounce) jar prepared mole sauce
- 1 teaspoon sugar (optional)
- 1 tablespoon toasted sesame seeds, for garnish

Wash the chicken pieces and pat dry. Season the chicken with salt and pepper. Heat the oil in the pressure cooker over medium-high heat and brown the meat on both sides. Deglaze the pot with the broth, scraping up all those crusty brown bits from the bottom. Lock the lid in place. Bring to 15psi over high heat and immediately reduce the heat to the lowest possible setting to stabilize and maintain that pressure. Cook for 6 minutes. Remove from the heat and use the natural release method before opening the lid. Transfer the chicken to a plate. Stir the mole sauce into the broth in the pressure cooker and simmer over medium heat. Whisk constantly until the mole is thoroughly blended into a smooth sauce. Taste and add the sugar, if desired. Return the chicken pieces to the pressure cooker and turn several times until the pieces are well coated and heated through. Arrange the chicken on serving plates and sprinkle the sesame seeds over the top. Pour the mole sauce into a separate bowl to be passed at the table.

honey-mustard chicken

To the raucous acclaim of hungry kids, we had our "chicken wings" nights with chicken drumettes and legs, and we served them with a variety of dipping sauces that came from whatever ingredients were at hand. Quick and easy to prepare, this is a fun midweek meal with maybe a green salad. On the weekend when you might have more time, serve this with coleslaw and/or potato salad. Whatever sides you choose, everyone will love this sweet and spicy chicken. • **SERVES 4**

Step One: COOK THE CHICKEN

2 pounds mixed chicken wings and legs

Place the cooking rack in the bottom of the pressure cooker and add ½ cup water. If using whole wings, cut off the tip at the last joint and freeze the pieces for later use in making chicken stock (see page 63). You can use the wings as is, or cut through the joint to separate them into two parts for easier—less messy—eating. Arrange the chicken pieces in loose layers so the steam can move freely. If using frozen chicken, make sure the wings are separated and not in a big frozen lump. Lock the lid in place. Bring to 15psi over high heat and immediately reduce the heat to the lowest possible setting to stabilize and maintain that pressure. Cook for 4 minutes. Remove from the heat and use the natural release method before opening the lid. Transfer the chicken to a plate. Pour off the water and wipe the pressure cooker dry.

Step Two: THE HONEY-MUSTARD GLAZE

1 tablespoon butter
1½ cups honey
1 tablespoon white wine vinegar
⅓ cup spicy mustard
2 teaspoons chili powder
½ teaspoon garlic powder
Pinch of cayenne pepper, or more to taste
Salt and freshly ground black pepper to taste
¼ cup finely sliced scallion tops, for garnish
2 cups ranch-style dressing or dipping sauce of your choice

Melt the butter in the pressure cooker over medium heat and stir in the honey, vinegar, mustard, chili powder, garlic powder, and cayenne pepper. Cook and continue stirring as the glaze thickens and clings to the spoon. Taste and adjust seasoning, adding salt and black pepper as needed. Add a few pieces of chicken at a time to the glaze. Use long-handled tongs to turn them several times to coat them with glaze. Arrange them on a serving plate. Repeat until all the chicken wings are covered with the glaze. Drizzle any remaining glaze over the chicken and then sprinkle the scallions on top. Serve everyone at the table a small, individual bowl of the dressing for their chicken.

Left: *Chocolate Cheesecake with Tart Cherry Topping* (see page 329)

Below: *Chunky Pinto Bean Dip* (see page 39)

Opposite: *Creole Beef and Rice* (see page 148)

Above: *Cranberry-Apple Pork Roast* (see page 193)

Above: *Fresh Tomato Soup with Grilled Cheese Croutons* (see page 72)

Opposite: *Hungarian Chicken Paprikash with Rice* (see page 139)

Opposite: *Navy Bean Soup with Butternut Squash and Chard* (see page 87)

Above: *Hungarian Goulash Over Mashed Potatoes* (see page 152)

Pulled Pork Sandwiches with Chipotle-Pomegranate Barbecue Sauce (see page 206)

spiced chicken curry

This is a simple, basic curry that won't shock those with sensitive palates. It's an easy dish to prepare and will fit nicely into most weekday menu plans. Most of the prep work is just measuring, and that offers a good opportunity to get even young children involved in a little hands-on kitchen learning. I like to serve this curry with basmati rice, and if you have two pressure cookers, this is the perfect time to use both. • **SERVES 6**

2 to 3 tablespoons vegetable oil
3 pounds assorted chicken pieces, such as legs, thighs, quarters, and/or breasts
2 medium onions, diced
8 cloves garlic, minced
1 teaspoon ground turmeric
1 tablespoon hot paprika
1 tablespoon curry powder
½ teaspoon ground ginger
½ teaspoon ground cinnamon
½ cup chicken broth
2 tablespoons fresh lemon juice
10 sprigs fresh cilantro, minced
3 Roma tomatoes, seeded and finely chopped
1 teaspoon salt, or to taste
½ teaspoon freshly ground black pepper
1 tablespoon cornstarch (optional)
½ cup plain yogurt
Fresh cilantro leaves, for garnish

Heat the oil in the pressure cooker over medium-high heat and brown the chicken a few pieces at a time. Set aside on a plate. Add the onions and cook to a golden brown color, adding the occasional teaspoonful of water as needed. Add the garlic, turmeric, paprika, curry powder, ginger, cinnamon, and continue to cook and stir until the spices are aromatic, taking care not to let them burn. Deglaze the cooker with the broth, scraping up all those crusty brown bits from the bottom. Stir in the lemon juice, minced cilantro, tomatoes, salt, and pepper, and then return the chicken to the pressure cooker. Lock the lid in place. Bring to 15psi over high heat and immediately reduce the heat to the lowest possible setting to stabilize and maintain that pressure. Cook for 8 minutes. Remove from the heat and use the natural release method before opening the lid. Transfer the chicken pieces to a serving platter and keep warm. Skim off any excess fat from the surface of the sauce.

If you prefer a thicker sauce, make a slurry using the cornstarch mixed in ¼ cup cold water and stir the mixture into the broth. Simmer gently over medium heat until the sauce starts to thicken. Slowly add the yogurt to the simmering sauce, and continue stirring until the sauce thickens to the desired consistency. Taste the sauce and adjust seasoning as desired. Garnish the chicken with the cilantro leaves and pass the curry sauce at the table to be spooned over the chicken.

stuffed chicken breasts with basil rice and tomato-alfredo sauce

This is a complete meal, with the meat and rice cooking in the pressure cooker while you cook the Alfredo sauce separately. The finished dish is one of those meals that looks like you spent hours in the kitchen. I've laid out these really detailed directions so it is very simple, but it looks so elegant that you'll want to serve it often. We begin with chicken breasts that are pounded thin . . . no excuse now, I've been telling you right along how useful a meat mallet is as a "stress-management" tool. Put the babies in a quiet room, send the dog outside, and turn up the TV while you get to whacking.

• **SERVES 4**

Step One: THE CHICKEN

4 skinless, boneless chicken breasts
Salt and coarsely ground black pepper
4 ounces provolone or mozzarella cheese, cut lengthwise into ½-inch logs
1 (7-ounce) jar roasted sweet red peppers, drained and cut lengthwise into ½-inch strips
½ cup fresh basil leaves, cut into thin strips
2 tablespoons Hungarian paprika
1 teaspoon dried thyme
4 teaspoons olive oil

Lay a chicken breast between two pieces of plastic wrap. Using the flat side of the meat mallet, gently pound each breast to an even ¼-inch thickness. Take care not to pound too hard or the meat may get too thin and tear. Season both sides of the meat with salt and black pepper. With the smooth side down, position a log of cheese lengthwise down the center of each breast. Place a strip of red pepper on each side of the cheese. Top each breast with one-quarter of the cut basil leaves and sprinkle with the paprika and thyme. Leave about a ¼-inch clear margin around the edges to help seal the roll so the melting cheese doesn't leak out. Tightly roll each breast lengthwise like a jelly-roll, tucking in the ends to close each roll, securing the seams with however many toothpicks you need. Brush 1 teaspoon oil over each of four squares of aluminum foil. Place one of the chicken rolls in the middle of each of the foil squares, and fold over the edges and ends tightly. Place the cooking rack in the bottom of the pressure cooker and add ½ cup water. Arrange two packets on the bottom layer, leaving space in between each for the steam to move freely for even cooking. Arrange the remaining two packets at right angles in a second layer, again leaving lots of space in between.

Step Two: THE RICE

1 cup white basmati rice, rinsed until the water runs clear
2 tablespoons butter
1 teaspoon chicken bouillon granules
½ cup fresh basil leaves, cut into thin strips

Select a 1½-quart stainless steel insert pan that will stack on top of the chicken rolls, and add the rice, 2 cups water, the butter, bouillon, and basil. Place the insert pan with the rice mixture on top of the chicken in the pressure cooker. Lock the lid in place. Bring to 15psi over high heat and immediately reduce the heat to the lowest possible setting to stabilize and maintain that pressure. Cook for 6 minutes. Remove from the heat and use the natural release method before opening the lid.

Step Three: THE SAUCE

1 (10-ounce) container refrigerated prepared Alfredo sauce
2 cups halved cherry tomatoes
½ cup fresh basil leaves, cut into thin strips
½ teaspoon freshly ground black pepper

Prepare the sauce while the chicken and rice cook. In a small saucepan, heat the Alfredo sauce, tomatoes, basil, and pepper over medium heat until hot and bubbly. Pour the sauce into a serving bowl. Lift the rice out of the pressure cooker, transfer to a separate serving bowl, and fluff with a fork. Using tongs, place the chicken packets on a cutting board and open them carefully. Cut each roll into 1-inch slices and arrange them on a serving plate.

stuffed turkey pinwheels with tomato-avocado salsa

Turkey is a great addition to your meal planning, and with a wide variety of cuts available, it's a versatile choice for many recipes. When I spotted turkey breast cutlets at my supermarket, I knew they would be perfect for pinwheels. I serve this dish with either white rice or mashed potatoes. If your pressure cooker is tall enough, you can use the tiered cooking method to cook the side dish at the same time. • **SERVES 4**

Step One: THE SALSA

For best results, make this salsa a couple of hours in advance to allow time for the flavors to marry. Keep refrigerated and serve cold.

1 (5-ounce) container prepared pesto sauce
1 tablespoon olive oil
1 tablespoon fresh lemon juice
1 large bunch basil, torn
2 scallions, minced
1 large avocado, pitted, peeled, and diced
3 Roma tomatoes, diced
Salt and freshly ground black pepper to taste

Reserve about ⅓ cup of the pesto sauce for the turkey pinwheels. Put the remaining pesto sauce in a glass or other nonreactive bowl and mix in the oil, lemon juice, basil, and scallions. Add the avocado and tomatoes, stirring gently until combined. Taste, adding salt and pepper as needed.

Step Two: THE TURKEY PINWHEELS

4 thin turkey breast cutlets
⅓ cup pesto sauce
4 slices prosciutto
½ cup thinly sliced fresh basil
4 slices Jarlsberg cheese
1 tablespoon paprika

Lay the turkey cutlets flat. Spread a thin layer of the pesto sauce on each cutlet. Divide the prosciutto and arrange the pieces on top of the turkey, then add the basil, and place the cheese on top. Starting from one of the short ends, roll up each of the cutlets. Use a sharp knife to cut each of the turkey rolls into 2-inch sections. Use kitchen string (it's easier) or toothpicks to secure each section to keep the pinwheels from unfurling as they cook. Lightly dust the sides of each pinwheel with the paprika. Pour ½ cup water in the pressure cooker and place the cooking rack in the bottom. Spray a perforated steaming basket with nonstick cooking spray and arrange the pinwheels cut side down in the basket. Don't crowd; if necessary, arrange a second layer, offsetting the pinwheels on top of the first layer. Lock the lid in place. Bring to 15psi over high heat and immediately reduce the heat to the lowest possible setting to stabilize and maintain that pressure. Cook for 4 minutes. Remove from the heat and use the natural release method before opening the lid. When done, snip the strings if necessary and remove before serving. Serve the hot turkey pinwheels with the chilled salsa on the side.

spice-rubbed turkey breast

When it comes to a quick meal, a turkey breast may be the most overlooked meat there is. A turkey breast is a great option for people who don't like dark meat, or for small families, couples, and singles who don't want something as large as a whole turkey. A pressure cooker makes it easy to serve up a delicious turkey breast any time you like, whether as the star attraction at a holiday feast or the main dish at your weekend dinner with rustic smashed potatoes and pan gravy. This recipe is very easy, and even beginner cooks and novice pressure cooker users will be able to cook a fabulous meal using the steam roasting technique. It is suitable for presentation at the table, where it will impress your family and whet their appetites as it's carved. If that isn't your style, it's just as quick and convenient to slice and serve in sandwiches alongside a mug of soup. Plan on using the leftovers in other recipes for salads, stews, or your favorite casserole. The leftover meat will freeze well, and don't forget the bones for making a rich stock. • **SERVES 10 TO 12**

Step One: THE SEASONED SPICE BLEND

½ teaspoon garlic powder
1½ teaspoons ground coriander
½ teaspoon ground cumin
½ teaspoon ground ginger
1½ teaspoons ground turmeric
1 tablespoon paprika
1½ teaspoons ground sage
1 teaspoon salt
½ teaspoon freshly ground black pepper

Mix all the ingredients in a spice shaker or a small plastic storage container with a tight-fitting lid. Use this spice blend to add much-needed color and flavor to poultry when they are pressure cooked without browning. The mix will keep for several months when stored in a cool, dark place.

Step Two: THE TURKEY ROAST

One 6- to 7-pound bone-in turkey breast
½ bunch fresh Italian parsley
6 fresh sage leaves
2 lemons, cut into wedges
1 celery heart with leaves, halved
2 onions, quartered
2 carrots, peeled, halved lengthwise, and quartered

Rinse the turkey breast inside and out and pat dry. Trim off any excess fat and skin. Sprinkle the spice blend on the meat surface, inside and out, spreading it around evenly with your fingers. Turn the turkey breast upside down and fill the open cavity with the parsley, sage, lemons, celery, onions, and carrots. Place the cooking rack in the bottom of the pressure cooker and add 1 cup water. Lay out two foil helper handles at right angles and center the turkey breast, folding up the ends to form a sling. Lift the turkey breast and place it in the pressure cooker. Lock the lid in place. Bring to 15psi over high heat and immediately reduce the heat to the lowest possible setting to stabilize and maintain that pressure. Cook for 22 minutes. Remove from the heat and use the natural release method before opening the lid.

Transfer the turkey breast to a roasting pan to collect the juices and tent with foil for about 10 minutes before carving. Discard the vegetables and return any accumulated juices to the pressure cooker. Use the broth to make gravy if desired, or use for making stock within the next 2 days. Alternatively, freeze and save for later.

Step Three: THE PAN GRAVY

2 tablespoons cornstarch
Salt and freshly ground black pepper to taste

Skim off any excess fat from the surface of the broth. Heat the broth to a simmer over medium heat. To thicken the broth, make a slurry using the cornstarch blended with ½ cup water. Stir the slurry into the broth, and use a wire whisk to blend as it thickens to the desired consistency. Taste and season with salt and pepper. Serve the gravy alongside the sliced turkey.

COOK'S NOTE: Frugal cooks will look for whole turkey breasts when they are on sale, and save the scraps and the carcass to freeze for making stock.

COOK'S NOTE: When cooking large pieces of poultry, don't rely on the color as a sign of doneness. After the pressure cooker has fully depressurized, use a food thermometer to accurately check that the meat has reached a safe temperature; for turkey the USDA recommends 165°F (74°C). If it isn't quite done, simply return to pressure for an additional 5 minutes, using the natural release to depressurize. Be careful not to overcook meats when using the pressure cooker. A few unnecessary minutes of extra cooking time will make the meat tough and dry.

---

barbecued boneless country-style pork ribs

Country-style "ribs" aren't really ribs; they're cuts of meat from the pork shoulder. The high fat content of these beauties keeps the meat moist and tender and adds a lot of great flavor. Without a bone, they can be quite a messy wrestling match to eat with just the fingers, but if you don't mind using a knife and fork, they're real good eatin', and you sure can't beat the price! Ribs that are cooked on the grill often get really dried out and tough, but by using the pressure cooker to partially cook and tenderize the meat first, the result is tender, moist ribs that have all the smoky flavor of the grill. Using the steam-roasting method, much of the fat will drain away in the pressure cooker so that these boneless ribs are ready for the grill or broiler in just minutes.

• **SERVES 6**

3 pounds country-style pork ribs
Salt and coarsely ground black pepper to taste
3 tablespoons vegetable oil
2 cups barbecue sauce of your choice

Trim the ribs of any excess fat. Rub salt and pepper into the meat. Heat the oil in the pressure cooker, brown the ribs on all sides, and set aside. Place the cooking rack in the pressure cooker and pour in 1 cup water. Place the ribs in a steaming basket to elevate and hold them well above the waterline. Lock the lid in place. Bring to 15psi over high heat and immediately reduce the heat to the lowest possible setting to stabilize and maintain that pressure. Cook for 12 minutes. Remove from the heat and use the quick release method before opening the lid.

Meanwhile, preheat a grill or the broiler. Pour the barbecue sauce into a shallow dish and add the ribs, turning the meat to coat all sides. Place the ribs on the hot grill, or alternatively put them on a pan under the broiler, basting and turning as needed until the sauce begins to caramelize, about 8 minutes.

cranberry-apple pork roast

When fresh cranberries appear in the produce section, grab a couple of extra packages and stash them in the freezer to use in recipes like this one all year long. Serve this pork with a substantial side dish like cooked noodles, Old-Fashioned Creamy Mashed Potatoes 101 (page 258), or Soft and Creamy Polenta (page 278), any of which will accommodate the flavorful sauce.

• **SERVES 4 TO 6**

Salt and freshly ground black pepper to taste
1 teaspoon garlic powder
3 to 4 pounds boneless pork roast
2 tablespoons olive oil
½ cup dry white wine
¼ cup apple cider vinegar
½ cup apple juice
1 cup fresh or frozen whole cranberries
2 Granny Smith or other tart apples, cored, peeled, and coarsely chopped

Rub salt and pepper and the garlic powder into the surface of the roast. Heat the oil in the pressure cooker over medium-high heat and brown the roast on all sides; set aside on a plate. Deglaze the pot with the wine, scraping up all those crusty brown bits from the bottom. Add the vinegar, juice, cranberries, and apples, stirring to mix. Place the pork in the pressure cooker. Lock the lid in place. Bring to 15psi over high heat and immediately reduce the heat to the lowest possible setting to stabilize and maintain that pressure. Cook for 22 minutes. Remove from the heat and use the natural release method before opening the lid. Transfer the pork roast to a carving board and slice the meat, then arrange it on a serving plate. Pour the sauce into a bowl to be passed at the table.

COOK'S NOTE: To thicken the sauce, mix 2 tablespoons cornstarch with ⅓ cup cold water. Add the slurry to the sauce in the pressure cooker and simmer over medium heat, stirring often as it thickens, but do not boil.

---

pork chops in meaty tomato sauce

Not only is this family-friendly recipe simple and easy, but it's also quick to fix and even faster to cook. Serve the chops and sauce over pasta (start cooking the pasta first that so it's ready at the same time as the sauce), or try it over Soft and Creamy Polenta (page 278). Add a mixed green salad and some garlic bread, and dinner is complete. • **SERVES 5**

- 2 tablespoons olive oil
- 5 bone-in pork chops, about ½ inch thick
- 8 ounces bulk Italian sausage or links with casings removed
- 1 cup dry red wine
- 1 small onion, chopped
- 1 small green bell pepper, seeded and chopped
- 3 cloves garlic, minced
- 1 teaspoon dried oregano
- 1 teaspoon dried basil
- 2 bay leaves
- ½ teaspoon red pepper flakes
- Salt and coarsely ground black pepper to taste
- 1 (14-ounce) can diced tomatoes with juice
- 1 (15-ounce) can tomato sauce
- 1 (6-ounce) can tomato paste
- 1 teaspoon sugar (optional)
- ½ cup grated Parmigiano-Reggiano cheese, for garnish

Heat the oil in the pressure cooker over medium-high heat and brown the chops on all sides; set aside on a plate. Add the sausage, breaking it up with a spatula until it is crumbly. Drain off any excess fat. Add the wine and deglaze, scraping up all those crusty brown bits from the bottom. Add the onion, bell pepper, and garlic, then the oregano, basil, bay leaves, red pepper flakes, and salt and black pepper. Stir in the tomatoes with juice. Return the pork chops and any accumulated meat juices to the pressure cooker. In a small bowl, mix the tomato sauce and the tomato paste until smoothly blended. Pour the tomato mixture on top of the chops, and do not stir. Lock the lid in place. Bring to 15psi over high heat and immediately reduce the heat to the lowest possible setting to stabilize and maintain that pressure. Cook for 6 minutes. Remove from the heat and use the natural release method before opening the lid. Lift out the pork chops and discard the bay leaves. Stir the sauce until the mixture is well blended. Taste and adjust seasonings, adding the sugar if needed. Garnish each serving with some grated cheese.

pork chops with baby potatoes and pearl onions

The little pearl onions have a sweet, pungent flavor that gives simple pork chops a burst of flavor that's sure to be enjoyed by the entire family. This recipe can easily be doubled if you need to feed bigger appetites. • **SERVES 4**

4 bone-in pork chops
1 teaspoon garlic pepper
1 tablespoon olive oil
½ cup chicken broth
8 to 10 baby potatoes, about 1½ inches in diameter, scrubbed
8 ounces pearl onions or small boiling onions, less than 1½ inches in diameter, peeled

Season both sides of the pork chops generously with garlic pepper, pressing the seasoning into the meat with your fingers. Heat the oil in the pressure cooker over medium-high heat and brown the chops on both sides. Deglaze the pot with the broth, scraping up all those crusty brown bits from the bottom. Add the potatoes next, then the onions and any remaining garlic pepper seasoning. Lock the lid in place. Bring to 15psi over high heat and immediately reduce the heat to the lowest possible setting to stabilize and maintain that pressure. Cook for 4 minutes. Remove from the heat and use the natural release method before opening the lid. Arrange the chops, potatoes, and onions on a serving platter. If desired, pass the remaining pan juices at the table.

pork tenderloin with creamy shallot-tarragon sauce and mashed sweet potatoes

Pork is remarkable for its universal appeal, and the pork tenderloin has become a trendy cut because it's a very versatile piece of meat that can be roasted, braised, or grilled. It is always delicious no matter how it is cooked, whether plain or cozied up with flavor-boosting spices, herbs, fruits, or vegetables to create tasty combinations. Shallots have a very distinct sweet flavor with an underlying taste of garlic, making them a great partner for pork. With the added bonus dish of creamy mashed sweet potatoes, this one-pot meal makes a great-tasting no-fuss meal.

• **SERVES 6**

Step One: THE PORK TENDERLOIN AND SWEET POTATOES

½ teaspoon salt
1 teaspoon coarsely ground black pepper
1 teaspoon garlic powder
½ teaspoon ground sage
2 pounds pork tenderloin
2 tablespoons vegetable oil
⅔ cup dry white wine
3 or 4 medium red-skinned sweet potatoes (about 2 pounds), scrubbed

Combine the salt, pepper, garlic powder, and sage. Season the pork with the mixture, pressing the spices into the meat with your fingers. Reserve any remaining spices. Heat the oil in the pressure cooker over medium-high heat and brown the pork on all sides. Set aside on a plate and deglaze the pot with the wine, scraping up all those crusty brown bits from the bottom. Return the pork and any accumulated juices to the pressure cooker and add any remaining spices. Arrange the sweet potatoes around the pork. Lock the lid in place. Bring to 15psi over high heat and immediately reduce the heat to the lowest possible setting to stabilize and maintain that pressure. Cook for 15 minutes. Remove from the heat and use the natural release method before opening the lid. Transfer the sweet potatoes and the pork to a cutting board and cover the meat with foil. When ready to serve, cut the pork tenderloin against the grain into ½-inch medallions.

Step Two: THE CREAMY SHALLOT SAUCE WITH TARRAGON

2 tablespoons butter
2 shallots, thinly sliced
1 teaspoon dried tarragon, or more to taste
1 cup heavy cream
Salt and freshly ground black pepper to taste

Bring the pan sauce to a boil over high heat, uncovered, and reduce by half. Melt the butter in a heavy skillet over medium heat, taking care not to let it burn. Add the shallots and sauté them until transparent. Add ½ cup of the reduced pan sauce, the tarragon, and cream, stirring well. Taste and adjust seasoning as needed with salt and pepper. Pour into a gravy boat and keep warm; spoon over the sliced pork at the table.

Step Three: THE MASHED SWEET POTATOES

4 tablespoons (½ stick) butter, softened
¼ cup packed dark brown sugar
1 teaspoon ground allspice
½ teaspoon ground nutmeg
Salt and freshly ground black pepper to taste

Peel the potatoes when they have cooled slightly. Put the pulp into the bowl of a stand mixer and add the butter, sugar, allspice, and nutmeg. Beat the mixture until smooth, and then season with salt and pepper. Spoon into a serving bowl.

braised pineapple pork chops with garlic-ginger glaze

I made this recipe on the spur of the moment, and it was one of those serendipitous events that just came together by happenstance. I had intended to make the pork chops with sweet teriyaki sauce—you should try them that way, too—to complement pineapple, but I grabbed the wrong bottle from the fridge. So I added the last little knob of ginger and, of course, garlic, and the sauce ended up having a wonderful sweet and salty combination that I loved. It was an easy-to-make dinner with just tiny a bit of prep work. Serve these with rice to keep to the Asian theme, or go with potatoes; either way makes for a very nice meal. • **SERVES 6**

Step One: THE MEAT

6 thin-cut pork chops
Salt and coarsely ground black pepper to taste
2 tablespoons olive oil
¼ cup dry white wine
¼ cup soy sauce
4 large cloves garlic, roasted (see page 252) and mashed to a pulp
1 tablespoon grated fresh ginger

Season the chops with salt and pepper. Heat the oil in the pressure cooker over medium-high heat and brown the chops on both sides. Add the wine, soy sauce, garlic, and ginger, stirring to mix. Lock the lid in place. Bring to 15psi over high heat and immediately reduce the heat to the lowest possible setting to stabilize and maintain that pressure. Cook for 4 minutes. Remove from the heat and use the natural release method before opening the lid. Transfer the meat to a serving plate.

Step Two: THE GLAZE

¼ cup honey
1 (20-ounce) can unsweetened pineapple chunks, well drained
1 teaspoon cornstarch
2 scallion tops, sliced, for garnish

Heat the sauce in the pressure cooker over medium heat and let it boil, uncovered, until reduced by half. Stir in the honey and continue cooking as the sauce gets thicker and begins to cling to the spoon. Reduce the heat and add the pineapple chunks and cornstarch, stirring until the pineapple is coated and the sauce is bubbling. Pour the pineapple chunks and the glaze over the pork chops and garnish with the scallions.

pork chops with pomegranate glaze

Fresh pomegranates start popping up in the produce aisle when the weather gets chilly, and they are usually available at a good price, so I like to stock up and use the intense, lip-smacking juice to rev up some new recipes. I like the seeds too. They're fun to eat—kids love 'em!—and they're just pretty as a garnish. Then there's the huge healthy-and-good-for-you factor, but pomegranates really taste so good, and that's the key factor in this recipe. Select pomegranates that are the heaviest for their size, as that is a good indicator of the juicy seeds inside. • **SERVES 4**

Step One: THE POMEGRANATE JUICE

2 or 3 pomegranates
Sweetener to taste (optional)
Pinch of salt (optional)

Before you can make juice, first you'll need to get all those seeds out of the pomegranates. To begin, use a sharp knife to cut off the "crown" end of the pomegranate and then score the rind, sectioning the fruit into quarters. Fill a large bowl with cold water and submerge the sections for 5 to 10 minutes. To keep the juice from splattering and staining your counter, skin, and clothing, break the pieces apart while they are underwater. Use your fingers to pick the seeds away from the pith and peel. The seeds will sink to the bottom of the bowl, while the pithy membranes will float to the top of the water for easier removal. Once the seeds are stripped from the pomegranate, give them a quick rinse in cold water and then they are ready for use. (Pomegranate seeds make a great snack, and they can be portioned out and stored in the freezer for later use.)

Reserve 2 to 3 tablespoons seeds for garnish. To extract the juice from the remainder of the seeds, put them into a food processor and process in on-off pulses for 15 to 20 seconds, or until you have a thick pulp. Strain the seed pulp through a fine-mesh strainer set over a bowl. Press the pulp with the back of a spoon to force out as much juice as possible. Taste the juice; it should be tart and not too sweet, but you can add a bit of sweetener to taste if desired, and a pinch of salt improves the flavor. The fresh pomegranate juice may be refrigerated in a covered container and used within 3 days, or frozen for up to 3 months.

(continued)

Step Two: THE PORK CHOPS

4 bone-in pork chops, cut about 1 inch thick
Salt and freshly ground black pepper to taste
1 to 2 tablespoons olive oil
½ cup chicken broth
1 cup fresh pomegranate juice

Season the chops generously with salt and pepper, pressing them into the meat with your fingertips. Heat the oil in the pressure cooker over medium-high heat and sear the chops on all sides to get a nice brown color. Deglaze the pot with the broth, scraping up all those crusty brown bits from the bottom. Stir in the pomegranate juice. Lock the lid in place. Bring to 15psi over high heat and immediately reduce the heat to the lowest possible setting to stabilize and maintain that pressure. Cook for 6 minutes. Remove from the heat and use the natural release method before opening the lid. Transfer the chops to a serving plate and keep in a warm oven while preparing the glaze.

Step Three: THE POMEGRANATE GLAZE

2 tablespoons balsamic vinegar
¼ cup honey

Skim off any fat from the surface of the broth in the pressure cooker. Bring to a boil over high heat, uncovered, then reduce to the heat to low and simmer, stirring often as it begins to reduce and thicken to a syruplike consistency, about 20 minutes. Stir in the vinegar and honey, and continue cooking the glaze until it coats your spoon. Taste and adjust the sweetness and tanginess to your preference. Using long-handled tongs, place each pork chop in the hot pomegranate glaze, turning several times until they are all evenly coated. Arrange the glazed pork chops on plates and garnish with a sprinkling of the reserved pomegranate seeds. Serve any remaining glaze in a small bowl to be passed at the table.

barbecued pork spareribs

Hey, how about some barbecued ribs? Oops, you forget to thaw them; that's too bad. What's that? . . . It's too hot to go stand outside over a flaming hot grill? . . . Yeah, I hate that, too. Sorry, no barbecue for you! Wait a second, my dears, we should have thought of this earlier: Let's use the pressure cooker! It's so easy, and it's so quick, that who knows, you might be cooking up a plate of barbecued ribs the middle of winter when the grill is buried in a snowdrift. Try this recipe and you'll have the tenderest barbecued ribs you have ever tasted! Forget boiling ribs—we want to keep all the flavor in those tender, succulent slabs, not boil it all out of them. To accomplish this wonder, we're going to do a little steam-roasting first, and then I'm going to give you a few different options for how to finish your barbecued ribs. Ready? • **SERVES 4 TO 6**

Step One: THE STEAM ROASTING

1 teaspoon salt
½ teaspoon freshly ground black pepper
1 teaspoon garlic powder
2 teaspoons chili powder
3 to 5 pounds pork spare ribs or baby back ribs

Mix the salt, pepper, garlic powder, and chili powder in small bowl. Cut the ribs into serving-size portions. Dust the spice mix on both sides of the ribs. The moisture from the pork should be enough to make the rub stick to the meat. Place the cooking rack in the bottom of the pressure cooker and add ½ cup water. Position the ribs vertically in the pressure cooker so the steam can move freely around them. Lock the lid in place. Bring to 15psi over high heat and immediately reduce the heat to the lowest possible setting to stabilize and maintain that pressure. Cook for 12 minutes. Remove from the heat and use the quick release method before opening the lid.

Step Two: THE BARBECUE

1½ cups barbecue sauce of your choice
2 tablespoons canola oil

At this point, the spare ribs are cooked and all they need is a coating of barbecue sauce and a bit of flame to glaze the surface. The quickest was to coat the ribs is to pour the barbecue sauce into a shallow pan and then dip the ribs into the sauce using tongs.

Preheat a grill or the broiler. To cook the ribs on a grill, brush the rack with the canola oil and coat the ribs with sauce before placing them on the grill. Just let them get a little caramelization started, but watch closely and don't let them burn. Turn, and

(continued)

baste with extra sauce until done to you liking. To use a broiler, brush the broiler rack with the canola oil and dip the ribs into the sauce. Position the broiler pan 6 inches from the heat source and broil until the sauce begins to caramelize, about 4 minutes. Turn the ribs and brush on more sauce, and broil for 2 to 3 minutes longer. Serve the ribs with any extra barbecue sauce on the side.

pork chops with garlicky mashed potatoes

This is one of my favorite quick meals because it's a very easy way to cook a main dish with a nice side dish at the same time. The pork chops are fork-tender and the garlic-flavored mashed potatoes make a perfectly delicious match. It's no secret that mashed potatoes taste better when they're made with lots of cream and butter, so don't skimp. Now, to make a good bowl of mashed spuds, you need to begin with drier, starchier types of potatoes; russet or Yukon gold are the best mashers. • **SERVES 4**

- 4 thin-cut bone-in pork chops
- Salt and coarsely ground black pepper to taste
- 2 tablespoons olive oil
- 1½ pounds russet potatoes, peeled and quartered
- 4 tablespoons (½ stick) butter, softened
- 2 tablespoons minced garlic or 6 to 8 cloves garlic, roasted (see page 252)
- ⅓ cup half-and-half or milk

Season the chops with salt and pepper. Heat the oil in the pressure cooker over medium heat, and cook the chops until browned on both sides. Set aside. Place the cooking rack in the bottom of the pressure cooker and add ½ cup water. Arrange the browned chops on the rack. Place the cut potatoes in a metal bowl and position it on top of the chops. Lock the lid in place. Bring to 15psi over high heat and immediately reduce the heat to the lowest possible setting to stabilize and maintain that pressure. Cook for 4 minutes. Remove from the heat and use the natural release method before opening the lid.

Transfer the potatoes to a mixing bowl and mash by whatever method you prefer. Add the butter first, then the garlic, and then salt and pepper to taste, fluffing with a fork. Add the half-and-half a little at a time, and whip with a fork to get the consistency you like. Adjust the seasonings as desired. Transfer the chops to a serving plate and serve with the potatoes.

shredded pork braised in guajillo chile sauce

This delicious velvety sauce has plenty of deep and complex flavors, which blend beautifully with the shredded pork. Guajillos are mild to moderate in heat with a pleasing taste that adds a spicy, earthy flavor to a basic red chili sauce, making it very versatile for lots of Tex-Mex recipes. Use the meat and sauce in sandwiches or burritos or in enchiladas. Serve it over a mound of mashed potatoes or rice, or add beans to turn it into chili (see the variation). • **SERVES 6**

8 dried guajillo chiles
3 to 4 pounds pork shoulder
2 teaspoons sea salt
2 to 3 tablespoons olive oil
2 medium onions, chopped
6 cloves garlic, finely minced
2 tablespoons ground cumin
1 cup dark beer
2 bay leaves
2 teaspoons dried Mexican oregano
1 (8-ounce) can tomato sauce

Remove the stems from the chiles and cut them open to take out the seeds and ribs. Heat a heavy dry skillet over medium heat to toast the chiles, turning them frequently as they start to change color. Watch closely as they turn crispy, taking care not to let them blacken or burn. Use a food processor to pulverize the toasted guajillo chiles; set aside.

Trim the excess fat from the pork shoulder and cut it into 2-inch cubes. Frugal cooks will want to freeze the bones and meat scraps for later stock making. Season the pork with the salt. Heat the oil in the pressure cooker and sear the meat in small batches, browning the cubes on all sides, then set aside on a plate. Add the onions and cook until they are soft and golden brown. Add the garlic, cooking until soft. Stir in the cumin and the pulverized chiles and let them sizzle until they become fragrant. Deglaze the cooker with the beer, scraping up all those crusty brown bits from the bottom. Return the meat and any accumulated juices to the pressure cooker. Stir in the bay leaves and oregano. Add the tomato sauce on top, and do not stir. Lock the lid in place. Bring to 15psi over high heat and immediately reduce the heat to the lowest possible setting to stabilize and maintain that pressure. Cook for 30 minutes. Remove from the heat and use the natural release method before opening the lid.

Preheat the broiler. Transfer the meat cubes to a baking sheet and shred with forks. Spread the shredded meat out on the sheet and place it about 6 inches from the broiler. Watch closely as the meat begins to crisp, turning the pieces over to get lots of crispy edges but taking care not to let them burn. Set aside. Meanwhile, skim off any excess fat from the surface of the guajillo chile sauce and discard the bay leaves. Use a hand-held blender to puree the sauce to a smooth consistency or puree in a blender. Bring the sauce to a boil over medium heat and cook uncovered, stirring often to prevent scorching, and reduce the sauce by half. Taste and adjust seasoning as desired. Return the crispy shredded meat to the sauce and stir until heated through.

Variation:

PORK AND GUAJILLO CHILI WITH BEANS

3 cups cooked beans of your choice, such as black, pinto, or kidney
1 cup sour cream, for garnish

Follow the directions up until the point where the pressure cooker is opened. Skim off any excess fat. If using canned beans, drain and rinse well. Add the beans to the sauce and simmer, uncovered, until the beans are heated through. Ladle the chili into bowls and top with a dollop of sour cream.

pulled pork sandwiches with chipotle-pomegranate barbecue sauce

Long after summer has slipped away and the weather is freezing cold and blustery, no one thinks much about a barbecue, right? I like the fast convenience of using my pressure cooker for all kinds of barbecued meats in the summer, but it's just as useful in the winter months to serve up pulled meat sandwiches for a weekend family lunch or to make a great big platter of sliders to munch on in front of the TV while cheering on your team. The spicy and tangy tartness of the barbecue sauce pairs up beautifully with pork and really creates extraordinary flavor. I like to serve this recipe with a nice coleslaw, which when you think about it is a perfect winter side dish, when cabbages are in season. If you want to try it my way, add a coleslaw topper over the pulled pork sandwich—delicious! • **SERVES 8**

Step One: THE MEAT

One 3- to 4-pound pork shoulder roast or Boston butt
Salt and freshly ground black pepper to taste
2 tablespoons olive oil
2 medium onions, diced
4 to 6 cloves garlic, minced
4 chipotle chiles in adobo sauce, seeded and finely chopped
1 (12-ounce) bottle of beer or 1½ cups beef or chicken broth
1 (8-ounce) can tomato sauce

Score the fat on the pork and season it generously with salt and pepper on all sides. Heat the oil in the pressure cooker, brown the pork on all sides, and set aside on a plate. Cook the onions and garlic, stirring often until slightly browned and softened, 6 to 10 minutes. Add the chiles and sauce. Deglaze the pot with the beer, scraping up any crusty brown bits from the bottom. Return the pork and any accumulated juices to the pressure cooker. Pour the tomato sauce over the top. Do not stir. Lock the lid in place. Bring to 15psi over high heat and immediately reduce the heat to the lowest possible setting to stabilize and maintain that pressure. Cook for 35 minutes. Remove from the heat and use the natural release method before opening the lid. Check for doneness; the pork should easily pull apart with a fork. If needed, return to pressure and cook for 6 minutes longer, using the natural release method before opening the lid. Transfer the pork to a cutting board and let it rest for 15 minutes or so to let the juices reabsorb. Cut away any excess fat before pulling the pork apart and shredding it into small, uniform pieces, then put it all back in the pressure cooker. Strain the broth, returning the pieces of onions and garlic to the pressure cooker.

Step Two: THE BARBECUE SAUCE

Prepare the barbecue sauce up to 2 days in advance if it's convenient, and then refrigerate in a tightly sealed container until needed, heating the sauce just before serving time. Otherwise, cook the sauce while the meat is cooking.

2 cups pomegranate juice
1 cup apple cider vinegar
1 cup dark brown sugar, or to taste
2 tablespoons spicy brown mustard

In a medium heavy saucepan, combine all the ingredients. Bring to a boil, then reduce the heat to low. Simmer uncovered, stirring often, until the mixture reduces to a thick syruplike consistency, about 20 minutes. It's ready when it sticks to and coats your spoon. Taste and adjust the sugar and vinegar to get the right amount of tangy sweetness you prefer.

Step Three: THE SANDWICHES

8 buns or rolls of your choice, lightly toasted
Dill pickles, for garnish

Add just enough barbecue sauce to coat all the meat; don't add too much or the sandwich buns will get soggy and fall apart. Heat the pork and sauce over low heat, stirring until it's piping hot. Place a generous mound of pork on each bun, top with dill pickles, and pass the extra sauce at the table.

COOK'S NOTE: The frugal cook will skim the fat from the strained meat broth and then freeze the broth for later use to add flavor to other recipes.

---

pulled pork for sandwiches

The pressure cooker makes fast work of turning the toughest cuts of meat so tender that they can easily be shredded with a fork. This is a simple recipe for making delicious pulled pork for use in a variety of sandwiches. Also use the tender shreds of meat in tamales, fajitas, or burritos. Freeze the meat for making soups and stews when time is short. Serve these sandwiches with crispy dill pickles and a side of fries or potato salad, if desired.

• **SERVES 6 (TWO-HANDED, HE-MAN-SIZE SANDWICHES)**

2 tablespoons olive oil
2 medium onions, chopped
2 green bell peppers, seeded and chopped
6 cloves garlic, minced
1 cup dry red wine
Salt and freshly ground black pepper to taste
4 pounds pork picnic shoulder, trimmed of excess fat
6 sandwich rolls, split and lightly toasted

Heat the oil in the pressure cooker over medium heat and add the onions, bell peppers, and garlic. Cook, stirring, until the onions are soft and translucent but not browned, about 4 minutes. Add the wine and 1 cup water, stirring to mix. Season the pork generously with salt and pepper on all sides. Position the pork in the pressure cooker. Lock the lid in place. Bring to 15psi over high heat and immediately reduce the heat to the lowest possible setting to stabilize and maintain that pressure. Cook for 35 minutes or until the pork shreds easily with a fork. Remove from the heat and use the natural release method before opening the lid. Transfer the pork to a cutting board and let rest for about 10 minutes. In the meantime, bring the sauce in the pressure cooker to a boil and cook, uncovered, until the liquid reduces by half. Pull the pork to shreds using two forks and then return to the pressure cooker to heat through. To serve, pile a generous amount of shredded pork on each roll. Serve the remaining broth in small bowls for dipping at the table.

pork chops and potatoes with pineapple salsa

Thick-cut pork chops and ordinary salsa go tropical spicy with the addition of pineapple, lime, cumin, and a little chile pepper to create a hearty, deep flavor. This dish not only tastes terrific, but it also looks pretty enough to impress everyone at your table. It's also really easy to prepare and is a quick weekday dinner recipe. • **SERVES 4**

4 bone-in pork chops, about ½ inch thick
Salt and freshly ground black pepper to taste
2 tablespoons olive oil
4 medium russet potatoes, scrubbed and halved
1½ cups chunky-style prepared salsa
1 cup chopped onion
1 teaspoon ground cumin
⅓ cup chopped fresh cilantro
1 tablespoon fresh lime juice
1 small serrano chile, seeded and minced (optional)
1 (8-ounce) can crushed pineapple in juice, drained

Rub the chops with salt and pepper. Heat the oil in the pressure cooker over medium-high heat Add the potatoes to the pressure cooker, cut side down, and let the surface get nicely browned. Transfer to a plate. Add the chops and brown the meat on all sides. Set aside on a plate, and deglaze the pot with water, scraping up all those crusty brown bits from the bottom. Stir in the salsa, onion, cumin, cilantro, lime juice, and the chile, if you want a bit of heat. Return the chops to the pressure cooker, and then add the pineapple on top, without stirring. Place the browned potatoes on top, cut side up. Lock the lid in place. Bring to 15psi over high heat and immediately reduce the heat to the lowest possible setting to stabilize and maintain that pressure. Cook for 6 minutes. Remove from the heat and use the natural release method before opening the lid. Arrange the chops and potatoes on individual serving plates. Stir the salsa and pineapple mixture to blend. Taste and adjust seasonings. Pour the salsa mixture into a small bowl to be passed at the table and spooned over the chops and the potatoes.

pork with red chili sauce

Tender bites of pork smothered in a red chili sauce . . . sound good? It is, and this is such a versatile recipe that I'm going to show you a few different ways that I use it to make different dishes. Do create your own new recipes, too, and let me know how they turn out. Serve this pork and sauce over fluffy white rice, with either black beans or pintos, topped with grated cheese and a spoonful of sour cream. I add some warm flour tortillas, too. • **SERVES 6**

2 pounds boneless pork sirloin
1 teaspoon salt
½ teaspoon freshly ground black pepper
2 tablespoons vegetable oil
2 medium onions, chopped
1 large green bell pepper, seeded and chopped
1 cup Mexican beer
2 cups Red Chili Sauce (page 302) or 2 (8-ounce) cans red chili sauce

Trim off any excess fat from the pork and then cut the meat into 1-inch cubes. Season the meat with the salt and black pepper. Heat the oil in the pressure cooker over medium-high heat and brown the pork in small matches, searing all sides. Set aside on a plate. Add the onions and cook until soft. Return the meat and any accumulated juices to the pressure cooker, and stir in the bell pepper and beer. Add the chili sauce on top, and do not stir. Lock the lid in place. Bring to 15psi over high heat and immediately reduce the heat to the lowest possible setting to stabilize and maintain that pressure. Cook for 18 minutes. Remove from the heat and use the natural release method before opening the lid. Skim off any excess fat from the surface. Taste and adjust seasoning as desired.

If you prefer a thicker sauce, simmer over medium heat uncovered, stirring often, for about 10 minutes or until the sauce reaches the desired consistency. Ladle the pork and sauce into a bowl and serve.

BONUS RECIPE

pork tacos with red chili sauce

- 24 (6-inch) corn or flour tortillas, warmed according to package directions
- 4 cups shredded lettuce
- 3 cups shredded Monterey Jack cheese
- 1 cup crema agria (Mexican-style sour cream) or sour cream

Cook the pork according to the directions. Fill the warm tortillas with the meat mixture, and add toppings as desired. Pass the chili sauce at the table and spoon it into the tacos as you eat them.

SERVES 6

amazingly simple spiral-sliced ham

This is the most ridiculously easy recipe ever! It's so simple that you'll want to cook a ham for dinner any day of the week. Spiral-sliced hams are very popular. They are already precooked, so they just need to be warmed up, but that can still take 45 minutes or more in the oven. Everyone loves ham, but who has time for that during the week? Of course, if you cook that spiral-sliced ham in the pressure cooker, you can serve a ham as your main course any day of the week. Add your favorite side dishes—maybe some mashed potatoes or barbecue beans. Plan on using the leftover ham in other recipes, and don't forget to save that meaty ham bone, too! • **SERVES 6**

4 pounds fully cooked spiral-sliced ham
¼ cup hot honey mustard

Place the cooking rack in the bottom of the pressure cooker and pour in ⅔ cup water. Use a basting brush to apply the mustard evenly over the surface of the ham. Place the ham in a steamer tray or use foil helper handles under the ham to place the ham on the rack. Lock the lid in place. Bring to 15psi over high heat and immediately reduce the heat to the lowest possible setting to stabilize and maintain that pressure. Cook for 14 minutes. Remove from the heat and use the natural release method before opening the lid. Cut the slices away from the bone and serve immediately.

braised flank steak with roasted garlic–wine reduction

The flank steak is a cut from the belly of a cow; it is lean meat with really good flavor, but it is also significantly tougher than other beef cuts. This means it takes to moist cooking methods such as braising, making it ideal for the pressure cooker. Flank steak used to be really inexpensive, but over time it has found its way into every sort of cuisine from Asian stir-fry to Mexican fajitas, and with its rising popularity, the price has gone up. It's still less expensive than today's premium prices for the more tender rib-eye or T-bone steaks, though. Depending on were you live, look for flank steak under various names like London broil and jiffy steak, or substitute a similar cut like skirt steak, which might be labeled as fajita meat or Philadelphia steak. A salad and mashed or baked potatoes are good accompaniments for this steak. • **SERVES 6**

Step One: THE ROASTED GARLIC

5 or 6 large, plump cloves garlic (do not peel)

Place the cooking rack in the pressure cooker and add ½ cup water. Put the unpeeled garlic cloves in a small ramekin and set it on top of the cooking rack. Lock the lid in place. Bring to 15psi over high heat, then immediately reduce the heat to the lowest possible setting to stabilize and maintain that pressure. Cook for 5 minutes. Remove from the heat and use the natural release method before opening the lid. Remove the garlic and, when cool enough to handle, snip off one end of each clove and pop out the buttery soft goodness inside. Mash to a smooth consistency with a fork and set aside.

Step Two: THE STEAK

1½ to 2 pounds flank steak, 1 to 2 inches thick
Salt and freshly ground black pepper to taste
1 tablespoon olive oil
1 cup dry red wine

Sprinkle the steak with salt and a generous amount of pepper. Heat the pressure cooker over medium-high heat and add the oil. When the oil is hot, brown the steak well on both sides. Add the wine. Lock the lid in place. Bring to 15psi over high heat, then immediately reduce the heat to the lowest possible setting to stabilize and maintain that pressure. Cook for 30 minutes. Remove from the heat and use the natural release method before opening the lid. Transfer the steak to a serving plate and keep warm.

(continued)

Step Three: THE SAUCE

1½ cups of the cooking broth
2 tablespoons cold butter

Skim off any excess fat from the surface of the broth and measure the needed amount, freezing any remaining broth for other uses. Pour the broth back into the pressure cooker and bring to a boil over medium-high heat, scraping up any browned bits on the bottom. Continue to boil, adding any meat juices that have accumulated under the steak. When the broth is reduced by half and looks thick and syrupy, after about 10 minutes, remove from the heat, and whisk in the mashed garlic and the butter, blending well.

To serve, thinly slice the meat, cutting against the grain, and arrange the slices on a serving platter. Drizzle the sauce over the slices and pass the remaining sauce at the table.

zinfandel-braised pot roast with carrots and parsnips

Pot roast is an American favorite, and it has become the menu staple that can be found on the proverbial family dinner table on any given Sunday. For a pot roast we generally use a cheaper cut of meat that requires several hours of cooking time as it slowly simmers to a tender stage. That's why a delicious pot roast was traditionally reserved for Sundays, when the family was home and there was time to cook it. That all changes when using a pressure cooker, and now we can serve up a big meal like this even on a weeknight. • **SERVES 8**

- 3½ pounds boneless beef chuck, trimmed of fat
- Salt and freshly ground black pepper to taste
- 2 tablespoons olive oil
- 1 cup beef broth
- 1 large onion, coarsely chopped
- 4 cloves garlic, smashed
- 1 cup Zinfandel or other robust dry red wine
- ⅓ cup finely chopped fresh sage
- 4 carrots, peeled and sliced into 1-inch pieces
- 4 parsnips, peeled and sliced into 1-inch pieces

Season the beef on all sides with salt and pepper. Heat the oil in the pressure cooker and brown the meat on both sides. Remove the beef and set it aside on a large plate. Deglaze the pot with the broth, scraping up all those crusty brown bits from the bottom. Return the beef to the pressure cooker along with any accumulated juices, and add the onion and garlic. Pour in the wine and add the sage. Lock the lid in place. Bring to 15psi over high heat and immediately reduce the heat to the lowest possible setting to stabilize and maintain that pressure. Cook for 25 minutes. Remove from the heat and use the quick release method before opening the lid. Spoon off the fat with a large spoon. Add the carrots and parsnips. Return to pressure and cook for 5 minutes longer. Remove from the heat and use the natural release method before opening the lid.

Carefully lift the beef out with tongs, set it on a carving surface, and cover loosely with foil to keep warm. Transfer the vegetables to a serving platter. Heat the remaining cooking liquid over medium-high heat, uncovered, and boil for about 10 minutes to concentrate the flavors. The juices will not be thick. Taste and adjust the seasoning with salt and pepper if needed. Cut the meat across the grain into thick slices and arrange on the platter with vegetables. Serve the wine sauce on the side.

savory herbed beef roast with wine sauce

A simple recipe for deliciously tender beef roast is all dressed up in an elegant wine sauce. A plain roast is fine, but this flavorful sauce is as much a part of the perfect meal as the meat. Best of all, it's a quick and easy sauce to make, and drizzled over the beef, it greatly enhances the flavor. Serve with side dish of mashed potatoes. • **SERVES 6**

Step One: THE HERB SEASONING

Salt to taste
2 teaspoons dried basil, crushed
1 teaspoon dried thyme, crushed
1 teaspoon dried Italian parsley, crushed
½ teaspoon coarsely ground black pepper

Combine all the seasonings in a small bowl.

Step Two: THE BEEF

3 to 4 pounds boneless beef round, rump, or bottom round roast
2 tablespoons olive oil
1 cup dry red wine
2 cloves garlic, minced
½ cup finely chopped onion

Dry the beef with paper towels and press the herb seasoning evenly into the meat with your fingers. Reserve any remaining herb seasoning. Heat the oil in the pressure cooker over medium-high heat and brown the beef on all sides. Transfer to a plate. Deglaze the pot with the wine, scraping up all those crusty brown bits from the bottom. Add the garlic, onion, and any remaining herb seasoning. Place the cooking rack in the bottom of the pressure cooker and center the roast on top. Lock the lid in place. Bring to 15psi over high heat and immediately reduce the heat to the lowest possible setting to stabilize and maintain that pressure. Cook for 25 minutes. Remove from the heat and use the natural release method before opening the lid. Transfer the roast to a platter and tent loosely with foil to rest.

Step Three: THE WINE SAUCE

2 tablespoons cold butter, cut into small pieces
Salt and freshly ground black pepper to taste
¼ cup chopped fresh chives, for garnish

Add the butter to the pan broth and bring to a boil over high heat, uncovered. Continue cooking, stirring frequently as the sauce reduces and begins to thicken, for about 10 minutes, or until it is thick enough to coat a spoon. Remove from the heat. Taste and adjust seasoning with salt and pepper. Stir in any accumulated juices from the meat plate.

Carve the roast into thin slices and arrange on a serving platter. Sprinkle with the chives. Spoon some sauce over the meat just before serving, and pass extra sauce at the table.

beef braised in picante roasted tomato and pepper sauce

When we lived in Spain, my mother fell in love with both the country and the cuisine of the region. When she discovered that smoked hot Spanish paprika was an essential ingredient in many popular Spanish recipes, pimentón de la Vera picante was quickly added to our spice collection. Made from dried and smoked hot chiles, this type of paprika releases its full color and flavor when it is heated; only then will it give your taste buds a proper jolt. Serve this with Kale Colcannon (page 256) or Soft and Creamy Polenta (page 278). I use a typical sofrito mix of aromatic vegetables, the flavor base for countless sauces, soups, and stews. • **SERVES 4**

Step One: THE MEAT

- 1½ to 2 pounds beef top or bottom round steak, about 1 inch thick, trimmed of fat
- Salt and coarsely ground black pepper to taste
- 1 to 1½ teaspoons hot smoked Spanish paprika (pimentón de la Vera picante)
- 2 tablespoons olive oil

Cut the beef into 4 serving-size portions and season lightly on both sides with salt and pepper. Sprinkle the paprika on both sides, rubbing the spice into the surface of the meat. Heat the oil in the pressure cooker over medium-high heat and brown the beef well on both sides. Set aside on a plate.

Step Two: THE SOFRITO

- 1 small onion, quartered
- ½ cup chopped fresh cilantro leaves
- 4 large fresh basil leaves
- 2 cloves garlic
- 1 tablespoon olive oil
- 1 cup dry red wine

Use a food processor to chop the onion, cilantro, basil, and garlic into pieces about the size of a pea. Heat the oil in the pressure cooker over medium-high heat and cook the mixture until the onions look translucent and soft, about 4 minutes. Deglaze the cooker with the wine, scraping up any crusty bits from the bottom.

Step Three: THE SAUCE

6 large Roma tomatoes, roasted (see page 299) and coarsely chopped
2 large chiles, such as Anaheim, poblano, or pasilla, roasted (see page 299) and coarsely chopped

Add the tomatoes and chiles to the pressure cooker. Return the meat and any accumulated juices to the pressure cooker. Lock the lid in place. Bring to 15psi over high heat and immediately reduce the heat to the lowest possible setting to stabilize and maintain that pressure. Cook for 15 minutes. Remove from the heat and use the natural release method before opening the lid. Spoon a little of the sauce on top of each serving.

mexican steak sandwiches

If you're a foodie, you love a well-stocked supermarket, and I could spend the whole day just browsing around the large and boldly colorful, sparkling clean Mexican *mercado* (supermarket) in my California town. The courteous and helpful *carnicero* (butcher) offers a huge selection of every sort of fresh meat imaginable. The freshly cut meats are displayed in a gleaming case that must be at least a hundred feet in length. One of the noticeable differences is that the Mexican cuts are much thinner than we are accustomed to seeing in American-style supermarkets. There are two reasons for this: First, as in many other countries, meat is not consumed as a large part of the diet in Latin America. Second, the wonderfully complex flavors of Mexican cuisine make the most of thin cuts of meat to stretch the food budget with traditional recipes that add delicious combinations of robust ingredients and piquant seasonings. This recipe is a bump up from the popular French dip sandwich with a little zestier flavor that comes from the addition of spicier Mexican ingredients. • **SERVES 4**

1 tablespoon olive oil
1 small onion, sliced
1 pound boneless beef chuck steak, less than ½ inch thick
1 teaspoon ground cumin
1 tablespoon chili powder
Salt and freshly ground black pepper to taste
½ cup flavoring liquid of your choice, such as beer, wine, coffee, stock, or other
1 teaspoon beef bouillon granules
1 green bell pepper, seeded and sliced
1 mild Mexican chile, such as Anaheim, poblano, or pasilla, seeded and sliced
2 jalapeño chiles, seeded and sliced
½ cup minced fresh cilantro
Mexican hot sauce to taste (optional)
4 hoagie rolls, lightly toasted
4 slices pepper Jack cheese

Heat the oil in the pressure cooker and cook the onion over medium-high heat until it begins to caramelize and become soft and brown. Slice the beef into ½-inch strips, 2 to 3 inches in length. Brown the beef in small batches, transferring each batch to a plate as it browns. Add the cumin, chili powder, and salt and black pepper to the pressure cooker. Add the flavoring liquid and bouillon, stirring to mix. Add all the bell pepper, chiles, and cilantro. Lock the lid in place. Bring to 15psi over high heat and immediately reduce the heat to the lowest possible setting to stabilize and maintain that pressure. Cook for 6 minutes. Remove from the heat and use the natural release method before opening the lid. Taste the broth and adjust seasonings to suite your taste, adding hot sauce if desired. Lay a toasted roll on each serving plate, and divide the steak and peppers between them. Top each sandwich with a slice of cheese and cut them in half on the diagonal. Portion the dipping sauce into small ramekins and place them on each plate.

essential roast beef and gravy

Love that beef roast, but hate cooking it all day in a hot oven? This one's for you, and look how simple it is! The pressure cooker makes life so much easier. Choose your favorite cut of beef chuck roast and plan on heaps of mashed potatoes for the gravy. • **SERVES 6**

3 pounds bone-in beef chuck roast, cut 2 inches thick
Salt and coarsely ground black pepper to taste
2 tablespoons olive oil
1 medium onion, diced
5 cloves garlic, smashed
1 (14-ounce) can beef broth
2 tablespoons cornstarch

Season the beef with salt and pepper. Heat the oil in the pressure cooker over medium-high heat and brown the beef on all sides. Transfer to a plate. Add the onion, reduce the heat to medium, and cook, stirring often, until soft and golden brown, about 5 minutes. Add the garlic and cook, stirring often, until it begins to change color, but take care not to overcook. Add the broth. Return the beef and any accumulated meat juices to the pressure cooker. Lock the lid in place. Bring to 15psi over high heat and immediately reduce the heat to the lowest possible setting to stabilize and maintain that pressure. Cook for 45 minutes. Remove from the heat and use the natural release method before opening the lid. Transfer the meat to a cutting board and tent with foil to keep warm.

Remove and discard the solids from the broth in the pressure cooker and skim off the fat or use a fat separator. Bring the broth to a rapid boil over medium-high heat until reduced by half, about 10 minutes. To thicken the broth, make a slurry using the cornstarch mixed with ⅓ cup water. Reduce the heat to medium and whisk the slurry into the broth, simmering gently until it's the desired consistency. Meanwhile, slice the roast and arrange on a serving platter. Pour the gravy into a serving bowl and serve alongside the meat.

wine-braised flank steaks with sage butter

This is one of my mother's favorite recipes; the braised meat just falls apart and melts in your mouth. The ingredients are simple, but the sage-infused butter adds an earthy flavor to the meat, making it very flavorful and incredibly rich. This is excellent entree to serve with hot noodles or mashed potatoes, and a green salad. • **SERVES 4**

Step One: THE SAGE BUTTER

6 tablespoons (3/4 stick) butter, softened
3 tablespoons finely chopped fresh sage leaves, plus a few sprigs for garnish
4 cloves garlic, roasted (see page 252) and mashed to a smooth pulp
1 tablespoon balsamic vinegar

At least 2 hours before serving, mix together the butter, sage, garlic, and vinegar until well blended. Cover tightly with plastic wrap and refrigerate until needed.

Step Two: THE MEAT

1½ to 2 pounds flank steak, about 1 inch thick, trimmed of excess fat
Salt and coarsely ground black pepper to taste
2 tablespoons olive oil
1 cup dry red wine
6 cloves garlic, roasted (see page 252) and mashed to a pulp
10 fresh sage leaves, snipped into small pieces

Season the steak with salt and pepper. Heat the oil in the pressure cooker over medium-high heat and brown the steak on all sides. Set aside on a plate. Deglaze the pot with the wine, scraping up all those crusty brown bits from the bottom. Mix the garlic and sage leaves with the wine. Return the steak to the pressure cooker along with any accumulated juices. Lock the lid in place. Bring to 15psi over high heat and immediately reduce the heat to the lowest possible setting to stabilize and maintain that pressure. Cook for 12 minutes. Remove from the heat and use the natural release method before opening the lid. Serve each portion of meat topped with a spoonful of the sage butter.

flatiron steak with chimichurri sauce

There's a doctoral dissertation waiting to be written about the confusing names for meats in the United States. Not only are there often several different names for the same cut, but many of them have no similar equivalent outside of the U.S. If that doesn't leave you scratching your head, then let me introduce you to the flatiron steak, or flatiron roast. This is a relatively new designer cut that is gaining in popularity because it is tasty and economical. If it isn't in your supermarket, substitute a thin-cut skirt steak. I use a spicy rub to add a flavor boost to the meat, which complements the cool taste of the fresh chimichurri sauce. • **SERVES 4**

Step One: THE CHIMICHURRI SAUCE

6 cloves garlic
1 cup fresh cilantro leaves
1 small shallot
2 tablespoons white wine vinegar
6 fresh oregano leaves or 2 teaspoons dried oregano
½ teaspoon red pepper flakes
½ teaspoon sea salt
Coarsely ground black pepper to taste
½ cup extra-virgin olive oil

Place the garlic in a food processor and pulse until finely chopped. Add the cilantro, shallot, vinegar, oregano, red pepper flakes, salt, and black pepper. Add the olive oil in a thin stream and process until smooth. Refrigerate in a tightly closed container until ready to serve.

Step Two: THE STEAK

1½ to 2 pounds flatiron steak, about ¾ inch thick, or substitute thin-cut skirt steak
1½ teaspoons ground cumin
1½ teaspoons sweet smoked Spanish paprika (pimentón de la Vera)
Salt and coarsely ground black pepper to taste
2 tablespoons olive oil

Season the steak with the cumin, paprika, and salt and pepper, rubbing the spices into both sides of the meat with your fingers. Heat the oil in the pressure cooker over medium-high heat and brown the meat on both sides. Set aside. Place the cooking rack in the bottom of the pressure cooker and add ½ cup water. Lay the meat on top of the rack, making sure that it is well above the waterline. Lock the lid in place. Bring to

(continued)

15psi over high heat and immediately reduce the heat to the lowest possible setting to stabilize and maintain that pressure. Cook for 8 minutes. Remove from the heat and use the natural release method before opening the lid. Transfer the meat to a cutting board and thinly slice the steak across the grain. To serve, spoon a generous dollop of the chimichurri sauce toward the side of each individual plate. Divide the steak slices and fan them out in a semicircle around the sauce.

beef chuck roast with a greek-inspired tomato sauce

This is an excellent way to turn an inexpensive chuck roast into a deliciously tender main dish. It has the added attraction of being beyond easy. I like it served with whipped potatoes, but for variety, try it with pasta or rice. • **SERVES 6 TO 8**

2 to 3 tablespoons olive oil
2 medium onions, chopped
Salt and coarsely ground black pepper to taste
3 pounds boneless chuck roast
1 cup dry red wine
1 tablespoon fresh oregano leaves
5 cloves garlic, minced
8 ounces fresh white mushrooms, washed and sliced
½ cup chopped fresh Italian parsley
1 (28-ounce) can diced tomatoes with juice
½ cup crumbled feta cheese
½ cup chopped pitted kalamata olives

Heat the oil in the pressure cooker over medium heat and cook the onions until they are golden brown and beginning to caramelize, about 5 minutes. Rub salt and pepper into the roast and brown it well on all sides. Set aside on a plate. Deglaze the pot with the wine, scraping up all those crusty brown bits from the bottom. Stir in the oregano, garlic, mushrooms, parsley, and tomatoes with juice. Return the roast to the pressure cooker along with any accumulated juices. Lock the lid in place. Bring to 15psi over high heat and immediately reduce the heat to the lowest possible setting to stabilize and maintain that pressure. Cook for 35 minutes. Remove from the heat and use the natural release method before opening the lid. Place the meat on a cutting board. Stir the cheese and olives into the tomato sauce and cover with a regular lid for about 4 minutes or until the cheese is blended into the sauce. Meanwhile, slice the meat and arrange on a platter. Taste the sauce and adjust the seasoning as needed. Serve the sauce in a separate bowl to be passed at the table.

taquería-style beef tacos with fresh california pico de gallo

Taquería is Spanish for "taco shop." They had humble beginnings in Mexico as street vendors, but now they've grown up and in my California neighborhood the traditional taquerías have moved into supermarkets and tiny restaurants tucked away in bustling strip malls in every neighborhood. Taquerías specialize in awesome tacos and burritos and many popular Mexican side dishes made from fresh ingredients and robust seasonings. My kind of food! Unlike American-style tacos, there is no cheese or other frilly fillings to get in the way of the meat. That's it—just a big pile of juicy, spicy meat and a squeeze of fresh lime served on small corn tortillas. That's typical of taquería food—the mini size makes the tacos easier to pick up and quickly devour in just a couple of bites. I've used a piquant sofrito mixture, the flavor base for countless Mexican dishes, and added a fresh salsa made with California avocados like the version that is served at my favorite taquería. • **SERVES 6 TO 8**

Step One: THE SOFRITO

1 dried ancho chile, seeded and halved
1 medium onion
20 sprigs fresh cilantro
1 mild Mexican chile, such as Anaheim, poblano, or pasilla, seeded and coarsely chopped
2 small jalapeño chiles, seeded and chopped
2 small tomatillos, papery husk removed and halved
6 cloves garlic
6 to 8 fresh oregano leaves

Pulverize the ancho chile in a food processor. Add the onion, cilantro, mild chile, jalapeños, tomatillos, garlic, and oregano, and pulse in short bursts until the sofrito mix looks uniformly chopped.

Step Two: THE CARNE ASADA

2 pounds flank steak
1 teaspoon salt
2 tablespoons olive oil
1 teaspoon sweet smoked Spanish paprika (pimentón de la Vera)
1 teaspoon ground cumin
⅓ cup dry red wine or dark Mexican beer
⅓ cup white vinegar
Juice of 2 medium limes

Season the steak with the salt. Heat the oil in the pressure cooker over medium-high heat and add the paprika and cumin, stirring as the spices begin to sizzle and become fragrant. Add the steak and turn once or twice to coat with the spices, and then brown the steak on both sides. Set aside on a plate. Add the sofrito mix and cook, stirring often, until the onions begin to brown, about 5 minutes. Deglaze the pot with the wine, scraping up all those crusty brown bits from the bottom. Add the vinegar and lime juice. Return the steak to the pressure cooker along with any accumulated juices. Lock the lid in place. Bring to 15psi over high heat and immediately reduce the heat to the lowest possible setting to stabilize and maintain that pressure. Cook for 20 minutes. Remove from the heat and use the natural release method before opening the lid. Transfer the steak to a cutting board and cut into thin strips. Strain the broth through a mesh sieve and discard the solids. Lay the meat in a shallow serving bowl and ladle some of the broth over the top to keep it moist. Freeze the remainder of that richly flavored broth for future use in your next pot of beans or chili.

Step Three: THE CALIFORNIA PICO DE GALLO

- Juice of 1 lime
- 2 avocados, pitted, peeled, and cubed
- 4 medium Roma tomatoes, diced
- 1 small white onion, finely diced
- 2 small jalapeño chiles, seeded and minced
- 1 small bunch fresh cilantro, leaves only, finely chopped
- Sea salt to taste

Prepare this fresh salsa while the meat is cooking. In a glass bowl or other nonreactive dish, drizzle the lime juice over the avocados to prevent discoloration. Add the tomatoes, onion, chiles, and cilantro, along with salt to taste. Toss gently to mix. Let the salsa stand at a room temperature until the meat is ready for serving. The recipe can easily be multiplied, but you will want to adjust the number of chiles to your taste.

Step Four: ASSEMBLING THE TACOS

- 1 package (at least 3 dozen; the count varies by brand) 4-inch mini corn tortillas
- 4 small limes, cut into wedges

Heat about 10 tortillas at a time in the microwave on High for about 35 seconds, or until they are warm and soft. Stack 2 tortillas on a plate and add a generous portion of the sliced beef with some of the spicy sauce. Squeeze a little lime juice on the meat and then spoon some of the pico de gallo on top. Fold the double tortillas over the filling, holding one end closed to keep everything inside while you quickly gobble from the open side. Repeat until everyone is stuffed.

COOK'S NOTE: Not all mainstream American supermarkets stock these mini tortillas. The 6-inch size that is carried by most are too unwieldy for taquería-style tacos, so trim them down to size using a 4-inch cookie cutter or kitchen scissors. Alternatively, if you have a Mexican eatery or market nearby, you should be able to find the 4-inch tortillas. Frugal cooks will want to save the tortillas scraps and either fry or bake them, adding a sprinkling of sea salt and then eating them with a dip while they are still warm.

---

flatiron steak with mashed potatoes and mushroom-wine gravy

Originally developed by the University of Nebraska and the University of Florida, this cut of beef, also sometimes labeled "flatiron roast," was marketed to the trendy upscale restaurant trade as a way for chefs to offer more profitable dishes. The flatiron steak has become so popular that it's now available as a designer cut in local supermarkets. Essentially a shoulder top blade roast weighing 2 to 3 pounds, this cut has a very good marbling, which makes it very flavorful. But the first thing you see is the large piece of connective tissue running down the middle, and because of that you might think it is going to be a tough piece of meat, but not so fast, my dears. All those upscale chefs knew a little trade secret about this cut of meat: It's the second most tender cut of beef, after the tenderloin. Yes, it's true; the flatiron is even more tender than a top sirloin, and in a pressure cooker, of course, this means fork-tender and melting in your mouth. • **SERVES 6**

- 2½ to 3 pounds flatiron steak
- 1 teaspoon garlic powder
- 1 teaspoon salt
- 1 teaspoon coarsely ground black pepper
- 2 tablespoons olive oil
- 1 cup chopped onions
- 1 cup dry red wine
- ½ cup strong brewed coffee
- 1 teaspoon beef bouillon granules
- 1 cup dried wild mushrooms, broken into small pieces
- 6 russet potatoes, peeled and cut into eighths
- 2 tablespoons Wondra flour
- ½ cup (1 stick) butter
- ⅓ cup milk

Season both sides of the steak generously with the garlic powder, salt, and pepper, pressing them into the meat with your fingertips. Heat the oil in the pressure cooker, brown the steak on all sides, and set aside on a plate. Cook the onions until they begin to turn golden brown. Deglaze the pot with the wine, scraping up all those crusty brown bits from the bottom. Add the coffee, bouillon, mushrooms, and 1 cup water, stirring to blend. Return the meat and any accumulated juices to the pressure cooker. Lock the lid in place. Bring to 15psi over high heat and immediately reduce the heat to the lowest possible setting to stabilize and maintain that pressure. Cook for 15 minutes. Remove from the heat and use the quick release method before opening the lid. Place the cut potatoes in a steamer tray and position the insert on top of the roast. Lock the lid in place and return to pressure, cooking for 4 minutes. Remove from the heat and use the natural release method before opening the lid. Transfer the potatoes to a bowl and transfer the roast to a cutting board.

To thicken the gravy, bring the broth to a simmer over medium heat and slowly sprinkle in the Wondra flour, whisking it into the broth until it's the desired consistency. Taste and adjust seasoning as desired.

Mash the potatoes by your preferred method. Add butter, and then milk, to reach the desired consistency, seasoning liberally with salt and pepper. Spoon the potatoes into a serving bowl. Slice the meat against the grain, and arrange the slices on a serving plate. Serve the mushroom gravy in a separate bowl to be passed at the table.

shredded barbecue beef brisket for sandwiches

My family loves tasty shredded beef sandwiches with lots of barbecue sauce. Thanks to the pressure cooker, I can serve these this any time of the year, regardless of the weather outside. I'm specifying a hickory-flavored liquid smoke that gives the meat a great, wood-grill flavor, but you can use any other variety you like. The recipe makes a lot of meat, so it's a nice choice for all those weekend sports fans who like to eat while cheering on their favorite teams. Serve it with coleslaw or potato salad, and maybe some baked beans, and you'll have a lot of happy people. • **SERVES 6 TO 8**

- 3 pounds beef brisket
- 1 to 1½ tablespoons barbecue spice rub
- 2 to 3 tablespoons olive oil
- 1½ cups beef broth
- 3 cups barbecue sauce of your choice
- 2 tablespoons Worcestershire sauce
- 3 teaspoons hickory-flavored liquid smoke
- 2 teaspoons garlic powder
- ½ teaspoon Louisiana-style hot sauce
- Salt to taste
- 8 sandwich rolls of your choice
- Dill pickles, for garnish (optional)

Rinse the brisket and pat dry. Rub the spice blend into the surface of the brisket, pressing it in with your fingertips. Heat the oil in the pressure cooker over medium-high heat and brown the meat on all sides. Deglaze the pot with the broth, scraping up all those crusty brown bits from the bottom. Lock the lid in place. Bring to 15psi over high heat and immediately reduce the heat to the lowest possible setting to stabilize and maintain that pressure. Cook for 55 minutes. Remove from the heat and use the natural release method before opening the lid. Check for doneness; the beef should pull apart with a fork. If needed, return to pressure for an additional 8 minutes or until the meat is easily shredded. Transfer the brisket to a cutting board. Drain the broth from the pressure cooker; the frugal cook will want to freeze this treasure for later use to add flavor to soups and other recipes. Shred the meat. Put the shredded meat and barbecue sauce in the pressure cooker, and stir in the Worcestershire sauce, liquid smoke, garlic powder, hot sauce, and salt to taste. With only a regular lid in place, cook over low heat until the meat is heated through, stirring often to prevent scorching the thick sauce. Serve on rolls with dill pickles, if desired.

COOK'S NOTE: I mention above that there is a lot of meat here, and it's delicious! So before mixing it with the barbecue sauce, feel free to set aside a portion to be used in salads, burritos, fajitas, gyros, soups, and casseroles.

---

apple and onion pot roast with gravy

Rely on your pressure cooker for pot roasts that are moist and tender. This recipe gets a nice flavor boost with a hint of apple flavor and the aroma of onions, which are blended into the gravy. Serve this beef roast with a side of mashed potatoes or with buttered noodles. • **SERVES 6 TO 8**

3 pounds boneless beef chuck roast
1 teaspoon salt
1 teaspoon freshly ground black pepper
1 teaspoon garlic powder
2 tablespoons olive oil
2 large onions, diced
½ cup apple juice
3 large tart apples, cored, peeled, and grated
1 (14-ounce) can beef broth
2 tablespoons cornstarch

Season the roast with the salt, pepper, and garlic powder. Heat the oil in the pressure cooker over medium-high heat and brown the beef on all sides. Set aside on a plate. Cook the onions until they begin to caramelize, stirring often, about 5 minutes. Deglaze the pot with the juice, scraping up any crusty brown bits from the bottom. Add the apples and broth, and stir to mix. Return the meat and any accumulated juices to the pressure cooker. Lock the lid in place. Bring to 15psi over high heat and immediately reduce the heat to the lowest possible setting to stabilize and maintain that pressure. Cook for 35 minutes. Remove from the heat and use the natural release method before opening the lid. Carefully lift out the roast to a serving platter and keep in a warm oven until ready to slice. Meanwhile, skim off any excess fat from surface of broth and then bring it to a boil. Cook, uncovered, until reduced to 2 cups, about 15 minutes.

To thicken the broth, mix the cornstarch in ⅓ cup cold water and stir it into the broth, simmering gently over low heat until it's the desired consistency. Taste and adjust seasoning. Carve the roast in thin slices and pass the gravy at the table.

corned beef with all the fixings

Corned beef and cabbage is one of my absolute favorite meals. For some people, corned beef and cabbage might be reserved for a special feast or only served on St. Patrick's Day. Traditionally, however, corned beef and cabbage is the quintessential New England boiled dinner. Cooked in a regular pot, a corned beef is usually boiled slowly for about 4 hours to draw out the excess salt and fat and get it tender enough to eat. That makes it a perfect choice for the pressure cooker, in which the cooking time is cut down to about 55 minutes.

The word *corn* in corned beef comes from an Old English usage that refers to a process of dry curing meat by packing it in coarse salt to draw the blood out of the meat, which preserved it back in the days before refrigeration. *Corn* describes the size and shape of the coarse rock salt used in the curing process, as it resembled a kernel of the grain. If you live in England, corned beef would be better known as a "corned silverside" or salt beef. In the United States, a corned beef is usually "pickled" or brined in salt water instead of dry cured in salt, but the name remains.

In the U.S., a corned beef is typically a brisket, rump, or round roast. The choice is between either the leaner flat or plank cut, which as its name implies is thinner and has a distinctive grain in the slices. The point cut is a rounder, thicker cut with more fat, and it may be priced a bit higher. Either cut will shrink by about one-third during cooking, so figure at least ⅓ pound per serving, or a more generous ½ pound if you have big appetites to feed. Be sure to add in the additional quantities needed if you plan to serve leftover corned beef in sandwiches and other recipes.

Include the condiments of your choice, such as spicy grainy mustard, horseradish, and or malt vinegar. I also add a loaf of good bakery rye bread, Irish soda bread, or dark pumpernickel (and be sure to pick up enough extra bread for sandwich making). • **SERVES 6**

Step One: THE SPICES

Usually a tiny packet of pickling spices is included in the corned beef package, and in most cases this isn't enough to actually add that distinctive flavor and aroma to the finished corned beef. If you want a deeper and more robust flavor in your corned beef, you can find premixed pickling spices in the spice aisle at most supermarkets, or try this custom blend that I use.

2 tablespoons pickling spices
1 teaspoon whole black peppercorns
½ teaspoon mustard seeds
¼ teaspoon celery seeds
½ teaspoon fennel seeds
2 large bay leaves
Pinch of red pepper flakes
½ teaspoon whole cloves
4 large cloves garlic, crushed

Tie all the spices into a square of cheesecloth. Alternatively, you may mix them together in a bowl and then add them loose to the pressure cooker, which is what I do.

Step Two: THE MEAT

Corned beef is usually sold in a shrink-wrapped package that contains some of the blood-tinged salt brine that was used in the curing process. Do not use the brine in the package to cook with. Place the package in a large colander in the sink, then cut it open and remove the packaging. Rinse the meat thoroughly to remove all the salty brine. A corned beef is usually boiled to draw out the salt and fat. You can use water, but I like to cook it in good, dark, stout ale to add flavor—and because a cold beer sure tastes good with a big corned beef sandwich the next day.

3 to 4 pounds corned beef brisket, your choice of flat or point cut, rinsed well and drained
1 pint stout or full-flavored beer, or use a combination of flavoring liquids such as beef broth or wine with water
The small seasoning packet packed with the meat, plus 3 cloves garlic, smashed, and 2 bay leaves, or use my spice blend (above)

Lay the brisket with the fattiest side up in the bottom of the pressure cooker. Add the stout and stir in the spices. Add additional flavoring liquid or water as needed to just cover the meat. Lock the lid in place. Bring to 15psi over high heat and immediately reduce the heat to the lowest possible setting to stabilize and maintain that pressure.

(continued)

Cook for 55 minutes. Remove from the heat and use the natural release method before opening the lid. Test for doneness using a meat thermometer; the internal temperature should be at least 160°F. Corned beef will have a natural pinkish-red color after cooking because nitrite is used in the curing process to give the meat its distinctive color, but this does not mean it isn't done, so don't rely on visual cues. The brisket should be fork-tender. If necessary, return to pressure for an additional 5 minutes and repeat the natural release. Transfer the brisket to a cutting board, cover it with foil and a folded towel, and let it stand for 10 to 15 minutes before slicing. This allows the meat to absorb its natural liquids, and it will continue to cook at the same time. Just before serving, carve the corned beef into thin slices across the grain and arrange them on a warmed platter.

Step Three: THE VEGETABLES

3 pounds assorted vegetables, such as carrots, red or white boiling potatoes, sweet potatoes, parsnips, turnips, rutabagas, Brussels sprouts, cabbage, and/or hard winter squash

While the meat is resting, it's time to cook the vegetables. Peel the vegetables as needed and cut the pieces to a similar size—I like hefty 2-inch chunks—so they cook uniformly. If using cabbage, cut into thick 2- to 3-inch wedges. Discard all but 2 cups of the cooking broth from the pressure cooker. Place the cooking rack in the pressure cooker and add all the vegetables. Lock the lid in place. Bring to 15psi over high heat and immediately reduce the heat to the lowest possible setting to stabilize and maintain that pressure. Cook for 4 minutes. Remove from the heat and use the quick or cold water release method before opening the lid. Using a slotted spoon, transfer the vegetables to serving bowls.

Serve some of the broth at the table to add flavor to the vegetables and beef. Refrigerate leftover brisket and vegetables separately for up to 4 days. Leftover corned beef may be frozen for up to 3 months.

beef brisket with potatoes, carrots, green beans and corn in onion sauce

This recipe is essentially a classier pot roast. The brisket is a beautiful piece of meat, but it's often overlooked. It's thick and large, very flavorful, and moderately priced for most budgets, but the downside is that a brisket is not just tough, but seriously tough—unless you have a pressure cooker. When you select a brisket, it should have a fair amount of fat on it, which helps make the meat come out significantly more succulent than when most of its fat is trimmed away. If your brisket is large, cut it into two more manageable pieces. The brisket cooks to perfect tenderness in the pressure cooker, and it tastes every bit as wonderful as it smells and looks. • **SERVES 6**

3 pounds beef brisket
Salt and freshly ground black pepper
2 tablespoons olive oil
2 medium onions, diced
2 tablespoons fresh Italian parsley
1 teaspoon dried thyme
2 bay leaves
4 cloves garlic, smashed
1 cup beef broth
2 tablespoons Worcestershire sauce
4 russet potatoes, peeled and each cut in 4 wedges
6 carrots, peeled and each quartered lengthwise
1 pound green beans, ends trimmed and cut into 2-inch pieces
4 ears fresh or frozen corn on the cob, cut into 3-inch pieces
2 tablespoons cornstarch

Season the brisket evenly on all sides with salt and pepper, pressing them into the meat with your fingertips. Heat the oil in the pressure cooker over medium-high heat and brown the meat on both sides. Set aside on a plate. Add the onions and cook, stirring often, until they start to turn golden in color, about 5 minutes. Meanwhile, make a bouquet garni by wrapping the parsley, thyme, bay leaves, and garlic in a cheesecloth and tying with kitchen string. Stir in the broth, Worcestershire sauce, and bouquet garni, and then arrange the meat and any accumulated juices in the pressure cooker. Lock the lid in place. Bring to 15psi over high heat and immediately reduce the heat to the lowest possible setting to stabilize and maintain that pressure. Cook for 55 minutes. Remove from the heat and use the natural release method before opening the lid. When the pressure cooker has depressurized, add the vegetables in the following order: potatoes, carrots, green beans, and corn. Return the cooker to high heat and bring up to 15psi. Cook for 4 minutes. Remove from the heat and use the quick release method before opening the lid. As soon as the pressure has dropped, transfer the vegetables from the cooker to a serving bowl. Transfer the brisket to a carving board

(continued)

to rest while you make the sauce. Discard the bouquet garni. Skim off any excess fat from the surface of the broth.

To thicken, make a slurry using the cornstarch mixed with ⅓ cup water. Slowly stir the mixture into the broth and simmer gently over medium heat until it's the desired consistency. Taste and adjust seasoning to taste. Ladle the onion sauce into a serving bowl to be passed at the table. Slice the brisket, or cut it into large portions as you like, and serve immediately.

COOK'S NOTE: Even though the recipe calls for only 1 cup of liquid, you'll have quite a bit of broth, as the meat and vegetables will produce an enormous amount of juices as they cook. If the quantity is more than you need or want to serve with the meal, before adding any thickener, portion some of it into freezer bags for later use in soups and stews.

---

meat loaf with mushroom gravy

Meat loaf is great, old-fashioned, home-style cooking at its best, tasty, satisfying, and economical. What's not to like? This is an easy-to-do weeknight dinner, and if there are any leftovers, use them to make sandwiches the next day. Partner this recipe with a side dish of potatoes. • **SERVES 4**

- 1½ pounds lean ground beef
- 1 small onion, finely chopped
- ⅔ cup soft bread crumbs
- 2 large eggs, lightly beaten
- 1 teaspoon salt
- ¼ teaspoon freshly ground black pepper
- 1 teaspoon ground sage
- 1 (15-ounce) can beef broth
- 1 cup dry red wine
- 3 cloves garlic, minced
- 8 ounces fresh white or cremini mushrooms, washed and sliced
- 2 tablespoons cornstarch

Place the beef, half the onion, the bread crumbs, eggs, salt, pepper, and sage in the bowl of a stand mixer with the paddle attachment. On a low setting, blend the ingredients into a smooth and uniform consistency for a finely textured meat loaf. As an alternative, place the ingredients in a 1-gallon plastic food bag and zip it closed. Knead the meat mixture through the bag until the ingredients are thoroughly mixed, and your hands will stay clean. Pack all the meat mixture into a springform pan or any pan that will fit in your pressure cooker. Tightly crimp a square of aluminum foil over the top of the pan. Add the broth, wine, garlic, the remaining onion, and the mushrooms to the pressure cooker. Place the cooking rack on the bottom and use foil helper handles to lower the meat loaf pan inside the pressure cooker. Lock the lid in place. Bring to 15psi over high heat and immediately reduce the heat to the lowest possible setting to stabilize and maintain that pressure. Cook for 20 minutes. Remove from the heat and use the quick release method before opening the lid. Carefully lift the meat loaf out of the pressure cooker and place it in a pie plate to catch any drips.

To thicken the broth, make a slurry using the cornstarch mixed in ⅓ cup water. Stir the slurry into the broth, simmering gently over medium heat until it's the desired consistency. Taste and adjust seasonings as desired. Pour the mushroom gravy into a small bowl to be passed with the meat loaf. Release the springform pan and slide the meat loaf onto a serving plate. Slice the meat loaf into wedges just as you would cut a cake, and serve with the mushroom gravy.

spinach-and-cheese-stuffed meat loaf

There's something about a meat loaf that seems to attract people. Maybe it's some fond childhood memories we all share, or that it's all meat and it goes so well with potatoes, or that it makes a great sandwich. This recipe happened quite by chance when I was going to use pesto for the stuffing but didn't have all the ingredients on hand. The spinach was a last-minute substitute—and it worked. • **SERVES 4 TO 6**

Step One: THE FILLING

- 1 (10-ounce) package frozen chopped spinach, thawed and well drained
- ½ cup shredded mozzarella cheese
- 3 tablespoons grated Parmesan cheese
- 1 teaspoon dried Italian herb blend
- ½ cup Italian seasoned dry bread crumbs

Place all the ingredients in a large bowl and blend into a smooth and uniform consistency. Set aside.

Step Two: THE MEAT

- 1½ pounds lean ground beef
- 2 large eggs, lightly beaten
- 1 small onion, diced
- 2 cloves garlic, minced
- ¾ cup Italian-style pasta sauce
- ¾ cup Italian seasoned dry bread crumbs
- 1 teaspoon salt
- ¼ teaspoon freshly ground black pepper
- ½ cup grated mozzarella or Parmesan cheese

Place the beef, eggs, onion, garlic, ½ cup of the pasta sauce, bread crumbs, salt, and pepper in the bowl of a stand mixer with the paddle attachment. On a low setting, blend the ingredients into a smooth and uniform consistency for a finely textured meat loaf. As an alternative, place the ingredients in a 1-gallon sealable plastic bag and zip it closed. Knead the meat mixture through the bag until the ingredients are thoroughly mixed, and your hands will stay clean.

Place the cooking rack in the bottom of the pressure cooker and add ½ cup water. Place a sheet of waxed paper on a clean work surface and pat the beef mixture into a rectangle about 7 by 10 inches. Spread the filling over the beef, leaving a margin of about ½ inch around the edges. Starting at the short end, roll the beef up jellyroll fashion. Press the beef mixture at both ends over the filling to seal. Place the roll, seam side down, in a 7-inch loaf pan or any insert pan that will fit within the diameter of your pressure cooker. Spread the remaining ¼ cup pasta sauce over the top of the meat loaf. Loosely cover the meat loaf pan with a square of foil. Use foil helper handles to position the pan in the pressure cooker. Lock the lid in place. Bring to 15psi over high heat and immediately reduce the heat to the lowest possible setting to stabilize and maintain that pressure. Cook for 20 minutes. Remove from the heat and use the quick release method before opening the lid. Carefully lift the meat loaf out of the pressure cooker and place it in a pie plate to catch any drips. Remove any fat that may have collected around the meat loaf. Transfer to a serving platter and cut into 1-inch-thick slices. Top with the cheese when serving.

stuffed mexican meat loaf with "baked" potatoes

Need a creative way to spice up your tired old meat loaf? Stuff it! Treat your family to this two-course meal of big baked potatoes and my Mexican-inspired meat loaf. With just enough piquant flavors from the cumin, peppers, and cilantro to make it interesting, this is an easy recipe that's suitable for a midweek dinner. Every Latin culture around the world has their own version of sofrito, and each region will have their own variations using local ingredients. When we lived in Spain, the sofrito mix was typically cilantro, onions, peppers, and garlic, all laboriously chopped by hand. In my area, the sofrito mix is often a blend of Southern California and Mexican cuisines, and it usually is made with cilantro, onions, mild chile peppers, and tomatoes, conveniently chopped in a food processor. The sofrito mixture can be altered to suit individual tastes as well as the ingredients available, but the purpose is to add a big boost of flavors to the finished dish.

Besides the delicious taste the sofrito adds to this meat loaf, there's a surprise inside with the melted cheese center. Complete the meal be adding a crisp salad and buttery crescent rolls.

• **SERVES 4**

1 pound lean ground beef
1 cup sofrito mix (equal amounts of diced onion, pasilla chile, and fresh cilantro)
⅔ cup ground corn chips
1 large egg
1½ teaspoons ground cumin
1 teaspoon salt
½ teaspoon freshly ground black pepper
Queso blanco (Mexican white cheese), cut 1 inch square and less than the length of the loaf pan
4 large russet potatoes, scrubbed
4 tablespoons (½ stick) butter
½ cup crema agria (Mexican-style sour cream) or sour cream
1 cup pico de gallo (page 45) or refrigerated prepared pico de gallo

Place the beef, sofrito mix, corn chips, egg, cumin, salt, and pepper in the bowl of a stand mixer with the paddle attachment. On a low setting, blend the ingredients into a smooth and uniform consistency for a finely textured meat loaf. As an alternative, place the ingredients in a 1-gallon sealable plastic bag and zip it closed. Knead the meat mixture through the bag until the ingredients are thoroughly mixed, and your hands will stay clean. Divide the meat mixture into two parts. Lightly spray a loaf pan, or any suitable metal or silicone pan that will fit in your pressure cooker, with nonstick cooking spray. Pack half the meat mixture into the pan. Place the cheese lengthwise down the middle of the meat mixture, leaving about ½ inch clear at each end to seal the ends and keep the cheese inside as it melts. Pack the remaining half of the meat mixture on top of the cheese, pushing it down firmly to merge the top and bottom halves and seal the edges all around the pan. Tightly crimp a square of aluminum foil over the top of the insert pan. Place the cooking rack on the bottom of the pressure cooker and use foil helper handles to lower the meat loaf pan inside. Lock the lid in place. Bring to 15psi over high heat and immediately reduce the heat to the lowest possible setting to stabilize and maintain that pressure. Cook for 9 minutes. Remove from the heat and use the quick release method before opening the lid. Carefully add the potatoes to the cooker, along the side of the loaf pan. If the potatoes are too large, place them in a steamer tray and sit it on top of the loaf pan. Return to pressure and cook for an additional 12 minutes. Remove from the heat and use the natural release method before opening the lid. Lift out the potatoes. Use a fork to make a dotted line from end to end and then push to open each potato by squeezing the ends toward the center using oven mitts or pot holders. Mash up the inside with a fork and season with salt and pepper. Top each potato with butter as desired and a dollop of crema agria. Carefully uncover the meat loaf and pour off any accumulated far and juices. Turn the meat loaf out on a serving plate and slice into serving portions. Arrange the slices and top with the pico de gallo. Serve hot.

porcupine meatballs

These little meatballs are an old-time classic pressure cooker recipe with many variations. No matter how they are customized, tweaked, or personalized, these meatballs are always a hit with the kids, and there's plenty to satisfy even the heartiest appetites. In this version, the porcupines are braised in your favorite pasta sauce. Serve them over a bed of fluffy white rice, or mix it up with mashed potatoes or cooked noodles. • **SERVES 4**

1 pound lean ground beef
½ cup long-grain white rice
½ cup minced onion
1 teaspoon salt
¼ teaspoon freshly ground black pepper
½ cup beef broth
1 teaspoon garlic powder
½ teaspoon red pepper flakes
2 teaspoons dried Italian herb blend
1 (26-ounce) jar tomato-based pasta sauce of your choice

Place the beef, rice, onion, salt, and black pepper in the bowl of a stand mixer with the paddle attachment. On a low setting, blend the ingredients into a smooth and uniform consistency, or mix by hand. Use a small ice cream scoop to quickly make the meatballs. Alternately, shape the meatballs by hand, making them 1 to 1½ inches in diameter. Add the broth, garlic powder, red pepper flakes, and herb blend to the pressure cooker, stirring well. Evenly distribute the meatballs around the bottom of the pressure cooker. Pour the pasta sauce on top, but do not stir. Lock the lid in place. Bring to 15psi over high heat and immediately reduce the heat to the lowest possible setting to stabilize and maintain that pressure. Cook for 6 minutes. Remove from the heat and use the natural release method before opening the lid. Transfer the porcupines and sauce to a serving dish.

lamb shanks in port wine sauce

When I was growing up, lamb shanks were a flavorful and very economical cut of meat. Like other shank cuts, they are tough and it takes several hours of cooking before they are tender enough to eat, unless you use a pressure cooker. My mom could feed four hungry children with a heap of lamb shanks, and I did the same, stretching my food budget and serving up delicious, fork-tender lamb. Nowadays it's no longer a poor man's dish, and the humble lamb shank has sky-rocketed to fame as celebrity chefs and fine restaurants dish up gourmet recipes highlighting this mouthwatering cut of meat. Serve these lamb shanks with a side of potatoes, polenta, or white beans. • **SERVES 4**

4 large lamb shanks, about 1 pound each
Salt and freshly ground black pepper to taste
2 to 3 tablespoons olive oil
1 large onion, diced
12 cloves garlic, smashed
1 tablespoon dried rosemary or 4 sprigs fresh rosemary
½ cup chicken broth
½ cup port wine
2 bay leaves
2 tablespoons tomato paste
3 tablespoons balsamic vinegar
1 tablespoon butter

Trim the excess fat from the shanks and season them with salt and pepper. Heat the oil in the pressure cooker over medium-high heat and brown the shanks well on all sides. Add the onion and cook until soft. Add the garlic and rosemary and continue to cook and stir until they are just lightly browned, taking care not to let them burn. Deglaze the cooker with the broth, scraping up all those crusty brown bits from the bottom. Stir in the wine and add the bay leaves. Dot the tomato paste on top of the liquid, but do not stir. Lock the lid in place. Bring to 15psi over high heat, and immediately reduce the heat to the lowest possible setting to stabilize and maintain that pressure. Cook for 35 minutes. Remove from the heat and use the natural release method before opening the lid. Transfer the lamb shanks to a serving plate. Discard the bay leaves and bring the wine sauce to a boil, uncovered, over high heat. Continue to cook and stir for about 8 minutes to reduce the sauce by half. When the sauce has thickened, whisk in the vinegar and butter. Taste and adjust seasoning as desired. Return the lamb shanks to the pressure cooker and turn them several times to coat with the sauce. Arrange the lamb shanks on plates and serve the remaining port wine sauce in a separate bowl.

greek-style lamb with traditional tzatziki

This spicy recipe is a personal favorite of mine. It takes a bit of planning, but there's no rush and you can leisurely do the prep work at your own pace over the span of a few days if that's more convenient. A well-seasoned dish of tender chunks of lamb and succulent caramelized onions is served with a traditional Greek tzatziki, a luscious sauce made of thick Greek yogurt mixed with cucumbers and garlic. This is a versatile recipe that is easily customized to suite your own tastes. To get you started with some serving suggestions, spoon the lamb over couscous, rice, or polenta, and or even smashed potatoes or noodles with a dollop of the tzatziki on top. Use it in a chilled salad with the tzatziki as a dressing. I like to make gyros with the leftovers, or you could try the lamb stuffed into toasted pitas with lettuce, sliced tomatoes, cucumbers, and crumbled feta cheese mixed with the creamy tzatziki. Keep it simple if you like, and just pile the big chunks of lamb and onions on a bun with a spoonful of the cool, creamy sauce on the side.

• SERVES 4 TO 6

Step One: THE TZATZIKI

This tangy Greek sauce begins with Greek yogurt, which is thicker than sour cream but richer and much more flavorful. This is delicious stuff, so good that you might be tempted to use it to replace regular sour cream in potatoes, dips, salad dressings, and any other recipes calling for sour cream or yogurt. Prepare the sauce well in advance to allow time for the flavors to marry.

1 large cucumber
2 cups Greek-style yogurt
4 cloves garlic, roasted (see page 252; more is better, but use any amount to suit your taste)
2 tablespoons chopped fresh dill weed or 1 teaspoon dried dill weed
Zest of 1 lemon
Salt and coarsely ground black pepper to taste

Peel the cucumber and cut it in half lengthwise. Use a spoon to scoop out all the seeds. Dice the cucumber, spread out on paper towels, and pat dry to adsorb excess moisture. Place the yogurt in a glass bowl. Gently fold in the cucumbers, garlic, dill, half the lemon zest, and salt and pepper. Cover and chill for a minimum of 2 hours; stir before serving.

Step Two: THE CARAMELIZED ONIONS

6 strips thick-cut bacon, chopped
3 large sweet onions, thinly sliced
2 tablespoons honey

Cook the bacon in a heavy skillet over medium-high heat until the fat is rendered and the bits are crisp. Transfer the bacon to paper towels to drain. Pour off and reserve all but 2 tablespoons of the bacon drippings , and cook the onions for about 15 minutes, or until they become soft and begin to change color. Lower the heat and add the honey, stirring often to prevent scorching as the onions turn a deep caramel color. Remove from the heat and set aside on a plate.

Step Three: THE LAMB

2 pounds boneless lamb, cut into 2-inch cubes
Salt and coarsely ground black pepper to taste
2 tablespoons bacon drippings (from the caramelized onions)
½ cup red wine
Juice of 1 lemon
4 cloves garlic, smashed and minced
½ teaspoon red pepper flakes
½ teaspoon ground nutmeg
One 2- to 3-inch cinnamon stick
5 whole cloves
10 whole black peppercorns

Season the lamb with salt and coarsely ground pepper. Heat the bacon drippings in the pressure cooker over medium-high heat and brown the lamb on all sides in small batches. Return the lamb, onions, and all their accumulated juices to the pressure cooker. Stir in the wine, lemon juice, garlic, red pepper flakes, and nutmeg. Make a bouquet garni, tying the cinnamon stick, cloves and peppercorns in a piece of cheesecloth, and push it below the liquid. Lock the lid in place. Bring to 15psi over high heat and immediately reduce the heat to the lowest possible setting to stabilize and maintain that pressure. Cook for 30 minutes. Remove from the heat and use the natural release method before opening the lid. Remove the bouquet garni. Use a slotted spoon to transfer the lamb to a plate. Turn the heat to medium and reduce the sauce by half. Add the lamb and the reserved bacon to the sauce, stirring to mix. Let the mixture simmer until heated through. Taste and adjust seasonings as needed. Serve the lamb with a dollop of tzatziki sauce, and sprinkle the remaining lemon zest on top.

(continued)

COOK'S NOTE: Greek yogurt seems to be everywhere these days, but if you can't find it, it's really easy to make at home: Line a wire strainer or colander with a double layer of cheesecloth and set it in a bowl. Add a 16-ounce container of plain, full-fat yogurt to the strainer and cover with plastic wrap. Let it drain in the refrigerator for at least 8 hours or overnight. The longer it sits, the thicker and firmer it becomes, and if you're very patient, in 24 hours you'll have a spreadable, creamy cheese for your toasted bagels . . . but that has nothing to do with this recipe, so moving on . . . Your homemade Greek-style yogurt is ready for use any time after the minimum 8 hours. Spoon the thickened yogurt into a tightly sealed storage container and keep refrigerated up to 1 week. The frugal cook will save the drained liquid (whey) for use within 3 days as a wholesome and nutritious substitute for part of the milk used in pancakes and baked goods.

braised lamb shanks with carrots and potatoes

Lamb shanks are a very economical cut of meat, but in addition to being a great budget stretcher, they have a fabulous flavor. This is so easy to make and doesn't take too much work to get everything all prepped, and then you just sit back and relax while the pressure cooker does that thing it does so well. These shanks are braised with fresh rosemary, garlic, and wine, and by adding baby carrots and tiny new potatoes, this becomes a delicious two-course meal. Of course, you can serve the meat with any other side dish such as polenta, or my family's favorite, roasted garlic mashed potatoes. However you decide to customize it, you'll need something to soak up the wonderful sauce. This is a fantastic meal for two, and it can easily be doubled for company. • **SERVES 2**

2 large lamb shanks, about 1 pound each, trimmed of fat
Salt and freshly ground black pepper to taste
1 large onion, diced
½ cup port wine
½ cup chicken stock
2 tablespoons tomato paste
12 cloves garlic, smashed flat
3 sprigs fresh rosemary, each about 3 inches long
2 cups baby carrots
8 to 10 baby red potatoes, about 1½ inches in diameter, scrubbed
1 tablespoon butter
1 tablespoon balsamic vinegar

Season the shanks with generous amounts of salt and pepper. Heat the oil in the pressure cooker over medium-high heat and brown the shanks on all sides. Set aside on a plate. Add the onion and cook until soft, stirring often as they begin to turn golden. Deglaze the pot with the wine, scraping up any crusty brown bits from the bottom. Blend the stock with the tomato paste, and pour the mixture into the pressure cooker, stirring well. Tie the garlic and rosemary in a small square of cheesecloth and place it in the broth. Return the meat and any accumulated juices to the pressure cooker. Lock the lid in place. Bring to 15psi over high heat and immediately reduce the heat to the lowest possible setting to stabilize and maintain that pressure. Cook for 35 minutes. Remove from the heat and use the quick release method before opening the lid. Add the carrots and potatoes, arranging them around the sides of the meat. Return to pressure for another 4 minutes. Remove from the heat and use the quick release method before opening the lid. Transfer the lamb shanks, carrots, and potatoes to a serving plate and keep warm in a low oven. Discard the garlic and rosemary. Skim off any excess fat from the surface of broth and bring it to a boil over medium-high heat. Reduce the sauce by half and then whisk in the butter and vinegar. Taste and adjust seasoning as desired. Serve the wine sauce in a separate bowl to be passed at the table.

side dishes

butter-braised cabbage

This super-simple side dish is not only full of flavor, but it's also quick and easy to make. The fresh, sweet, buttery cabbage is a great accompaniment to any pork or ham entree and pairs nicely with spicy sausages as well. • **SERVES 4 OR 5**

1 head green cabbage head
4 tablespoons (½ stick) butter
Salt and coarsely ground black pepper to taste
¼ teaspoon ground nutmeg
½ cup chicken broth

Discard the tough or blemished outer leaves of the cabbage. Cut the head of cabbage into quarters, and remove the tough core. Coarsely chop the cabbage. Melt the butter in the pressure cooker over medium-high heat and add salt and pepper, the nutmeg, broth, and cabbage. Lock the lid in place. Bring to 15psi over high heat and immediately reduce the heat to the lowest possible setting to stabilize and maintain that pressure. Cook for 3 minutes. Remove from the heat and use the cold water release method before opening the lid. Use a slotted spoon to transfer the cabbage to a serving bowl.

Variation:

BRAISED SWEET RED CABBAGE

Substitute 1 head red cabbage for the green cabbage, and replace the chicken broth with apple juice.

honey-glazed herbed baby carrots

A quick and tantalizingly sweet way to serve carrots with just a hint of dill. It's sweet and savory at the same time, and the aroma of the thyme and dill will tickle your taste buds. • **SERVES 4**

1 pound baby carrots
2 tablespoons butter
1 teaspoon dried dill weed
1 teaspoon dried thyme
½ cup honey
Salt to taste

Add ½ cup water to the pressure cooker. Place the carrots in a steamer tray. Place the tray in the cooker, using a cooking rack if needed to elevate it above the water level. Lock the lid in place. Bring to 15psi over high heat and immediately reduce the heat to the lowest possible setting to stabilize and maintain that pressure. Cook for 3 minutes. Remove from the heat and use the quick release method before opening the lid. Lift out the carrots, pour off the water, and wipe the pressure cooker dry. Melt the butter in the pressure cooker over medium heat. Add the dill weed and thyme, frying for a couple of minutes until they become fragrant. Add the honey and salt, stirring to blend. Cook and continue stirring as the glaze thickens and clings to the spoon. Add the cooked carrots to the glaze, turning gently until they are all well coated with the honey mixture and heated through. Spoon the carrots and any remaining glaze into a serving bowl.

glazed carrot and cranberry compote

This is a lovely and festive dish to serve with weekday dinner on a chilly winter day or as part of your holiday menu. Not only is it vividly colored with bright orange and deep red, but it also has a sweet and tangy flavor that will wake up your taste buds and spice up your meal. This is a quick and easy side that requires almost no prep work if you use prepackaged baby carrots.

• **SERVES 4 TO 6**

- 1 cup apple cider
- 1 pound baby carrots or 4 to 5 regular carrots, peeled and cut into ½-inch slices
- 1½ cups fresh or frozen whole cranberries
- 1 tablespoon butter
- ¼ cup packed light brown sugar
- 2 tablespoons maple syrup
- ½ teaspoon ground nutmeg
- Pinch of salt

Pour the cider into the pressure cooker and add the carrots and cranberries. Lock the lid in place. Bring to 15psi over high heat and immediately reduce the heat to the lowest possible setting to stabilize and maintain that pressure. Cook for 3 minutes. Remove from the heat and use the quick release method before opening the lid. Use a slotted spoon to transfer the carrots and cranberries to a serving bowl. Bring the apple cider in the pressure cooker to a boil over medium heat and stir occasionally until it is reduced by half, about 10 minutes. Stir in the butter, sugar, maple syrup, nutmeg, and salt, and continue stirring and cooking until the glaze begins to get sticky and coat the spoon. Return the carrots and cranberries to the pressure cooker and stir gently to coat them with the glaze. Serve immediately.

five-minute roasted garlic

If you're a garlic lover, you probably enjoy garlic in pretty much all its forms, but raw garlic is two to four times stronger in flavor than roasted garlic. When cooked, garlic becomes soft and easy to spread. It also develops a richer and milder flavor and adds a wonderful aroma to many recipes. Still, many people are reluctant to it use it because conventional methods for roasting garlic include lots of added oil and lots of waiting while the garlic cooks in the oven for up to an hour. Using my quick and easy way to make roasted garlic in the pressure cooker, now you can have all the roasted garlic you'll ever want in just a few minutes. Use it immediately by just squeezing the pulp out of a clove and spreading it on fresh or toasted bread, or adding it to salad dressings or baked potatoes, as well as any recipe that call for garlic.

3 to 4 large heads garlic

Remove the papery skin from the garlic heads and select the largest and plumpest cloves. Remove the papery skins from the cloves, but do not peel. Place the cooking rack in the pressure cooker and add ½ cup water. Arrange the unpeeled garlic cloves in a single layer in a perforated metal steamer tray that will fit inside your pressure cooker. Set the tray of garlic on top of the cooking rack. Lock the lid in place. Bring to 15psi over high heat and immediately reduce the heat to the lowest possible setting to stabilize and maintain that pressure. Cook for 5 minutes. Remove from the heat and use the natural release method before opening the lid. Remove the garlic and set aside until cool enough to handle. Using kitchen scissors, snip off the flatter end off each clove and squeeze out the buttery soft roasted garlic pulp inside. Mash the pulp to a smooth consistency with a fork and use immediately, or refrigerate in a tightly sealed container to use as needed. Keeps for about 1 week.

BONUS RECIPE

roasted garlic butter

Use this handy spread for bruschetta, tapas, garlic bread, potatoes, or for adding some flavor to steamed vegetables or meats.

½ cup (1 stick) butter
2 to 4 cloves garlic, roasted (see page 252), depending on your taste

Slice the butter into pats, put them in a small glass bowl, and let them soften to room temperature. When the butter is soft, squeeze in the garlic pulp and mash with a fork until it is smoothly blended. Pack the garlic butter into a tightly sealed container and refrigerate for up to 1 week.

MAKES ½ CUP

---

garlicky green beans and summer squash

This is quick, simple, and gorgeous food with lots of bright, fresh colors and tender but still crisp summer vegetables. Taking only three minutes to cook in a pressure cooker, it's a good recipe for those days when the temperature makes spending a lot of time in front of the stove an unwelcome chore. There's not a lot of prep time needed to get this dish on the table, and I've included a bonus recipe so you can make this versatile dish two ways. • **SERVES 4**

Step One: THE GARLICKY SAUCE

4 tablespoons (½ stick) butter
½ teaspoon dried thyme
1 shallot, finely chopped
4 cloves garlic, finely minced
¼ cup chopped pimientos

Melt the butter in a large skillet over medium heat and add the dried thyme. Stirring often, cook the shallot and garlic in the butter until soft and translucent, but do not brown. Add the pimientos and remove from the heat.

Step Two: THE VEGETABLES

1 pound green beans, ends trimmed
1 pound yellow summer squash, ends trimmed and cut into ½-inch-thick slices

Place the cooking rack in the pressure cooker and add ½ cup water. Add the green beans and the yellow summer squash. Lock the lid in place. Bring to 15psi over high heat and immediately reduce the heat to the lowest possible setting to stabilize and maintain that pressure. Cook for 3 minutes. Remove from the heat and use the cold water release method before opening the lid.

Step Three: THE FINALE

Salt and coarsely ground black pepper to taste

Heat the skillet with the garlic sauce over medium heat. Drain the beans and squash and then add them to the sauce, stirring gently until well coated and heated through. Add salt and pepper as desired. Spoon the vegetables into a serving dish, using a rubber spatula to get all the sauce. Serve immediately.

BONUS RECIPE

garlicky green bean and summer squash salad

2 cups halved cherry tomatoes
1½ cups Italian vinaigrette dressing
⅓ cup crumbled feta cheese

Prepare the recipe as directed, adding cherry tomatoes and your favorite Italian salad dressing to the finished recipe. Refrigerate in a tightly closed container and chill for several hours to allow the vegetables to marinate. Serve chilled with a sprinkling of feta cheese on each portion.

SERVES 4

kale colcannon

There are many regional variations on the Irish colcannon theme, a rustic dish made from coarsely mashed potatoes and cabbage. The Dutch have their *stamppot*, in Germany it's *Gruenkohl*, and the English version is called "bubble and squeak." By whatever name you call it, this dish has enough personality to stand up to all kinds of personal touches, so don't hesitate to make it your own by adding sour cream, sautéed leeks, onions, chives or garlic, or bits of leftover ham, sausage, or bacon.

My grandma was fond of kale, or "farmer's cabbage" as she called it, but today, many folks are likely to think of kale as just an ornamental decoration for supermarket display cases or the plate garnish that we toss aside at restaurants. With its ruffled, deep green leaves and mild flavor, kale is more than just a pretty vegetable, though. It's a great way to introduce greens to your dinner table.

• **SERVES 5**

Step One: THE VEGETABLES

2 pounds russet potatoes, peeled and cut into 1½-inch cubes
1 bunch kale, ribs removed and leaves cut into pieces
4 or 5 cloves garlic (do not peel)

Pour ½ cup water into a large pressure cooker. Place the potatoes in a perforated steaming basket and lower it into the bottom of the pressure cooker as the lower tier. If necessary, use a cooking rack to elevate the potatoes above the waterline. Place the kale into a plain insert pan without holes, and crimp a square of aluminum foil around the rim to cover the top. Arrange the insert pan with the kale as the second tier on top of the potatoes. Place the garlic on top of the foil covering the kale. Lock the lid in place. Bring to 15psi over high heat, then immediately reduce the heat to the lowest possible setting to stabilize and maintain that pressure. Cook for 4 minutes. Remove from the heat and use the natural release method before opening the lid.

Step Two: SMASH THE POTATOES

½ cup (1 stick) butter, softened
Salt and coarsely ground black pepper to taste
⅓ cup hot milk

Snip off the flattest end of each roasted garlic clove, pop out the buttery soft goodness inside, and mash to a smooth consistency. Transfer the potatoes to a mixing bowl and smash them with a potato masher or use your own preferred method, taking care to leave the potatoes with a coarse texture. To use a stand mixer with the paddle attachment, just pulse the power, taking care not to overwork the potatoes or you'll go from rustic, coarsely smashed potatoes to a glob of gluey potato starch in the blink of an eye. Add the mashed garlic, the softened butter, salt, and a very generous amount of black pepper to the potatoes. Add only enough milk to get the desired consistency and mix gently.

Step Three: SAUTÉ THE KALE

2 tablespoons butter

Melt the butter in a skillet over medium heat. Add the cooked kale and cook, stirring, as it wilts down to about a quarter of its volume, about 3 minutes. Gently fold the pieces of kale into the smashed potatoes, taste for seasoning, and adjust as desired. Transfer to a serving dish.

old-fashioned creamy mashed potatoes 101

Mashed potatoes are an American staple. Nothing beats a big bowl of fluffy, buttery spuds. It's the starch that gives mashed potatoes that highly prized, fluffy texture, so choose potatoes with a high starch content. There are several good varieties, like Yukon golds or yellow Finns, which have a butter-yellow interior, but the russet potato (also called the Idaho or baking potato) remains the most popular choice and is readily available throughout the year in any supermarket. Mature potatoes get a little drier and starchier as they age, and that makes them mash up even lighter and fluffier.

The pressure cooker excels at cooking potatoes, but when potatoes are drowned and boiled in water, they become soggy and waterlogged, and that makes for wet, sticky mashed potatoes. Knowing that dry potatoes make for lighter, fluffier mashed potatoes, use my PIP cooking method to elevate the cut potatoes above the waterline and allow them to cook in the superheated steam.

Once the potatoes are cooked, use your preferred method to quickly mash the dry potatoes with generous amounts of salt and pepper while they are still hot. My elderlies always made the best mashed potatoes by using an old-fashioned wire-mesh utensil that came as a giveaway hidden in a sack of cornmeal. Some cooks swear by a potato ricer to make the smoothest potatoes. With caution not to overwork the potatoes and end up with gluey spuds, I use a big stand mixer. You don't absolutely need to add butter to mashed potatoes, but it does add flavor and a lovely, unctuous mouthfeel. Add softened butter while mashing the potatoes. Avoid margarines, as they contain water, which will make your potatoes gooey and wet. As an alternative to butter, drizzle a couple of tablespoons of excellent-quality extra-virgin olive oil over the potatoes as you mash them. This is particularly good with added herbs, garlic, or strong cheeses.

A touch of milk or cream gives mashed potatoes a creamy, silky smooth texture that everyone loves, but add too much and you'll have potato soup. The exact amount needed depends not only on the texture of the potatoes, but also on the creaminess you desire. The trick is to add milk sparingly when the potatoes are almost completely mashed, using only enough to reach the perfect consistency. Finally, add any extra ingredients, like cheese, at the end, gently folding them into the mashed potatoes until just blended. • **SERVES 6**

- 4 large Idaho baking potatoes (about 2 pounds), peeled and cut into 2-inch pieces
- ⅓ cup milk
- 4 tablespoons (½ stick) butter, softened, plus more for garnish (optional)
- Salt and coarsely ground black pepper to taste

Pour ½ cup water into the pressure cooker and place the cooking rack on the bottom. Put the potatoes in a steamer tray and place it on top of the cooking rack. Lock the lid in place. Bring to 15psi over high heat and immediately reduce the heat to the lowest possible setting to stabilize and maintain that pressure. Cook for 4 minutes. Remove from the heat and use the natural release method before opening the lid. Lift out the potatoes, drain the water from the pressure cooker, and wipe it dry. Heat the milk in a heatproof glass container in a microwave oven on High until scalded. Put the cooked potatoes back in the pressure cooker and add the softened butter, salt, and a very generous amount of black pepper. Use a potato masher or whatever method you prefer to mash the potatoes to a smooth consistency. To use a stand mixer with the paddle attachment, just pulse the power, taking care not to overwork the potatoes. Slowly add small amounts of hot milk to get the desired creaminess. Transfer the mashed potatoes to a serving bowl and garnish with a pat of butter on top if desired.

COOK'S NOTE: Scalding milk is heating milk to a point where small bubbles start to appear around the edges and it's just about to reach the boiling point. This can be done in a saucepan on the stove as well as in the microwave.

---

rosemary buttered red potatoes

This is the simplest, but most elegant, potato dish ever! Do add a couple of sprigs of rosemary to your shopping list for this recipe; any extras freeze well and can be used in other recipes. The tantalizing aroma of rosemary will fill your kitchen and make your mouth water. • **SERVES 4**

8 medium red potatoes, scrubbed and each cut into about 6 wedges
3 tablespoons butter
1 heaping tablespoon fresh rosemary, finely minced, or 1½ teaspoons finely crushed dried rosemary
Salt and coarsely ground black pepper to taste

Pour ½ cup water into the pressure cooker. Place the cooking rack in the bottom. Place the potato wedges in a steamer tray and set it on top of the rack. Lock the lid in place. Bring to 15psi over high heat and immediately reduce the heat to the lowest possible setting to stabilize and maintain that pressure. Cook for 4 minutes. Remove from the heat and use the quick release method before opening the lid. Lift out the potatoes and drain the water from the pressure cooker. Heat the butter in the pressure cooker over medium heat and add the rosemary, letting it sizzle until it's fragrant. Add the potato wedges and salt and pepper, stirring gently to lightly fry them to a delicate light gold color. Spoon the potatoes into a serving bowl and drizzle any remaining butter and rosemary over the top.

cracked potatoes with rosemary and garlic butter sauce

Garlic lovers, rejoice! These red potatoes get a big flavor boost from mellow roasted garlic and fresh rosemary. Not only do these potatoes smell divine, but they also look heavenly. Flattened, the red skins crack open to reveal the white potato inside, and it's all topped off with melting herbed garlic butter and sliced scallions. • **SERVES 8**

Step One: THE ROSEMARY BUTTER SAUCE

Prepare this at least 2 hours in advance of serving to allow the flavors to marry.

4 cloves garlic, roasted (see page 252) and mashed to a pulp
1 tablespoon minced fresh rosemary or 1 teaspoon dried crushed rosemary
½ cup (1 stick) butter, softened

Mix the garlic pulp and rosemary with the softened butter. Scoop the butter mixture onto a sheet of waxed paper and form it into a log shape. Refrigerate in a tightly sealed container until needed.

Step Two: THE CRACKED POTATOES

Choose rounded potatoes about the size of your closed fist for this dish.

8 medium red potatoes, scrubbed
Salt and coarsely ground black pepper to taste
3 scallion tops, thinly sliced

Pour ½ cup water into the pressure cooker and place the cooking rack in the bottom. Arrange the potatoes on the rack. Lock the lid in place. Bring to 15psi over high heat and immediately reduce the heat to the lowest possible setting to stabilize and maintain that pressure. Cook for 8 minutes. Remove from the heat and use the natural release method before opening the lid. Transfer the potatoes to a cutting board. Using a solid rolling pin or a heavy pan, flatten each potato, cracking the top open while leaving the bottom intact. Arrange on a serving plate and season generously with salt and pepper. Unwrap the chilled rosemary-garlic butter and cut into ½-inch slices. Place a pat of the butter mixture on top of each cracked potato and sprinkle with the scallions. Pass any remaining rosemary-garlic butter pats at the table.

COOK'S NOTE: Want more? Fry 6 bacon strips until crisp. Crumble the bacon and sprinkle on top of the potatoes. Want "the works"? Add grated sharp cheddar cheese and a dollop of sour cream.

---

red potatoes and brussels sprouts in garlic-dill butter

A simple dish that pairs two companionable old friends in an interesting herbed sauce makes for a flavorsome side dish that will match up with any meat. It's very quick and easy to prepare, and it's always nice to serve two different vegetables in one dish. • **SERVES 4**

- 10 small red potatoes (about 2 inches in diameter), scrubbed and halved
- 10 large Brussels sprouts, trimmed
- 3 to 4 tablespoons butter
- 2 tablespoons minced fresh dill weed
- 1 tablespoon minced garlic
- Salt and coarsely ground black pepper to taste

Place the cooking rack in the bottom of the pressure cooker and add ½ cup water. Using a steaming basket or tray, arrange the potatoes on the bottom, and then add the Brussels sprouts on top. Lock the lid in place. Bring to 15psi over high heat and immediately reduce the heat to the lowest possible setting to stabilize and maintain that pressure. Cook for 3 minutes. Remove from the heat and use the cold water release method before opening the lid. Lift out the vegetables, pour the water out of the pressure cooker, and wipe dry. Melt the butter in the pressure cooker over medium heat and add the dill weed and garlic. Add the potatoes and toss until they fully coated with the butter and herbs. Add the Brussels sprouts and salt and pepper, gently turning to coat with the butter mixture. Spoon into a serving bowl and pour the remaining sauce over the top.

fingerling potatoes and swiss chard

Swiss chard is easy to prepare and amazingly flavorful, and with all its many colorful variations, it's beautiful, too. When I made this with gorgeous little purple potatoes and brilliant rainbow chard, it reminded me of a birthday party. This dish has so few ingredients that it's embarrassingly simple, but it sure is a delicious and nutrient-rich side dish that will make a bright and fresh addition to any meal. • **SERVES 4**

1 bunch Swiss chard
1 to 1½ pounds fingerling potatoes, scrubbed and cut into ⅛-inch-thick slices
1 medium red onion, thinly sliced
Salt and coarsely ground black pepper to taste
2 tablespoons butter, melted (optional)

Separate the chard stalks from the leaves. Cut the stalks into 1-inch pieces and freeze for later use in stocks and soups. Place the cooking rack in the bottom of the pressure cooker and add ½ cup water. Place the potatoes and onion in a steamer basket and position it on the cooking rack. Stack the chard leaves and roll them up lengthwise, making a cigar shape. Cut the roll of leaves into 1-inch sections and add the strips to the steamer basket. Lock the lid in place. Bring to 15psi over high heat and immediately reduce the heat to the lowest possible setting to stabilize and maintain that pressure. Cook for 3 minutes. Remove from the heat and use the natural release method before opening the lid. Immediately transfer the vegetables to a serving bowl, and add salt and pepper and the butter, if desired. Toss gently to blend and serve hot.

double-cheese scalloped potatoes with bacon

As far as I'm concerned, the pressure cooker is the only way to make tender scalloped potatoes in a wonderful creamy sauce. This is simply old-fashioned comfort food, the sort of side dish that goes perfectly with almost any meat-based main dish. • **SERVES 6**

Step One: THE CHEESE SAUCE

6 strips bacon
2 tablespoons butter
3 tablespoons all-purpose flour
1 cup heavy cream or milk
Generous dash of Louisiana-style hot sauce
½ teaspoon salt
½ teaspoon freshly ground black pepper
1 cup shredded sharp cheddar cheese
½ cup grated Parmesan or Pecorino Romano cheese

In a skillet, cook the bacon until crisp. Set aside on paper towels to drain. Reserve 2 tablespoons bacon fat in the skillet and discard the rest. Heat the bacon fat over medium heat and add the butter. When the butter is melted, stir in the flour, making a smooth pastelike consistency. Continue cooking and stirring for about 1 minute or until the raw flour taste is gone. Whisk in the cream, hot sauce, salt, and pepper, stirring constantly. Add both cheeses and continue stirring until melted. The sauce will look thin at first, but it will thicken as you stir. Thin the sauce with a little milk if it becomes too thick.

Step Two: THE POTATOES

4 russet or Yukon gold potatoes, scrubbed and thinly sliced
1 cup diced onions

Use nonstick cooking spray to coat the inside of a 1½-quart stainless-steel or silicone insert pan that will fit loosely inside your pressure cooker. Layer about one-third of the potatoes into the prepared insert pan, followed by a thin layer of onions, then spoon in about one-third of the cheese sauce. Repeat the alternating layers, pouring the remaining cheese sauce on top when the insert pan is full. Shake the pan to settle the layers and evenly distribute the sauce mixture. Spray the underside of a square of aluminum foil with cooking spray and tightly crimp it over the top of the insert pan. Make 3 or 4 small slits around the edge of the foil to allow steam to escape. Place the rack in the bottom of the cooker and add 1½ cups water. Use foil helper handles to lower the dish into the pressure cooker. Lock the lid in place. Bring to 15psi over high heat and immediately reduce the heat to the lowest possible setting to stabilize and maintain that pressure. Cook for 25 minutes, or until the potatoes are tender when tested with a fork. Remove from the heat and use the natural release method before opening the lid. Sprinkle the crumbled bacon bits on top just before serving.

COOK'S NOTE: To quickly and easily cut the potatoes into uniformly thin slices so they will cook evenly, use a kitchen mandoline or the slicing attachment on a stand mixer.

---

sherried sweet potato and apple mash

Mashed sweet potato concoctions are a nice alternative to standard white potatoes. Both the starchier lighter-skinned and the red-skinned types will make a great mash, but in this recipe the sweeter red variety complements the tartness of the apples and lemon. Pair this dish with the richness of a good pork roast or extra-thick chops, or with some lovely lamb chops. • **SERVES 5 OR 6**

3 large red-skinned sweet potatoes, peeled and cut into 2-inch cubes
2 Granny Smith or similar tart cooking apples, peeled, cored, and chopped
2 tablespoons butter, plus more if desired
Zest and juice of 1 small lemon
¼ cup firmly packed light brown sugar
½ teaspoon ground cinnamon
¼ cup good-quality dry sherry (not the so-called cooking sherry)
Salt and freshly ground black pepper to taste

Add ½ cup water to the pressure cooker. Place a steamer tray in the bottom, using a cooking rack if necessary so that it is raised above the waterline. Add the cubed potatoes and chopped apples to the steamer tray. Lock the lid in place. Bring to 15psi over high heat and immediately reduce the heat to the lowest possible setting to stabilize and maintain that pressure. Cook for 6 minutes. Remove from the heat and use the quick release method before opening the lid. Lift out the apples and potatoes and drain the water out of the pressure cooker. Melt the butter in the pressure cooker over medium-high heat. Add the lemon juice and half the zest, sugar, cinnamon, and sherry. Bring the mixture to a boil and cook for about 3 minutes, stirring as it begins to thicken. Scoop the apples and potatoes back into the pressure cooker and mash by whatever method you prefer until they are smooth and creamy. Add more butter if desired. Taste the potatoes and add salt and pepper as needed. Transfer the mixture to a heated serving dish and sprinkle the remaining lemon zest on top.

COOK'S NOTE: To use a stand mixer with the paddle attachment, place the apples and potatoes in a prewarmed mixing bowl and slowly add the hot butter and sherry mixture, briefly pulsing the mixer on and off in short bursts until they are nice and smooth. Take care not to overdue it when using an electric mixer or the potatoes will become sticky.

COOK'S NOTE: Substitute apple juice or chicken broth for the sherry if you prefer. The taste will be somewhat different, but you will still make a flavorful and tasty dish.

---

mashed sweet potatoes with butter pecan streusel

With their high vitamin content, complex carbohydrates, and fiber, sweet potatoes are a very nutritious addition to your meal planning. This dish is just sweet enough to pair beautifully with pork or poultry, but it's easily customized if you like a bit more sweetness. Sweet potatoes are moist and soft, so it takes very little time to mash them, and if you have a potato ricer handy, you don't even need to peel them. This is a huge time-saver that makes this dish a good choice for a delicious weeknight side dish. The topping is one of those handy, make-ahead staples that I like to make in larger batches to use on all kinds of desserts, hot cereals, and waffles, and did I mention that you can also use it to top yogurt or fruit crumbles? Of course not, this is a pressure cooker recipe, so let's get cooking! • **SERVES 6 TO 8**

Step One: THE BUTTER PECAN STREUSEL

⅓ cup all-purpose flour
⅓ cup old-fashioned rolled oats
⅓ cup packed dark brown sugar
½ teaspoon salt
3 tablespoons cold butter, diced
½ cup chopped pecans

Preheat the oven to 350°F. Cover a baking sheet with aluminum foil. Stir together the flour, oats, sugar, and salt in a bowl. Add the butter, rubbing it in with your fingertips until the mixture has a crumbly texture. Mix in the pecans. Spread out the topping mixture in a thin layer on the prepared baking sheet, patting it even. Bake for 10 minutes or until the topping is lightly toasted. Cool on the baking sheet. The streusel may be made a day ahead. Cover tightly and refrigerate until needed, and then rewarm in a heavy skillet.

Step Two: THE SWEET POTATOES

4 large red-skinned sweet potatoes (2 to 2½ pounds), scrubbed
⅓ cup dark brown sugar
4 tablespoons (½ stick) butter, melted
½ rounded teaspoon ground cinnamon
Salt and coarsely ground black pepper to taste

Place the cooking rack in the bottom of the pressure cooker and add ⅔ cup water. Arrange the potatoes on the rack. Lock the lid in place. Bring to 15psi over high heat and immediately reduce the heat to the lowest possible setting to stabilize and maintain that pressure. Cook for 14 minutes. Remove from the heat and use the quick release

(continued)

method before opening the lid. Mash the potatoes while they are still hot. If using a potato ricer, there is no need to remove the skins. Cut each sweet potato in half horizontally, and then cut each half into two sections. Place a section into the ricer, cut side down, and close the handles to push the pulp through the holes. Open up the ricer and pluck out the skin that was left behind. Repeat until all the potatoes are done. If you are using a potato masher or any other method, carefully peel off the skins (they will come away in large sheets), then mash to a smooth consistency.

Dissolve the sugar in the melted butter. Stir the butter mixture and cinnamon into the potatoes and season with salt and pepper. Spoon the mashed sweet potatoes into a serving bowl and sprinkle the streusel over the top. Serve immediately.

perfect white rice

For some reason folks are afraid to try to make rice. Well, here's my simple, foolproof method for cooking long-grain white rice in a pressure cooker. Try this and you will be looking for recipes just so you can serve rice as a side dish. Just imagine, no stirring, no more burned rice, and best of all, it is so quick and easy! You'll get perfect results when using my PIP method. • **SERVES 4**

1 cup long-grain white rice
½ teaspoon salt
Coarsely ground black pepper to taste

Put the rice in a 1-quart stainless-steel bowl that will fit inside the pressure cooker and fill it with cold water to rinse the rice. Swish your fingers around to stir the rice, drain, and repeat 2 or 3 times, until the water runs clear. Drain well and return to the bowl. Position the cooking rack in the bottom of the pressure cooker and pour in ½ cup water. Use foil helper handles under the rice insert bowl to help position it on the cooking rack. Pour 1⅔ cups water into the rice bowl and add the salt and pepper. Lock the lid in place. Bring to 15psi, and reduce the heat to the lowest setting that will just maintain that pressure. Cook for 4 minutes. Remove from the heat and use the natural release method before opening the lid. Remove the bowl from the cooker using the helper handles. Fluff the rice with a fork before serving.

COOK'S NOTE: For a more savory rice with additional flavor, substitute stock or broth for the water, or stir 1 teaspoon bouillon granules into the rice. Add flavorful seasonings that complement your menu, like ¼ cup soy sauce or lemon juice. Include aromatics such as 1 tablespoon minced garlic or ginger or ½ cup chopped fresh cilantro or onion. Other herbs and spices, such as 1 teaspoon thyme, dill, or cumin, may also be added to enhance this basic rice recipe.

---

pine nut rice pilaf

Rice pilaf is just a gussied-up version of plain rice with some interesting ingredients that add flavor and color. The crunchy nuts are the real surprise in this recipe. • **SERVES 4**

2 tablespoons butter
1 medium onion, finely chopped
1 stalk celery, finely chopped
1 cup long-grain white rice
1 teaspoon poultry seasoning
1 teaspoon dried thyme
1 teaspoon salt
¼ teaspoon freshly ground black pepper
1 carrot, peeled and diced
8 ounces fresh white mushrooms, washed and sliced
2½ cups chicken broth
½ cup pine nuts, toasted

Melt the butter in the pressure cooker over medium heat. Cook the onion and celery until soft. Add the rice and stir until it looks translucent. Add the poultry seasoning, thyme, salt, pepper, carrot, and mushrooms. Stir in the broth. Lock the lid in place. Bring to 15psi over high heat and immediately reduce the heat to the lowest possible setting to stabilize and maintain that pressure. Cook for 4 minutes. Remove from the heat and use the natural release method before opening the lid. Fold in the pine nuts and serve.

savory herbed three-grain pilaf

If you're looking for a change from ordinary potatoes or regular rice, this is an easy and very tasty alternative, and what's even better, there's no tedious chopping or stirring. This is a deliciously fragrant recipe that fills the air with the scent of herbs, and the irresistibly nutty flavor and hearty texture of the barley and the combination of wild and brown rice makes this a great dish to accompany poultry, pork, or beef. • **SERVES 2**

- ½ teaspoon dried thyme
- ½ teaspoon dried marjoram
- ½ teaspoon dried oregano
- ½ teaspoon garlic powder
- ¼ teaspoon coarsely ground black pepper
- 1 teaspoon chicken bouillon granules
- 2 tablespoons wild rice
- ¼ cup long-grain brown rice
- ¼ cup pearl barley
- 1 (14-ounce) can chicken broth
- ½ cup dry white wine

Place the cooking rack in the pressure cooker and add 1 cup water. Using a 1½-quart stainless-steel insert bowl that will fit within your pressure cooker, add the thyme, marjoram, oregano, garlic powder, pepper, bouillon, wild rice, brown rice, and barley. Stir in the broth and wine. Place the insert bowl with the grain mixture in the pressure cooker. Lock the lid in place. Bring to 15psi over high heat and immediately reduce the heat to the lowest possible setting to stabilize and maintain that pressure. Cook for 15 minutes. Remove from the heat and use the natural release method before opening the lid. Transfer to a serving dish and fluff with a fork before serving.

parmesan-carrot risotto

This is an impressive and gourmet-quality side dish that looks gorgeous, tastes marvelous, and is inexpensive to make; plus it's easy and fast. It has a nice color presentation with the bright orange carrot bits, so what's not to love? You don't even need to buy the pricey risotto rice such as the traditional Arborio. I have tested risottos with medium-grain rice like Cal-Rose and Asian pearl rice, and the yields were just as creamy and delicious. Use a food processor to cut down your prep time and add this risotto to any midweek meal. • **SERVES 6**

4 tablespoons (½ stick) butter
1 medium red onion, diced
1¼ cups short- or medium-grain white rice
½ cup dry white wine
2½ cups chicken broth
4 medium carrots, peeled and grated
½ teaspoon ground nutmeg
Salt and coarsely ground black pepper to taste
½ cup grated Parmesan cheese

Melt 2 tablespoons of the butter in the pressure cooker over medium heat. Add the onion and cook until soft and translucent but not brown, about 4 minutes. Add the rice, stirring until it looks translucent. Pour in the wine and broth. Add the carrots and nutmeg, season with salt and pepper, and stir to mix. Lock the lid in place. Bring to 15psi over high heat and immediately reduce the heat to the lowest possible setting to stabilize and maintain that pressure. Cook for 7 minutes. Remove from the heat and use the quick release method before opening the lid. Stir in the remaining 2 tablespoons butter and the cheese. Taste and adjust seasonings as needed. Serve immediately.

COOK'S NOTE: The rice will continue to absorb the sauce as it sits. If you have any leftovers, heat ⅓ cup chicken broth in a small saucepan and then stir in the remaining risotto to return it to a creamy consistency. Add additional broth, a spoonful at a time, stirring until the rice is heated through and has a nice creamy consistency again.

---

risotto with asparagus

Most people are reluctant to try cooking risotto because they think that it is a labor-intensive dish requiring constant stirring while adding the necessary ingredients in precise amounts like some mad alchemist. Here's the trick: Once you use a pressure cooker to make a perfect risotto quickly and easily without stirring, you'll want to serve this Italian specialty all the time. • **SERVES 4**

- 1 pound thin asparagus spears
- 1 tablespoon butter
- 1 tablespoon olive oil
- 3 cloves garlic, minced
- 1 shallot, diced
- 1 cup Arborio or similar short-grain white rice
- ½ teaspoon dried thyme
- ½ cup dry white wine
- 2¼ cups chicken broth
- ½ cup grated Parmesan cheese
- Salt and freshly ground black pepper to taste

Hold each asparagus stalk at the base and bend it gently until it snaps in half. Save and freeze the tougher bottom part for making stock or soup. Cut the tip of the asparagus spear into 2-inch sections. Melt the butter in the pressure cooker over medium heat and add the oil. Add the garlic and shallot, cooking until soft and translucent but not brown, about 4 minutes. Add the rice and thyme, stirring frequently until the rice is opaque. Pour in the wine and chicken broth. Lock the lid in place. Bring to 15psi over high heat and immediately reduce the heat to the lowest possible setting to stabilize and maintain that pressure. Cook for 7 minutes. Remove from the heat and use the quick release method before opening the lid. Immediately add the asparagus pieces and stir to mix. Cover with a regular lid and let the pressure cooker sit for 5 minutes. Stir in the cheese. Taste and add salt and pepper as needed. Serve immediately.

COOK'S NOTE: The rice will continue to absorb the creamy sauce as it sits. If you have any leftovers, heat ⅓ cup chicken broth in a small saucepan and then stir in the remaining risotto. Add additional broth, a spoonful at a time, stirring until the rice is heated through and has a nice creamy consistency again.

COOK'S NOTE: If thin, baby asparagus spears are not available, substitute regular asparagus. To make the larger spears tender, bring a pot of salted water to a boil and add the asparagus. Blanch for 2 minutes and then drop the spears into a bowl of ice water to preserve their beautiful bright green color and keep them crisp-tender. Do not overcook.

---

risotto with fresh tomatoes and herbs

Risotto is the crown jewel of rice recipes. It's creamy and delicious with butter and cheese, and it offers an infinite variety of creative choices to customize it to any taste. From the basic, no-frills version to a gloriously decadent dish, risotto can be anything you like. Unlike the original saucepan version, the pressure cooker not only makes risotto faster, but it also eliminates the constant stirring. In this recipe, you'll get that classic risotto creaminess combined with the fresh flavors of tomatoes and herbs. • **SERVES 6**

1 tablespoon butter
1 tablespoon olive oil
½ cup diced onion
3 large cloves garlic, finely minced
1½ cups Arborio or similar short-grain white rice
½ teaspoon dried thyme
½ cup dry white wine
3½ cups chicken broth
½ cup grated hard Italian cheese, such as Pecorino Romano, aged Asiago, or Parmesan
2 cups diced Roma or cherry tomatoes
½ cup finely chopped fresh herbs of your choice, such as basil, oregano, and/or sage
Salt and freshly ground black pepper to taste

Melt the butter in the pressure cooker over medium heat and add the oil. Add the onion and garlic, and cook until soft and translucent but not brown, about 4 minutes. Add the rice, stirring until it looks transparent. Stir in the thyme, wine, and broth. Lock the lid in place. Bring to 15psi over high heat and immediately reduce the heat to the lowest possible setting to stabilize and maintain that pressure. Cook for 7 minutes. Remove from the heat and use the quick release method before opening the lid. Immediately add the cheese, stirring until it melts into a creamy sauce. Add the fresh tomatoes and herbs, stirring to mix. Taste and add salt and pepper as needed. Serve immediately.

COOK'S NOTE: The rice will continue to absorb the creamy sauce as it sits. If you have any leftovers, heat ⅓ cup chicken broth in a small saucepan and then stir in the remaining risotto to return it to a creamy consistency.

---

risotto with corn and rainbow chard

A lot of the flavor in risotto comes from the cheese, so use a good-quality, well-aged, hard Italian cheese. The taste and aroma of freshly grated Pecorino Romano cheese, or a good Parmigiano-Reggiano or aged Asiago, will go a long way toward boosting the flavor of any risotto, and it's especially useful when adding mild ingredients like chard. • **SERVES 6**

2 tablespoons olive oil
½ cup diced onion
1½ cups Arborio or similar short-grain white rice
4 cloves garlic, roasted (see page 252) and mashed to a pulp
½ teaspoon freshly cracked black pepper
1½ cups frozen corn kernels
3½ cups chicken stock
½ cup white wine
1 cup grated Pecorino Romano or any hard Italian cheese
Salt and freshly ground black pepper to taste
1 bunch rainbow chard, ribs trimmed and leaves thinly sliced

Heat the oil in the pressure cooker over medium heat and cook the onion until soft and translucent, but do not brown. Add the rice, stirring to coat with the oil until it looks transparent. Stir in the garlic, pepper, corn, broth, and wine. Lock the lid in place. Bring to 15psi over high heat and immediately reduce the heat to the lowest possible setting to stabilize and maintain that pressure. Cook for 7 minutes. Remove from the heat and use the quick release method before opening the lid. Immediately add the grated cheese, stirring until it melts into a creamy sauce. Taste and adjust seasoning as desired. The rice may look a little soupy at this stage, but it will continue to absorb liquid and become creamier as it sits. Briefly bring the rice to a simmer over medium heat and fold in the chard. Remove from the heat and cover with a regular lid for about 2 minutes or until the chard starts to wilt but still retain their bright color. Serve immediately.

Variation:
RISOTTO WITH TOMATOES AND BABY SPINACH

Omit the corn. Substitute 1 (8- to 10-ounce) package fresh baby spinach leaves and 2 cups diced cherry tomatoes for the chard. Cook as directed. After the cheese is added, briefly bring the rice to a simmer over medium heat and then fold in the spinach and tomatoes. Remove from the heat and cover with a regular lid for about 2 minutes or until the spinach starts to wilt but still retains the bright color. Serve immediately.

easy-cheesy rice and corn

The title should say it all! Perk up plain white rice with this creamy, cheesy, rice-and-corn combination to tempt even the most finicky eaters. Not only it super easy to prepare, but it's also a very pretty and colorful dish that goes well with a pork or chicken. • **SERVES 4**

1 cup long-grain white rice
1 cup frozen corn kernels
Salt and freshly ground black pepper to taste
1 teaspoon chicken bouillon granules
½ teaspoon dried thyme
½ cup sour cream
1½ cups shredded sharp cheddar cheese
½ cup sliced scallion tops

Put the rice in a 1½-quart stainless-steel bowl that will fit inside the pressure cooker and fill it with cold water to rinse the rice. Swish your fingers around to stir the rice, drain, and repeat 2 or 3 times, until the water runs clear. Drain well and return to the bowl. Position the cooking rack in the bottom of the pressure cooker and pour in ½ cup water. Use foil helper handles under the rice insert bowl to help position it on the cooking rack. Add the corn to the rice, along with salt and pepper, the bouillon, and the thyme. Pour 1⅔ cups water into the rice bowl and stir to blend. Lock the lid in place. Bring to 15psi and reduce the heat to the lowest setting that will just maintain that pressure. Cook for 4 minutes. Remove from the heat and use the natural release method before opening the lid. Combine the sour cream and the cheese with rice mixture. Cover the pressure cooker with a regular lid and let it stand for about 5 minutes for the cheese to melt. Remove the rice bowl from the cooker using the helper handles and spoon the creamy mixture into a serving bowl. Gently fold in the scallions. Taste and adjust seasonings as desired. Serve immediately.

Variation:

EASY-CHEESY RICE AND CORN WITH PEPPERS

Substitute pepper Jack cheese for the cheddar. Stir 1 (4-ounce) can chopped and drained green chiles into the cooked rice along with the cheese.

cilantro and lime rice

A delicious combination of fresh lime juice and cilantro wakes up plain rice and appeals to your taste buds. Serve as is with salt and pepper, or add a bit of butter if desired. This is a good side dish to serve with a Mexican main dish. It's also a flavorsome addition to wraps and burritos and any salads that call for rice. For this PIP recipe, you will need a stainless-steel insert pan or bowl that will fit inside your pressure cooker. • **SERVES 4 TO 6**

1 cup long-grain white rice
1 teaspoon chicken bouillon granules
Zest and juice of 1 large lime
½ cup chopped fresh cilantro leaves
Salt and freshly ground black pepper to taste

Place a cooking rack in the pressure cooker and pour in 1 cup water. Place the rice, 1½ cups water, the bouillon, lime juice, and cilantro in the insert pan. Put the pan of rice on the rack inside the pressure cooker. Lock the lid in place. Bring to 15psi over high heat and immediately reduce the heat to the lowest possible setting to stabilize and maintain that pressure. Cook for 4 minutes. Remove from the heat and use the natural release method before opening the lid. Transfer the rice to a serving bowl and add the lime zest and salt and pepper. Fluff the rice with fork and serve steaming hot.

soft and creamy polenta

Polenta should be a regular menu recipe in your kitchen repertoire. It's made from coarsely ground cornmeal, and with its bright yellow color and fresh corn flavor, it makes an ideal base for all kinds of vegetables, sauces, and meats. Polenta is very versatile, taking on any flavor it's cooked with, and so every batch can be personalized to reflect your tastes or complement the main dish. Dished up right from the stove with just butter and cheese, it can be a simple rustic food, or it become a pillow for seasoned tomato sauce, garlicky greens, or what have you. Plain or all dressed up with extras, polenta can be served as part of a main dish, a quick side dish, or chilled and fried for breakfast. I use the PIP cooking method to ensure perfect results with no stirring and no fuss. • **SERVES 4**

4 cups vegetable or chicken broth
1 cup polenta or stone-ground coarse cornmeal
½ cups dry white wine
2 cloves garlic, minced
½ teaspoon dried thyme
4 tablespoons (½ stick) butter, melted
¼ cup heavy cream
½ cup shredded Gruyère cheese
Salt and freshly ground black pepper to taste

Place the cooking rack in the pressure cooker and add 1 cup water. Add the broth to a 1½-quart stainless-steel insert bowl that will fit within your pressure cooker, and slowly whisk in the polenta. Add the wine, garlic, thyme, and butter. Use foil helper handles to place the bowl in the pressure cooker. Lock the lid in place. Bring to 15psi over high heat and immediately reduce the heat to the lowest possible setting to stabilize and maintain that pressure. Cook for 5 minutes. Remove from the heat and use the natural release method before opening the lid. Stir the cream and cheese into the polenta until well blended. If the polenta seems too thin, cover the pressure cooker with a regular lid and wait a few minutes for it to thicken. The polenta should be soft and smooth, but if you want it creamier still, stir in 1 or 2 tablespoons more cream. Taste and add salt and pepper if desired. To serve, spoon a generous mound of polenta onto each plate.

cheesy mexican cornbread

I love cornbread, so if I'm serving up a big pot of spicy beans, there's always going to be a plate of cornbread to go along with it. I love Mexican food, too, and while there are many different variations of cornbread, this one is loaded with all kinds of extra-spicy goodies that really pop up the flavor, making it a perfect accompaniment for your next pot of beans. Don't worry, if you don't have a source for Mexican cheese, just substitute pepper Jack cheese, or cheddar cheese if you prefer. To cook this PIP recipe, you will need a plain, flat-bottomed, stainless-steel or silicone insert pan that will fit within your pressure cooker. • **SERVES 4 TO 6**

2 tablespoons butter, softened, for greasing the insert pan
2 large eggs
¼ cup bacon drippings
⅔ cup buttermilk
1 cup drained canned whole kernel corn
1 (4-ounce) can chopped green chiles
⅓ cup minced fresh cilantro
1⅓ cups cornmeal
⅔ cup all-purpose flour
1 teaspoon baking powder
1 teaspoon baking soda
1 teaspoon salt
½ teaspoon red pepper flakes
1 teaspoon dried Mexican oregano
1½ cups cubed queso fresco

Generously grease and flour a stainless-steel or silicone insert pan that will fit within your pressure cooker. In a small bowl, whisk the eggs, and then blend in the bacon drippings, buttermilk, corn, chiles, and cilantro. In a large bowl, mix together the cornmeal, flour, baking powder, baking soda, salt, red pepper flakes, and oregano. Add the liquid ingredients to the dry ingredients and stir until just barely blended, and then fold in the cheese cubes. Pour the batter into the prepared pan, filling about two-thirds full to allow room for it to rise. Cover the cornbread pan with a greased lid or crimp a greased square of aluminum foil over the top to make a tight seal. Add ⅔ cup water to the pressure cooker and put a cooking rack in the bottom. Use foil helper handles to place the pan on top of the rack. Lock the lid in place. Bring to 15psi over high heat, then immediately reduce the heat to the lowest possible setting to stabilize and maintain that pressure. Cook for 16 minutes. Remove from the heat and use the natural release method before opening the lid. Remove the insert pan from the cooker and let it cool on a wire rack for about 5 minutes. Then run a small sharp knife around the edge to loosen the sides before inverting the cornbread on a plate. Cut into wedges and serve with lots of butter.

macaroni and cheese times three

It's safe to say that homemade macaroni and cheese is a popular family meal that is enjoyed by everyone from the youngest toddler to the most venerable oldster. Rich and creamy—you know what I'm talking about!—this is the down-home cookin' stuff that your mama used to make. This version gets a huge time savings in the pressure cooker and ups the gooey deliciousness with not one, not two, but three different kinds of cheese. Say goodbye to your diet for this dinner and you're guaranteed that every mouthful will be pure macaroni-cheesy bliss. • **SERVES 4**

Step One: THE MACARONI

2 tablespoons butter
1 onion, minced
2 cloves garlic, minced
2½ cups elbow macaroni
2 cups chicken stock
Salt and freshly ground black pepper to taste

Melt the butter in the pressure cooker over medium-high heat and cook the onion and garlic, stirring frequently until the onions start to get soft, about 3 minutes. Add the macaroni, chicken stock, and salt and pepper. Stir to mix. The liquid should just barely cover the pasta. Lock the lid in place. Bring to 15psi over high heat and immediately reduce the heat to the lowest possible setting to stabilize and maintain that pressure. Cook for 6 minutes. Meanwhile, start the cheese sauce. Remove from the heat and use the natural release method before opening the lid.

Step Two: THE CHEESE SAUCE

4 tablespoons (½ stick) butter
1 teaspoon paprika
2 to 3 tablespoons all-purpose flour
1 cup heavy cream
1 cup shredded sharp cheddar cheese
1 cup crumbled Gorgonzola cheese
1 cup shredded Havarti cheese
⅓ cup milk (optional)
Pinch of cayenne pepper, or more to taste
Salt and a lot of freshly ground black pepper
½ cup fresh Italian parsley leaves, finely chopped

Melt the butter in a saucepan over medium heat and stir in the paprika and flour to make a smooth paste. Very gradually whisk in the cream, using a whisk to prevent lumps. Cook, stirring frequently as the mixture becomes thick and creamy, about 15 minutes. Slowly add the three cheeses, stirring frequently until the cheeses are melted. If the cheese sauce is too thick, add the milk, a little at a time until the sauce is the desired consistency. Add the cayenne pepper, salt and black pepper, and the parsley. Taste and adjust seasonings. Fold the cheese sauce into the cooked macaroni. Cover with a regular lid and let stand for 5 minutes, as the sauce will continue to thicken. Serve immediately.

Pork Chops, Sauerkraut, and Potatoes (see page 145)

Right: *Salpicón de Res: Shredded Beef Salad* (see page 60)

Below: *Risotto with Tomatoes and Sausage* (see page 121)

Opposite: *Shortcut Barbecued Chicken* (see page 160)

Opposite: *Shortcut Green Chile and Corn Chowder* (see page 157)

Above: *Shortcut Beef Pot Roast with Mushroom Gravy* (see page 167)

Right: *Spiced Chicken Curry* (see page 185)

Below: *Smoky Beef-and-Bacon Pinto Bean Chili* (see page 116)

Opposite: *Spiced Apple Brown Betty* (see page 308)

Taqueria-Style Beef Tacos with Fresh California Pico de Gallo (see page 226)

fresh tomato sauce

This is a simple marinara sauce that will turn ripe tomatoes into a fresh batch of tomato sauce for dinner. You can freeze leftovers for later use. Enjoy this fresh sauce over your favorite pasta, or try it with spaghetti squash. • **SERVES 4**

Step One: PEEL THE TOMATOES

If you're lucky enough to have a food mill, you can skip this step. Just follow the directions for your mill, which is usually to quarter the tomatoes and put small batches through the mill. For everyone else, let's get started on those tomatoes.

3 pounds Roma or similar ripe pulpy tomatoes

Pour about 4 cups water into the pressure cooker and bring to a boil with only a regular lid. Place a large bowl of ice water nearby. Meanwhile, make a small X in the bottom of each tomato. Plunge 2 or 3 tomatoes into the boiling water for about 30 seconds, or until the skins begin to loosen. Using a slotted spoon, transfer the tomatoes to the ice water and let sit in the water for 1 minute before transferring to a large plate. Starting at the X, use a sharp paring knife to peel away and discard the skins. Use a teaspoon to scoop out the seeds. Chop the tomatoes and reserve any juice.

Step Two: THE SAUCE

1 tablespoon extra-virgin olive oil
1 medium onion, diced
6 cloves garlic, roasted (or to taste; see page 252) and mashed to a smooth paste
½ teaspoon sugar
2 sprigs fresh basil or 2 teaspoons dried basil
2 sprigs fresh thyme or 2 teaspoons dried thyme
Salt and coarsely ground black pepper to taste
½ cup tomato juice
½ cup dry red wine
¼ cup tomato paste

(continued)

Drain the pressure cooker. Heat the oil in the pressure cooker over medium-high heat and cook the onion until soft. Add the garlic, stirring it into the oil just until fragrant. Add the peeled tomatoes and any accumulated juices, sugar, basil, thyme, and salt and pepper, and stir in the tomato juice. In a measuring cup, mix the wine and tomato paste until smooth, and pour over the top without stirring. Lock the lid in place. Bring to 15psi over high heat and immediately reduce the heat to the lowest possible setting to stabilize and maintain that pressure. Cook for 8 minutes. Remove from the heat and use the natural release method before opening the lid. Adjust the consistency of the sauce if it is very juicy by allowing it to simmer longer without a lid. Taste and adjust seasoning as desired.

COOK'S NOTE: This sauce will have chunks of tomatoes, but if you would like a smoother version, use a handheld blender or pulse the sauce in a food processor fitted with the steel blade.

---

zesty tomato-herb sauce

This is a good old-fashioned sauce using fresh tomatoes and herbs that's quick and easy to prepare. I don't peel the tomatoes because I have this guilty memory of my grandma's lecture about all that "good stuff" that would be thrown away—you know the one, right? Of course, you can certainly peel your own tomatoes if you want to . . . I'm calling for a lot of fresh herbs in this recipe because I wanted an intense flavor to match the tomatoes. Now a word about tomatoes: The juicier the tomatoes, the thinner the sauce, so pulpier tomatoes are best. Don't get all flustered if you don't have any. Just use whatever tomatoes are available and do not add their juices; it will still taste wonderful in whatever recipe you use it. • **SERVES 4**

2 tablespoons extra-virgin olive oil
1 large onion, minced
6 cloves garlic, crushed
1 cup finely chopped fresh basil
½ cup finely chopped fresh oregano
½ teaspoon red pepper flakes
½ cup dry red wine
3 pounds Roma tomatoes, seeded and diced
1 teaspoon salt
½ teaspoon freshly ground black pepper
1 (6-ounce) can tomato paste
1 to 2 teaspoons sugar (optional)

Heat the oil in the pressure cooker over medium-high heat and cook the onion until soft and translucent, about 4 minutes. In the following order, add the garlic, basil, oregano, red pepper flakes, wine, and tomatoes, and do not stir. Sprinkle on the salt and black pepper. Spread the tomato paste on top and do not stir. Lock the lid in place. Bring to 15psi over high heat and immediately reduce the heat to the lowest possible setting to stabilize and maintain that pressure. Cook for 10 minutes. Remove from the heat and use the natural release method before opening the lid. Use a handheld blender to puree the sauce to a smooth consistency. Taste and adjust seasonings, adding sugar if desired to mellow out the tartness of the tomatoes.

Variation:

ZESTY TOMATO-HERB SAUCE WITH RICOTTA CHEESE

After you release the pressure, add 1 (16-ounce) container ricotta cheese to the sauce and simmer over low heat, uncovered, stirring often until the sauce is creamy and heated through.

creamy vodka sauce with prosciutto

When I first heard about vodka sauce, I was skeptical and thought it was just a gimmick. Okay, the color of vodka sauce is distinctly pink due to the added cream, and it's lovely to look at, but seriously, I mean, what was the point in adding perfectly good booze to perfectly fine pasta sauce? I was really puzzled, until I actually ate some. Oh boy, was I ever wrong. It's tricky to explain, but once the alcohol actually burns off, the essence that remains adds a beautiful depth of flavor to the creamy tomato sauce. This sauce is always delicious on any type of pasta, ravioli, or tortellini, and it's great on sautéed shrimp as well (see the bonus recipe). • **SERVES 4**

2 tablespoons butter
1 shallot, minced
1 small onion, diced
4 cloves garlic, minced
½ cup finely chopped fresh basil leaves
10 sprigs fresh Italian parsley, finely chopped
½ teaspoon red pepper flakes
1 cup vodka
1 cup chicken broth
2 tablespoons chopped capers
4 ounces prosciutto, chopped
2 pounds Roma tomatoes, seeded and diced
Salt and freshly ground black pepper to taste
2 tablespoons tomato paste
1 cup heavy cream
½ cup grated Pecorino Romano or any hard Italian grating cheese
1 to 2 teaspoons sugar (optional)

Heat the butter in the pressure cooker over medium-high heat and cook the shallot and onion until soft, about 4 minutes. Add the garlic, basil, parsley, red pepper flakes, vodka, and ½ cup of the broth, and continue cooking, uncovered, until the liquid is reduced by half; this will take about 8 minutes. In the following order, add the capers, prosciutto, chopped tomatoes, and salt and pepper, and then spread the tomato paste on top, and do not stir. Lock the lid in place. Bring to 15psi over high heat and immediately reduce the heat to the lowest possible setting to stabilize and maintain that pressure. Cook for 6 minutes. Remove from the heat and use the natural release method before opening the lid. Depending on your personal preferences, you can either leave the sauce chunky, or use a handheld blender to puree it to a smooth consistency. Stir in the cream and cheese, simmering over low heat, uncovered, stirring often until the sauce is smooth and creamy and heated through. Taste and adjust seasonings, adding sugar if desired to mellow out the tartness of the tomatoes.

BONUS RECIPE

vodka shrimp

Serve this over cooked fettuccine.

1½ pounds jumbo shrimp (about 23 to the pound)
4 tablespoons (½ stick) butter
3 cloves garlic, smashed
Pinch of ground cloves

If necessary, peel and clean the shrimp, running a small knife down the back to reveal the dark vein and pulling it out. Rinse well and pat dry. Heat the butter in a skillet over medium heat and add the garlic and shrimp and a good dash of ground cloves. Sauté the shrimp, turning occasionally, until they turn pink, about 5 minutes. Discard the garlic. Add the shrimp and butter in the skillet to the cooked Creamy Vodka Sauce and stir gently to blend.

SERVES 4

tomato-spinach sauce

Yes, I know, you're already making faces and wondering why you have to peel tomatoes for this recipe. Well, you don't, not really, but I'm going to include the directions anyway, because the sauce will have a smoother texture and the flavor won't be affected in the event the peel is bitter. The sauce will look more appetizing, too, because tomato skins do not break down as fast as the pulp. It's not that the food police will come knocking at your door, but you will have all those little rolls of tomato skin floating around in your sauce to get stuck in your teeth and the kids' braces. Well, you can see where I'm going, right? Serve this fresh sauce over your favorite cooked pasta, ravioli, or tortellini, or use it in any recipe that calls for tomato sauce. • **SERVES 4**

Step One: THE TOMATOES

2½ pounds Roma tomatoes

Bring a saucepan of water to a boil. Meanwhile, prepare a large bowl of ice water and place it near the stove. Remove the stems from the tomatoes if necessary, and cut a shallow "X" only through the peel at the top and bottom of each tomato. When the water is boiling, put 2 or 3 tomatoes in the water. Quickly remove the tomatoes with a slotted spoon or a fork and plunge them immediately into the ice water bath. The skin will split along the knife cuts, making it easy to pull the peel off with your fingers or a knife. Cut the tomatoes in half lengthwise and scoop out the seeds, and then dice them small and set aside in a bowl to capture the juices. Continue with all the tomatoes.

Step Two: THE SAUCE

¼ cup olive oil
1 medium onion, diced
6 cloves garlic, minced
¼ cup fresh basil, chopped
¼ cup fresh oregano, chopped
¼ cup fresh Italian parsley, chopped
One 4-inch sprig fresh rosemary
¼ teaspoon red pepper flakes
Salt and freshly ground black pepper to taste
1 cup dry red wine
1 bunch fresh spinach, chopped
3 tablespoons tomato paste
½ cup grated Pecorino Romano or any hard Italian grating cheese
1 to 2 teaspoons sugar (optional)

Heat the oil in the pressure cooker over medium-high heat and cook the onion until soft. Stir in the garlic, basil, oregano, parsley, and rosemary, and fry until they are fragrant. Add the red pepper flakes and salt and black pepper. Deglaze the pressure cooker with the wine, scraping any crusty bits from the bottom. In the following order, add the peeled tomatoes and any accumulated juice, the spinach, and then dot the tomato paste across the top without stirring. Lock the lid in place. Bring to 15psi over high heat and immediately reduce the heat to the lowest possible setting to stabilize and maintain that pressure. Cook for 10 minutes. Remove from the heat and use the natural release method before opening the lid. Stir in the cheese and simmer over low heat until the sauce is evenly blended. Taste and adjust seasonings, adding sugar if desired to mellow out the tartness of the tomatoes.

greek tomato, spinach, and olive sauce

Like many recipes, this one was the happy result of necessity. The pressure cooker makes it easy to prepare meals on the fly using the ingredients you have on hand to create something quick and delicious for dinner. The kalamata, or Greek olive, is a meaty brine-cured olive with a distinct taste and appearance, which is usually found at the deli counter in most supermarkets. Serve this fresh sauce over—what else?—fresh or homemade pasta or tortellini, or try it with spaghetti squash. • **SERVES 2 OR 3**

2 tablespoons olive oil
1 medium onion, diced
6 cloves garlic, minced
¼ cup finely chopped fresh basil
3 tablespoons chopped fresh oregano
½ cup halved and pitted kalamata or similar brine-cured olives
¼ cup drained capers
1½ pounds Roma tomatoes, diced
¼ teaspoon red pepper flakes
1 tablespoon balsamic vinegar
½ cup dry red wine
1 bunch fresh spinach, chopped
1 cup crumbled feta cheese
⅓ cup heavy cream
Salt and coarsely ground black pepper to taste

Heat the oil in the pressure cooker over medium-high heat and cook the onion until soft and translucent, about 4 minutes. Add the garlic, basil, and oregano, stirring as they sizzle and become fragrant. Stir in the olives, capers, tomatoes, red pepper flakes, vinegar, and wine. Add the spinach on top and do not stir. Lock the lid in place. Bring to 15psi over high heat and immediately reduce the heat to the lowest possible setting to stabilize and maintain that pressure. Cook for 5 minutes. Remove from the heat and use the quick release method before opening the lid. Stir in the cheese and cream over low heat until melted and heated through. Taste and adjust seasonings as desired, adding salt and coarsely ground black pepper only if necessary.

bellissimo bolognese sauce

Whether it's called *bolognese* in Italian, or *bolognaise* by its French name, this beautiful meat-based sauce is perfect with your favorite pasta. There are many variations on this classic sauce, and it's sometimes lumped in with other tomato-based sauces, but authentic recipes should only have a small amount of tomato. The one thing all the conventional recipes have in common is an incredibly long simmering time, and that lengthy cooking time is more likely to get a pass in a busy household. The pressure cooker means that this sauce will earn a well-deserved place in your menu planning, so try this sauce on all your favorite pasta dishes from spaghetti and ziti to lasagna, and even pizza. • **SERVES 6**

2 tablespoons olive oil
2 large onions, chopped
2 teaspoons dried basil
2 teaspoons dried oregano
1 teaspoon fennel seeds, crushed
1 teaspoon dried thyme
8 ounces ground beef
8 ounces ground pork
8 ounces Italian bulk pork sausage
2 tablespoons balsamic vinegar
1 cup dry white wine
6 cloves garlic, minced
3 carrots, peeled and grated
2 stalks celery, minced
½ cup minced fresh Italian parsley
Salt and coarsely ground black pepper to taste
½ teaspoon red pepper flakes (optional)
1 (15-ounce) can tomato sauce
¼ cup grated Parmesan cheese
½ cup half-and-half
1 to 2 teaspoons sugar (optional)

Heat the oil in the pressure cooker over medium-high heat and cook the onions until softened but not browned, about 4 minutes. Add the basil, oregano, fennel seeds, and thyme to the hot oil, stirring as they start to sizzle and fry. Add the ground meats and sausage, stirring and crumbling the meat, until well browned. Drain off any excess oil. Add the vinegar and wine, scraping up any brown bits from the bottom of the pressure cooker. Stir in the garlic, carrots, celery, parsley, salt and black pepper, and the red pepper flakes if desired. Add the tomato sauce last, but do not stir. Lock the lid in place. Bring to 15psi over high heat and immediately reduce the heat to the lowest possible setting to stabilize and maintain that pressure. Cook for 15 minutes. Remove from the heat and use the natural release method before opening the lid. Stir the mixture until thoroughly blended. Bring the sauce to a simmer over medium heat, uncovered, and continue to cook to until most of the liquid has evaporated. Add the grated Parmesan and half-and-half, stirring the mixture until well blended. Taste and adjust seasonings, adding the sugar if desired.

spicy tomato sauce with hot italian sausage

Tomato sauces are powerful weapons in your culinary arsenal, so to speak. Using a pressure cooker, they are quick and easy to make from common ingredients, and they can be readily tailored to suit your own taste preferences. Tomato sauces are so versatile in pasta dishes, pizza, chili, soups, and many other recipes that I like to keep my freezer well stocked. It's a perfect solution for those nights when I absolutely can't make myself start chopping and mincing, but I can manage to pull a flavorful tomato sauce out of the freezer and still serve up a nice meal.

This particular sauce has a really nice, spicy bite to it that imparts a pleasant heat with every mouthful. It's one of my favorite red sauces, because it isn't so hot that the wonderful flavors are masked, but it will definitely keep you from dozing off. Serve it over linguine or fettuccine or any pasta of choice, add some garlic bread and maybe a crunchy romaine salad, and dinner is served. And do freeze any leftovers for more of those nights when you don't feel like dicing and slicing. • **SERVES 6**

1 tablespoon olive oil
1½ pounds hot bulk Italian sausage or links with casings removed
1½ cups diced onions
1 small fennel bulb, diced (about 1 cup)
4 large cloves garlic, minced
1½ teaspoons anise seeds
2 tablespoons dried oregano
1 tablespoon dried basil
1 teaspoon dried marjoram
1½ cups dry red wine
½ teaspoon red pepper flakes
3 bay leaves
2 teaspoons salt
½ teaspoon freshly ground black pepper
10 sprigs fresh Italian parsley, minced
2 cups sliced fresh, canned, or dried mushrooms
1 (28-ounce) can diced tomatoes with juice
1 (28-ounce) can crushed tomatoes
1 (14-ounce) can tomato sauce
1 (6-ounce) can tomato paste
1 (14-ounce) can pitted black olives, drained and sliced
1 to 2 teaspoons sugar (optional)
Grated Parmigiano-Reggiano or Pecorino Romano cheese, for garnish

Heat the oil in the pressure cooker over medium-high heat and brown the sausage, breaking it up with a wooden spoon until it is evenly crumbled. Stir in the onions, fennel, and garlic, and cook until the onions are soft but not browned, about 4 minutes.

Add the anise seeds, oregano, basil, and marjoram, cooking and stirring until the spices become fragrant. Deglaze the pressure cooker with the wine, scraping up any crusty brown bits from the bottom. Add the red pepper flakes, bay leaves, salt, black pepper, parsley, mushrooms, and diced tomatoes with juice, and then stir in 1½ cups water, mixing well. In the following order, add the crushed tomatoes and the tomato sauce on top of the other ingredients in the pressure cooker, and do not stir. Next, dot teaspoonfuls of the tomato paste across the surface; no stirring. Lock the lid in place. Bring to 15psi over high heat and immediately reduce the heat to the lowest possible setting to stabilize and maintain that pressure. Cook for 12 minutes. Remove from the heat and use the natural release method before opening the lid. Stir in the black olives. Remove the bay leaves. Taste and adjust seasoning as needed, adding sugar if the tomatoes have a bitter aftertaste. Top each serving with a generous amount of grated cheese.

creamy herbed tomato sauce with garlicky italian meatballs

Garlic lovers, this recipe is for you—everyone else take warning! There is a powerful influence of garlic in this delicious sauce. Everyone loves meatballs, and if you haven't tried my Five-Minute Roasted Garlic (page 252), use it in this recipe. I like a mixture of ground beef and sausage for meatballs, but you can get creative and try ground veal, lamb, chicken, or turkey. If it's convenient, the meatballs may be made up to a day in advance to allow the flavors to marry. Serve over pasta, with garlic bread and a simple green salad with an Italian vinaigrette and, of course, an excellent dry red wine. • **SERVES 4 OR 5**

Step One: THE MEATBALLS

- 4 Italian sausage links, casings removed
- 8 ounces ground beef
- 1 large egg, beaten
- ½ cup soft bread crumbs
- 4 cloves garlic, roasted (see page 252) and mashed to a pulp
- ½ cup minced onion
- ½ cup minced green bell pepper
- 2 teaspoons dried oregano
- 1 teaspoon dried basil
- 3 tablespoons olive oil

Use a stand mixer with the paddle attachment to evenly mix the sausage meat and beef to a smooth consistency. Add the egg, bread crumbs, garlic, onion, bell pepper, oregano, and basil. Alternatively, keep your hands clean by placing the ingredients in a large plastic freezer bag and kneading until it is thoroughly mixed. Use a small ice cream scoop to quickly make the meatballs or shape by hand, making them 1 to 1½ inches in diameter. Heat the oil in the pressure cooker over medium-high heat and lightly brown the meatballs in small batches. Set aside on a plate.

Step Two: THE SAUCE

2 tablespoons olive oil
1 medium onion, diced
8 cloves garlic, minced
1 tablespoon minced fresh rosemary or 1 teaspoon crushed dried rosemary
3 tablespoons minced fresh oregano or 1 tablespoon crushed dried oregano
2 tablespoons minced fresh basil or 2 teaspoons crushed dried basil
10 sprigs fresh cilantro, minced
1 cup dry red wine
2 bay leaves
½ teaspoon red pepper flakes, or to taste
1 (15-ounce) can diced tomatoes with juice
1 (28-ounce) can crushed tomatoes
1 (15-ounce) can tomato sauce
3 tablespoons tomato paste
½ cup ricotta cheese
¼ cup heavy cream
1 teaspoon sugar, or more to taste (optional)
Salt and coarsely ground black pepper to taste
Grated Parmigiano-Reggiano cheese, for garnish

Heat the oil in the pressure cooker over medium-high heat and cook the onion until soft and translucent, about 4 minutes. Add the garlic, rosemary, oregano, basil, and cilantro, stirring until they become fragrant. Deglaze the pot with the wine, scraping up all those crusty brown bits from the bottom of the pressure cooker. Return the meatballs to the pressure cooker and stir in the bay leaves and red pepper flakes. In the following order, add the diced tomatoes with juice, the crushed tomatoes, the tomato sauce, and the tomato paste, but do not stir. Lock the lid in place. Bring to 15psi over high heat and immediately reduce the heat to the lowest possible setting to stabilize and maintain that pressure. Cook for 8 minutes. Remove from the heat and use the natural release method before opening the lid. Simmer the sauce over low heat, uncovered. Remove bay leaves. Blend in the ricotta cheese and cream. Taste and adjust seasonings as desired, adding sugar if the tomatoes seem too bitter, and salt and pepper only if needed. Garnish each serving with a generous amount of grated cheese.

red mole sauce

Mole means "sauce," and typical of Mexican cuisine, it is redolent with a variety of peppers and aromatic spices. There is no single recipe for making a mole sauce because the ingredients vary by season, locale, and the personal preferences of the cook. Mole can be thick or thin, green or red or a deep brick color, and it's all good. The chile peppers chosen for the mole sauce can be mild or hot or somewhere in between, depending on your own tastes and the ingredients available in your market. A mole sauce usually starts with common types of dried chile peppers, including the "holy trinity" of Mexican chiles, ancho, mulato, and pasilla peppers. The secret ingredient that adds a richer and deeply complex flavor to the mole is Mexican chocolate, a blend of ground cacao, cinnamon, and sugar that comes in round disks. All moles are very time-consuming and it's not uncommon to find recipes with 30 ingredients that take all day to prep and cook, so it is usually reserved for special occasions such as weddings and big holiday feasts. However, with the convenience of a pressure cooker, this mole is cooked in about half an hour, and the finished sauce is a combination of sweet, spicy, and pleasantly hot flavors. Mole is served with everything from poultry and red meats to vegetables and even seafood. • **SERVES 4**

Step One: THE DRIED CHILES

For more information about dried chile peppers and how to work with them, read the How-To Primer on Dried Chile Peppers on page 297.

4 dried ancho chiles, seeded and chopped
2 dried mulato chiles, seeded and chopped
4 dried pasilla chiles, seeded and chopped
4 to 6 dried cascabel chiles, seeded and chopped (optional)

Place the chopped ancho, mulato, and pasilla chiles in the pressure cooker. Use the dried cascabel chiles as well if you want a hotter version. Pour ½ cup water into the pressure cooker, adding additional water as necessary to cover the chiles. Lock the lid in place. Bring to 15psi over high heat and immediately reduce the heat to the lowest possible setting to stabilize and maintain that pressure. Cook for 15 minutes. Remove from the heat and use the natural release method before opening the lid.

Step Two: THE TOASTED SPICES

2 tablespoons sweet smoked paprika
1 tablespoon hot smoked Spanish paprika (pimentón de la Vera picante)
½ teaspoon ground cloves
2 teaspoons ground cumin

While the chiles are cooking, heat a dry, heavy cast-iron skillet over medium-high heat. When the skillet is hot, add both types of paprika, the cloves, and cumin, stirring constantly, until the spices begin to change color and become fragrant. Be careful not to let them burn. Immediately transfer the spices to a plate, spreading them out to cool. Add the spices to the dried pepper mixture in the pressure cooker.

Step Three: THE SAUCE

1 cup strong brewed coffee
1 large onion, roasted (see page 299) and chopped
4 large tomatillos, roasted (see page 299) and chopped
4 large Roma tomatoes, seeded, roasted (see page 299), and chopped
½ cup raisins or diced prunes
3 cloves garlic, chopped
10 sprigs fresh cilantro, finely chopped
1 teaspoon dried Mexican oregano
3 tablespoons creamy peanut butter
1 ounce Mexican chocolate, grated; or 1 ounce unsweetened chocolate, grated, plus ½ teaspoon ground cinnamon and 1 teaspoon sugar
1 (10-ounce) can tomato puree
1 to 1½ cups crushed plain tortilla chips
Salt to taste

Stir the coffee, onion, tomatillos, tomatoes, raisins, garlic, cilantro, and oregano into the pressure cooker. In a small bowl, mix the peanut butter, chocolate, and tomato puree and spread the mixture over the top of the other ingredients in the pressure cooker, but do not stir. Lock the lid in place. Bring to 15psi over high heat and immediately reduce the heat to the lowest possible setting to stabilize and maintain that pressure. Cook for 12 minutes. Remove from the heat and use the natural release method before opening the lid. Stir to combine all the ingredients. Use a handheld blender to puree the mixture until it's very smooth. For a thicker mole, stir in some of the crushed tortilla chips, a little at a time, simmering over medium heat until the sauce reaches the desired consistency. Taste, adding salt and adjusting the seasonings as desired. Refrigerate the finished mole in a tightly covered container overnight to allow the flavors to develop, or portion out and freeze until ready to use. The sauce will thicken more after it is chilled, and it can be thinned by adding small amounts of water until it reaches the right consistency.

pork and artichoke ragoût

Pork is always a good buy. It's easy to cook, and it's versatile enough that it fits into any type of cuisine, so I like to come up with new ways to incorporate pork in my recipes. I look for ideas that will have a quick prep time so that the recipe can be managed on a weeknight for busy people but still offer real food that's flavorful and appealing. I like this pork and artichoke sauce. It's wonderful on your favorite type of cooked pasta—I recommend fettuccine—or polenta, and I love to eat the leftovers as is, like a soup! • **SERVES 4**

2 boneless pork chops
Salt and coarsely ground black pepper to taste
2 tablespoons olive oil
1 small onion, chopped
6 plump cloves garlic, finely chopped
1 tablespoon smoked paprika
½ teaspoon red pepper flakes
1 tablespoon dried oregano
2 teaspoons dried basil
½ cup dry white wine
8 ounces fresh white mushrooms, washed and sliced
2 tablespoons chopped capers
2 tablespoons minced fresh Italian parsley
1 (28-ounce) can diced tomatoes with juice
1 (15-ounce) can tomato sauce
3 tablespoons tomato paste
½ cup drained and sliced canned pitted black olives
½ cup drained and chopped canned artichoke hearts
1 to 2 teaspoons sugar (optional)
¼ cup grated Parmigiano-Reggiano cheese

Season the pork chops with salt and black pepper. Heat the oil in the pressure cooker over medium-high heat and brown the meat on both sides. Transfer to a plate. Add the onion to the pressure cooker and cook until soft and translucent. Meanwhile, cut into chops into ½-inch cubes. Next, add the garlic, paprika, red pepper flakes, oregano, and basil, stirring until they become fragrant. Deglaze the cooker with the wine, scraping up all those crusty brown bits from the bottom. Add the mushrooms, capers, parsley, the diced tomatoes with juice, and the cubed pork, stirring to mix. In the following order, add the tomato sauce and then spread the tomato paste on top, but do not stir. Lock the lid in place. Bring to 15psi over high heat and immediately reduce the heat to the lowest possible setting to stabilize and maintain that pressure. Cook for 6 minutes. Remove from the heat and use the natural release method before opening the lid. Stir in the black olives and artichoke hearts and simmer the sauce over low heat, uncovered, until it is heated through. Taste and adjust seasonings as desired, adding sugar if the sauce seems too bitter. Garnish each serving with a generous amount of grated cheese.

A HOW-TO PRIMER ON

dried chile peppers

Many people who enjoy Mexican cuisine are intrigued by the spicy flavors but mystified by the endless varieties of sizes, shapes, and colors of the chile peppers that are the characteristic seasoning in most recipes. Dried chile peppers are available in many supermarkets, where they might be stocked with the selection of Mexican ingredients, in the spice aisle, or sometimes in the produce section. You've probably looked at all those strange and mysterious packages of dark, wrinkled peppers, but you hurried on because you had no idea what to do with them. Oh, my dears, they are like black gold in the kitchen, so go back and grab a bunch, hug them to your bosom, and take them home.

The "holy trinity" of dried chiles in many Mexican recipes is made up of the pasilla, the ancho, and the mulato chiles, all of which are fairly mild. There are many different varieties of dried chiles, from wicked little dried-up pointy things to large rounded ones, and all of them are shriveled, wrinkled, and darkly twisted. In addition, there are often different names for the fresh and dried varieties, so it can be confusing.

Then there's that dreaded "hotness" factor, probably the chief misconception that most people have about chile peppers. While there are some pepper varieties that are definitely in the oh-my-god-I'm-gonna-die category, in our recipes we're looking for chiles that are sweet and mild with just enough heat to add spicy flavor without being overwhelming. The actual heat is concentrated in the veins or ribs near the seed heart, and that can be easily removed. As a precaution, you might want to wear protective food-handling gloves when working with either fresh or dried chiles. And remember not to touch your eyes or mouth, babies, and pets and other helpless critters.

Dried chiles should keep for up to a year when stored in a cool, dry place in an airtight container. If possible, buy loose rather than packaged chiles so that you can examine them closely. Dried chiles should have a rich (not dusty) and uniform color, and unbroken skins, and they should still be pliable, not dried to a brittle crisp.

So let's start with the heart-shaped ancho chiles. The name means "wide," and it is a brownish-black, flat pepper, the largest and the sweetest of the dried chiles. It is the dried version of the mild poblano, which is the "people" pepper, so popular that it accounts for nearly one-fifth of all chiles eaten in Mexico. The ancho has hints of raisin and plum with a nice medium heat. You can grind the whole dried pod in a blender, with or without the seeds depending on your heat preference.

California chiles are dried Anaheim chiles, another very mild pepper that you might see labeled as "chile verde." California chiles are oblong and dark red or brown. These peppers can vary somewhat, with some having a sweet flavor and others having more of a spicy bite.

Cascabel peppers are sometimes labeled as "rattlesnake chiles" because the dried seeds rattle inside the pepper when shaken. *Cascabel* means "little round bell," and these are dark blood-red chiles that look like large, dark cherries. They are moderately hot and make a good addition to recipes such as chili, where a little more heat is desired.

Chipotle chiles are dried and smoked large jalapeños that are sold both dried and canned in adobo, a rich and smoky reddish brown sauce. Dark brown and wrinkled, they have a deep smoky flavor and are moderately hot with a sweet, slightly chocolate aftertaste.

Guajillo, meaning "little gourd," is a beautiful russet red dried chile that has a delicate spicy flavor with a slight smokiness that makes it a favorite in Mexican cooking.

Mulato chile peppers are made from poblanos that have been left to ripen to a rich brown color before being dried. This extra ripening adds to the richly complex flavors with a moderate heat. They look much like the ancho, but they are darker and sweeter, with an earthy undertone.

New Mexico chiles are dark red and look much like California chile peppers in appearance. The dried New Mexico chiles are often used in decorative wreaths and strings of peppers. They have a sweet, earthy flavor and are mild in taste, with just enough of a bite to add lots of flavor to a recipe without too much heat.

Pasilla chiles are dried chilaca peppers. They are long and thin with black, wrinkled skin and a mild taste.

Some recipes will call for toasting the dried chiles—yeah, that's a head-scratcher, ain't it?—but trust me, this little extra step really does add a unique flavor that gives the chiles a much richer, deeper, and more pronounced taste—and that's what all this cooking stuff is about, right? Even if the recipe doesn't specifically call for toasted chiles, the flavor bonus often makes it worth doing anyway.

To toast a few dried chile peppers, heat a heavy, ungreased skillet over medium heat until it is very hot. Place the whole chile peppers in the skillet in a single layer without crowding, and let them cook just until they start to get little darker spots and the chiles become fragrant. Watch them very closely, turning as needed and taking care not to let them burn; this only takes a few seconds if your pan is hot enough. Lay them on a wire rack to cool.

To toast a larger quantity of dried chiles, place them in a single layer on a baking sheet in a preheated 350°F oven for 5 to 8 minutes. Monitor them carefully, as the time it takes for the chiles to become fragrant can vary considerably. Turn the chiles often to prevent burnt spots, which will make them taste bitter. They should remain pliable and not be allowed to become brittle. Transfer the chiles to a wire rack to cool as soon as they become fragrant. When they are cool enough to handle, you can store the toasted dried chile peppers in a tightly closed glass jar, or prepare them for use in your recipes.

To use any type of dried chiles in a recipe, first cut off the top off each pepper to remove the stem. Then split the pod open and scrape out the seeds and ribs with a flat knife. The ribs inside the pepper have the highest concentration of capsaicinoids, the hottest part of the chile, and the seeds are hot because they are connected to the ribs. I usually remove all the seeds but leave some part of the inner ribs, but you can do something else depending on your taste preference.

Next, the dried chile is ready to be chopped or pulverized. For larger pieces, chop the dried chiles or snip with kitchen scissors to make pieces that are about the size of a lima bean. To pulverize, use a mortar and pestle for small amounts, or place the seeded chiles in a plastic food bag, cover with a kitchen towel, and give it a few whacks with a meat mallet . . . see, I told you those things were useful! Alternatively, put the dried peppers in a food processor and pulse just until the pieces are about the size of a lentil. Take care or you'll grind the dried chiles into powder, which may be useful for some recipes, but for most, the smaller pieces are best.

Any extra dried chile peppers can be stored in a tightly closed glass jar in a cool, dark place for up to a year. To save time, I process a large quantity of dried chile peppers and keep a supply of toasted and untoasted on hand to use when needed.

A HOW-TO PRIMER ON

roasted tomatoes, peppers, onions, and tomatillos

Roasted tomatoes and peppers add a succulent sweetness and deeper flavor to many recipes. They are available in jars and cans in every supermarket, but you can save a lot of money by roasting these fresh vegetables at home. Not only is it remarkably easy to roast tomatoes and peppers, but it's foolproof, too. The whole process takes only a few minutes and no special kitchen equipment is required. Besides tomatoes and any variety of pepper, you can also roast onions and tomatillos. Since I've included some recipes in this book that use roasted tomatoes and peppers, I thought I should include the directions. There are many other ways to proceed, and you may already have your own method, but for those who don't, here's how I do it:

To fire-roast just 1 or 2 tomatoes or peppers, use a gas burner (sorry, electric just won't work) on your stove, or fire up your grill. Hold a whole tomato or pepper with long-handled tongs and rotate it over the flame until the surface is evenly blistered and charred. Set aside in a bowl and cover tightly with plastic wrap; let cool before removing the seeds and skin.

To roast several fresh tomatoes, start with Roma or Italian-type pulp tomatoes, as they have more meat and less juice and seeds than other varieties. Firm cherry tomatoes may also be used. Slice the tomatoes in half lengthwise and scoop out the seeds. Lay the halves cut side down in a single layer on a baking sheet and brush them with a light film of canola oil or any oil with a high smoke point.

To roast several peppers, choose any variety of sweet peppers or mild or hot chiles. Slice in half lengthwise and scoop out the seeds. Lay the halves cut side down in a single layer on a baking sheet and brush them with a light film of canola oil or any oil with a high smoke point.

For both tomatoes and peppers, position the oven rack at the highest slot beneath the broiler. Place the pan of vegetables under the broiler until the skins start to blister and blacken. Rotate the pan for even roasting and monitor them closely to prevent too much charring. Use long-handled tongs to remove the tomatoes/peppers from the pan as they finish. This should take 5 to 10 minutes. Place the charred tomatoes/peppers in a bowl and cover with plastic wrap until cool. Tomatoes don't need to be peeled. When the peppers are cool enough to handle, the skins should peel away easily. Use the backside of a knife to scrape off any last stubborn bits.

To prepare tomatillos for roasting, peel off the papery outer husk and cut them in half. To prepare onions for roasting, remove the skin and outer layer from the onions and cut them in half. Lay the tomatillo and onion halves cut side down in a single layer on a baking pan and brush the surface with a light film of canola oil or any oil with a high smoke point. Place the pan under the broiler until the surface starts to char. Rotate the pan for even roasting and monitor them closely to prevent too much charring. Use long-handled tongs to turn the tomatillos and onions and finish roasting them on the other side. Place the roasted tomatillos and onions on a plate to cool before using in your recipe.

COOK'S NOTE: Wear disposable plastic gloves when handling hot peppers to protect your skin.

COOK'S NOTE: When the price is right, buy extra quantities of fresh tomatoes and peppers for roasting. They can be frozen flat and then portioned out and packaged, ready for use at another time.

guajillo chile sauce

This is an amazingly useful chile sauce with a really authentic and robust-but-not-too-hot flavor that is wonderfully smoky. Use this sauce in all your favorite Tex-Mex recipes, including enchiladas, chili, posole, tamales, and Mexican rice. Boost the flavor of taco and burrito fillings, dried bean dishes, shredded meat sandwiches, and braised meats. Try the sauce as a spicy dip for shrimp cocktails, or mix it into bean dip for an extra punch. I even use it in breakfast burritos . . . with lots of shredded cheese, of course. • **SERVES 4**

10 to 12 dried guajillo chiles, seeded
2 to 3 tablespoons olive oil
2 medium onions, chopped
8 large cloves garlic, roasted (see page 252)
1 tablespoon ground cumin
½ teaspoon ground cloves
4 cups vegetable, chicken, or beef broth or stock
2 bay leaves
2 teaspoons dried Mexican oregano
2 teaspoons sea salt
Juice of 2 small limes
1 to 2 teaspoons sugar (optional)

Heat a heavy cast-iron skillet over medium heat to toast the chiles. Lay them flat in the hot skillet, skin side up. You may need to do this in batches. Press them flat with a metal spatula as they begin to crackle and start to change color. Watch closely and do not allow them to blacken or burn, as that will change the taste from sweet and smoky to bitter. Flip the chiles as they darken and toast the other side. Place the toasted chiles in a food processor and pulse to pulverize and chop the toasted chiles to a coarse, mealy appearance.

Heat the oil in the pressure cooker over a medium setting and cook the onions until they are soft and golden brown. Add the cooked onions, garlic pulp, cumin, and cloves to the ground chiles in the food processor and blend, adding just enough broth to make a smooth puree, scraping down the sides of the container often. Heat the oil remaining in the pressure cooker and add the puree, stirring constantly. Watch closely as the puree reduces, adjusting the heat as necessary as the chile mixture begins to darken. You want to see the puree slowly change to a distinctive brick red paste over 6 to 8 minutes, so keep stirring and be patient. Deglaze the cooker with the remaining broth, scraping up all the browned bits from the bottom. Stir in the bay leaves, oregano, and salt. Lock the lid in place. Bring to 15psi over high heat and immediately reduce the heat to the lowest possible setting to stabilize and maintain that pressure. Cook for 8 minutes. Remove from the heat and use the natural release method before opening the lid. Remove the bay leaves. Stir in the lime juice. Taste and adjust seasoning as desired. Add the sugar in small increments if the sauce has a bitter aftertaste.

red chili sauce

Red chili sauce is a "mother sauce" and should be made in quantity and then portioned out and tucked away in the freezer for later use as needed. Another good reason to make it in advance is to allow extra time for all the complex flavors to get well acquainted before you use it. If you enjoy Mexican cuisine, there are probably a couple of big cans of this sauce in your pantry, ready to add unique taste to a long list of popular Mexican dishes. My homemade version begins with a variety of mild dried chile peppers, and the end result is a pungent, flavor-packed sauce that you will use in recipes for Spanish rice, enchiladas, chili con carne, tamales, huevos rancheros, dipping sauce for quesadillas . . . hungry yet? Red chili sauce is also excellent as a sauce over sliced chicken, pork, or beef, and for shredded meat sandwiches. • **SERVES 4**

Step One: MAKE THE CHILE PEPPER BLEND

4 large dried ancho, California, mulato, or pasilla chiles
2 large dried guajillo chiles
2 small dried chipotle chiles
1 or 2 dried cascabel chiles (optional for those who like more heat)

Wear protective gloves while handling the chiles. Lightly toast the whole dried ancho and guajillo chiles (see page 297). When cool enough to handle, cut the chiles open lengthwise and remove the stems, seeds, and ribs. Cut all the chiles into small pieces with scissors or a knife. Place the pieces in a blender and process in batches until they are all a uniform, powdery texture. Set aside the powdered chile blend.

Step Two: MAKE THE SAUCE

3 to 4 tablespoons vegetable oil
1 large sweet onion, diced
6 plump cloves garlic, minced
2 teaspoons ground cumin
1 teaspoon dried oregano, crushed
½ cup strong brewed coffee
2 teaspoons balsamic vinegar
1 teaspoon salt, or to taste
4 large Roma tomatoes, peeled and diced (see page 286)
2 tomatillos, papery husks removed and diced
10 sprigs fresh cilantro, minced
3 tablespoons tomato paste
1 teaspoon sugar, or to taste

Heat the oil in the pressure cooker over medium-high heat and cook the onion until soft. Add the garlic, cumin, oregano, and the powdered chile blend, stirring as the mixture sizzles and becomes fragrant. Deglaze the cooker with the coffee, scraping up all those crusty brown bits from the bottom. Stir in the vinegar and salt. In the following order, add the tomatoes, tomatillos, and cilantro, but do not stir. Then dot the tomato paste over the top, and do not stir. Lock the lid in place. Bring to 15psi over high heat and immediately reduce the heat to the lowest possible setting to stabilize and maintain that pressure. Cook for 10 minutes. Remove from the heat and use the natural release method before opening the lid. Stir the mixture to mix. Using a handheld blender, puree the sauce to a smooth consistency. Taste and adjust the seasonings, adding sugar if the tomatoes are bitter. For a thicker texture, allow the sauce to simmer over low heat without a lid, stirring often to prevent burning. Continue cooking until the sauce is reduced to the desired consistency, about 8 minutes. The sauce will darken slightly, developing a nice rich color as the spices cook. Refrigerate in a tightly closed container for use within a few days, or portion into freezer bags and store for later use.

desserts

poached plums with brown sugar sauce and bourbon cream

This jazzed-up recipe was inspired by the simple, rustic dessert dishes that were popular in days gone by, when fruits in season were poached with a little sugar or syrup. Often these were whole fruits, such as large peaches, apricots, and plums—and did I mention you left the pits in?—and it was an inexpensive, no-fuss, fast, and easy way to put a sweet dessert on the table. I chose whole plums for this because they are naturally sweet and juicy and pretty to look at, and they seem to be a little neglected these days. Poached plums turn all soft and pudgy, just oozing with juicy sweetness. They also look spectacular nestled in a bowl of vanilla ice cream or sitting on top of a slice of pound cake. Served with a spoonful of brown sugar sauce and a dollop of bourbon-infused whipped cream on top, this old-fashioned dessert goes from simple to spectacular.

• **SERVES 4 TO 8**

Step One: THE BOURBON CREAM

Make this topping in advance to allow the flavors to blend.

1 cup heavy cream
1 tablespoon bourbon
½ cup sour cream
½ cup packed light brown sugar
⅛ teaspoon salt

Add the cream and bourbon to the bowl of a stand mixer and use the whisk attachment to beat at medium speed until fluffy and doubled in volume. Fold in the sour cream, brown sugar, and salt until combined. Cover with plastic wrap and refrigerate for at least 4 hours or until ready to serve. Stir before spooning the cream onto individual servings of plums.

(continued)

Step Two: THE PLUMS AND BROWN SUGAR SAUCE

½ cup sweet port or other sweet dessert wine
8 plums (any variety)
1 cinnamon stick
1 tablespoon butter
⅓ cup packed light brown sugar
1 tablespoon lemon zest
A few long strands of lemon peel, for garnish

Pour the port into the pressure cooker and add the plums and the cinnamon stick. Lock the lid in place. Bring to 15psi over high heat and immediately reduce the heat to the lowest possible setting to stabilize and maintain that pressure. Cook for 4 minutes. Remove from the heat and use the quick release method before opening the lid. Using a slotted spoon, transfer the plums to a plate. Heat the wine in the pressure cooker over medium-high heat, uncovered, and boil until it is reduced by half. Discard the cinnamon stick. Add the butter and brown sugar, stirring as the sugar dissolves and the sauce thickens. Add the lemon zest and return the plums to the pressure cooker, turning them until coated with the sauce. Serve in individual bowls, topped with the brown sugar sauce and a spoonful of the bourbon cream.

fresh figs poached in spiced wine

There were two huge and very old fig trees on my grandma's ranch. Every year they were loaded with bushels of figs that we ate fresh and still warm from the sun. My mom would haul a box of figs home and make cookies for us, and this dessert. Sometimes she served these poached figs with vanilla ice cream, and sometimes with whipped cream. Both are wonderful. • **SERVES 4**

2 cups sweet red wine
1 cup sugar
Zest and juice of 1 lemon
2 sprigs basil
1 bay leaf
1 cinnamon stick
1 teaspoon whole black peppercorns
8 fresh figs, with stems
Whipped cream, for garnish

Place the wine, sugar, lemon zest and juice, basil, bay leaf, cinnamon stick, and peppercorns in the pressure cooker. Simmer over medium heat, stirring, until the sugar is dissolved. Place the figs in the pressure cooker. Lock the lid in place. Bring to 15psi over high heat and immediately reduce the heat to the lowest possible setting to stabilize and maintain that pressure. Cook for 6 minutes. Remove from the heat and use the quick release method before opening the lid. Gently remove the figs and divide among dessert bowls. Scoop out and discard the spices. Simmer the wine sauce over medium heat until it is reduced and begins to thicken and cling to the spoon. Spoon some of the sauce over each serving of figs. Add a dollop of whipped cream just before serving.

spiced apple brown betty

A brown betty is a simple American dessert that dates back to colonial times. It's a rustic, homey dish of spiced fruit layered between buttered crumbs. The most familiar version is the popular apple brown betty, made with tart apples. Almost any other type of fruits or berries can be used to make this dish, and you may certainly use any custom fruit mix to match to your own tastes. Served warm in cold weather or chilled in the summer, this sweet and tart dessert is beautiful with a splash or milk or cream, or a scoop of good vanilla ice cream . . . oh my!

My secret here is the homemade toasted bread crumbs from the thicker, crustier end slices saved from several loaves of bread. Use any variety of white or wheat bread, and then toast them with the sugar until they begin to caramelize, creating a richer flavor. • **SERVES 4 TO 6**

Step One: THE TOASTED BREAD CRUMBS

7 slices stale bread
1½ tablespoons butter
¼ cup sugar
½ cup old-fashioned rolled oats

Preheat the oven to 400°F. Tear the bread into pieces and pulse in a food processor with the butter and sugar until coarsely ground. Spread the bread crumb mixture and the oats in a thin, even layer on a baking sheet. Toast in the oven until the mixture turns golden brown, about 5 minutes. Watch closely, stirring occasionally to prevent burning. Remove from the oven and break up any clumps with a fork. Reserve ½ cup of the toasted mixture to use as a topping.

Step Two: THE SPICED APPLES

1 tablespoon butter, softened, for greasing the insert pan, plus 2 tablespoons, melted
4 tart apples, such as Granny Smith or Braeburn, cored and sliced
Zest and juice of 1 lemon
½ teaspoon salt
⅔ cup packed dark brown sugar
1 teaspoon ground cinnamon
¼ teaspoon ground nutmeg

Butter a stainless-steel insert pan that will fit within your pressure cooker. In a bowl, toss the apples, lemon juice and zest, salt, brown sugar, cinnamon, and nutmeg. Place alternate layers of apples and bread crumbs into the insert pan, ending with apples on top. Pour the melted butter over the ingredients and cover the bowl securely with aluminum foil or a tight-fitting lid. Add ½ cup water to the pressure cooker and position the cooking rack in the bottom. Use foil helper handles to place the insert pan on the cooking rack. Lock the lid in place. Bring to 15psi over high heat and immediately reduce the heat to the lowest possible setting to stabilize and maintain that pressure. Cook for 10 minutes. Remove from the heat and use the natural release method before opening the lid. Lift the pan out of the pressure cooker and remove the covering immediately. Spoon into individual dessert dishes and sprinkle some of the reserved crumb mixture on top. Serve warm.

Variation:

CHERRY BROWN BETTY

Omit the lemon juice and zest and the cinnamon. Substitute granulated sugar for the dark brown sugar. Substitute 2 cups halved fresh sweet cherries for the apples. Cook as directed.

caramel apple streusel

In the fall, my grandma would sometimes make us warm and gooey caramel apples as a special treat. While we all trooped outside with our sticky prizes, she would also make a caramel apple dessert for our dinner. Her original recipe is lost to time, but like many women of her day, she probably made it on the fly using whatever ingredients she had on hand. I created this dessert from my memory of those crisp fall days spent at her farm, and it's been a longtime family favorite. This is a lovely pressure cooker dessert, and best served warm with vanilla ice cream.

• **SERVES 4 TO 8**

Step One: THE APPLES

4 Granny Smith apples, peeled, cored, and thinly sliced
½ cup sugar
1 tablespoon all-purpose flour
1 teaspoon ground cinnamon
4 tablespoons (½ stick) butter, melted
1 tablespoon fresh lemon juice

In a medium bowl, toss the apples with the sugar, flour, cinnamon, butter, and lemon juice. Use nonstick cooking spray to coat the inside of a 1½-quart stainless-steel or silicone insert pan that will fit loosely inside your pressure cooker. Spread the mixture evenly in the pan.

Step Two: THE STREUSEL

1½ cups all-purpose flour
1 cup packed dark brown sugar
1 cup quick-cooking oats
½ cup finely chopped walnuts
1 cup (2 sticks) butter, softened

In a bowl, mix all the ingredients until just barely moistened. Spoon the mixture evenly over the apples.

Step Three: THE CARAMEL SAUCE

1 (14-ounce) package individually wrapped caramels
1 (5-ounce) can evaporated milk

Unwrap the caramels and put them in a heavy saucepan with the evaporated milk. Cook over low heat, stirring frequently, until all the caramels have melted and the mixture has a smooth consistency. Drizzle about half the caramel sauce over the top of the apples and streusel, reserving the remaining half. Spray the underside of a square of aluminum foil with cooking spray and tightly crimp it over the top of the insert pan. Make 3 or 4 small slits around the edge of the foil to allow steam to escape. Place the rack in the bottom of the cooker and add 1½ cups water. Use foil helper handles to lower the insert pan into the pressure cooker. Lock the lid in place. Bring to 15psi over high heat and immediately reduce the heat to the lowest possible setting to stabilize and maintain that pressure. Cook for 6 minutes. Remove from the heat and use the quick release method before opening the lid. Spoon the apple streusel into dessert bowls, add a scoop of vanilla ice cream and a spoonful of the warm caramel sauce, and serve immediately.

berry bread pudding with raspberry coulis sauce

Naturally you must begin with stale, day-old bread, but the secret to making a luscious bread pudding is using the right type of bread. Look for a heavy, dense bread and avoid thinly sliced breads with coarse, porous textures, as they simply cannot hold enough milk for a decent pudding. This is important because the better the bread, the more milk and egg mixture will soak in, which will make the pudding smoother and more cakelike. According to my grandmother's recipes, the crusts "must" be removed before making bread pudding. She was quite adamant about that, but if you prefer a more rustic type of bread pudding, then leave the bread whole. Served with the fruit sauce, this is a wonderful combination of tartness and sweetness. • **SERVES 6**

Step One: THE COULIS SAUCE

1 cup unsweetened raspberry fruit spread
2 tablespoons sugar (optional; the sauce should be more tart than sweet)
2 tablespoons Grand Marnier, Cointreau, triple sec, or orange curaçao

Place the fruit spread in a small bowl and stir in the sugar if desired. Add the Grand Marnier and stir until the mixture is smooth. Set aside until ready to serve. The raspberry sauce may be refrigerated for up to 1 week.

Step Two: THE PUDDING

5 tablespoons butter, softened
2 cups milk, or use a combination of milk and heavy cream, plus more if needed
4 large eggs, lightly beaten
2 teaspoons vanilla extract
½ cup sugar
1 teaspoon ground nutmeg
Pinch of salt
8 thick slices stale bread
2 cups fresh or frozen blackberries or raspberries

Use 1 tablespoon of the butter to grease the inside of a 1½-quart metal ring mold, Bundt pan, or pudding mold, as well as the inside of the lid or a sheet of aluminum foil to cover it. In a large bowl, mix together the milk, eggs, vanilla, sugar, nutmeg, and salt. Spread the bread slices with the remaining 4 tablespoons butter and then stack them up. Cut through the stack of bread, making 1-inch cubes. Put all the bread cubes into the bowl with the milk mixture, pushing them beneath the liquid. Wait about 10 minutes for the bread to soak up as much of the milk as possible. Add more milk, if needed. Continue adding more milk as long as the bread will absorb it; this might take as long as a half an hour. The bread should be almost dissolved into a batterlike consistency for this recipe. Place a layer of berries in the bottom of the ring mold. Add about half of the bread batter, and then another layer of berries, and then the remaining batter. Cover the pudding mold tightly with the lid, or crimp the square of aluminum foil over the top of the insert pan. Place the rack in the pressure cooker and add 1 cup water. Using foil helper handles, lower the pudding mold into the cooker. Lock the lid in place. Bring to 15psi over high heat and immediately reduce the heat to the lowest possible setting to stabilize and maintain that pressure. Cook for 25 minutes. Remove from the heat and use the natural release method before opening the lid. Carefully lift the pudding out of the cooker and remove the covering.

To serve, run a knife blade around the inside of the pan to loosen the sides, and place a serving plate over the top. Quickly invert the pan to unmold the pudding. Slice the pudding as you would a cake. Place a spoonful of the coulis sauce on each dessert plate, making a decorative pattern if you like. Add a slice of the bread pudding and serve warm.

chocolate custard

No boxed custard here! None of those mixes tastes as delicious as an old-fashioned, silky, chocolaty, wholesome custard made from real eggs, milk, and good-quality chocolate. • **SERVES 4**

- 2 tablespoons butter, softened, for greasing the custard cups
- 2 ounces bittersweet chocolate, grated
- 2 cups milk
- 2 large eggs
- ½ cup sugar, or to taste
- ½ teaspoon salt
- 1 teaspoon vanilla extract
- Whipped cream, for garnish

Butter 4 (6-ounce) custard cups. Reserve 1 teaspoon of the grated chocolate for a garnish, and add the remaining chocolate to the milk. Scald the milk on the stovetop, stirring to make sure all the chocolate is melted and the mixture is well blended. Beat the eggs with an electric mixer. Add the sugar and salt, blending well. Very slowly pour the hot milk mixture into the egg mixture with the mixer on medium speed, adding a little at a time in a thin stream. Add the vanilla. Fill the custard cups about two-thirds full with the custard mixture. Securely cover each custard cup with a square of aluminum foil. Place the cooking rack in the pressure cooker and add 1 cup water. Arrange the custard cups in the pressure cooker, stacking in two offset layers if necessary. Lock the lid in place. Bring to 15psi over high heat and immediately reduce the heat to the lowest possible setting to stabilize and maintain that pressure. Cook for 4 minutes. Remove from the heat and use the quick release method before opening the lid. Lift out the custards and loosen the foil to allow the steam to escape. Refrigerate for at least 4 hours.

To serve, run a thin knife blade around the sides of the cups and unmold on small dessert plates. Top with whipped cream and sprinkle some of the reserved grated chocolate on top of each custard.

caribbean coconut-mango rice pudding

SERVES 4

1 (15-ounce) can cream of coconut (not coconut milk)
1 (12-ounce) can evaporated milk
1 teaspoon almond extract
1 teaspoon ground cardamom
1 cup long-grain white rice
⅔ cup sweetened flaked coconut
2 tablespoons dark rum
1 mango, peeled, pitted, and pureed
½ cup chopped macadamia nuts

In a 2-quart insert bowl that will fit within your pressure cooker, stir 2¾ cups water, the cream of coconut, evaporated milk, almond extract, and cardamom until combined. Add the rice. Place the cooking rack in the pressure cooker and add ½ cup water. Place the bowl on the rack and lock the lid in place. Bring to 15psi over high heat and immediately reduce the heat to the lowest possible setting to stabilize and maintain that pressure. Cook for 8 minutes. Remove from the heat and use the natural release method before opening the lid.

While the pudding cooks, toast the coconut: Heat a small, heavy skillet over medium heat. Add the coconut and cook for 4 to 5 minutes, stirring constantly, or until the coconut is lightly browned. Transfer to a plate to cool.

Stir the rum into the pudding. Press a sheet of plastic wrap onto the surface of the pudding and refrigerate until chilled. Spoon a layer of rice pudding into dessert parfait glasses, followed by a layer of the pureed mango. If your glasses are tall enough, add a second layer of pudding and mango. Sprinkle the toasted coconut and macadamia nuts on top before serving.

orange-almond poppy seed cake with orange glaze

There were acres and acres of orange groves on my grandmother's California farm. One of the chores we had as children was collecting the ripe oranges that fell off the trees. The perfect ones went to the farmer's co-op market, and the rest we ate or squeezed for juice. There was always a big glass jar of pulpy fresh orange juice in the fridge, and every now and then Grandma would make this cake. This is a PIP recipe, and you will need a 6-cup Bundt pan, or a 1½-quart ring mold, or a traditional pudding mold that will fit within your pressure cooker, turning it into a mini oven.

Select Valencia oranges whenever possible for this cake. It is one of the sweet oranges and well known for its tangy, pulpy juice. The next best orange to use would be the navel orange, but don't stop there: Try your own customized versions substituting other citrus fruits like lemons, tangerines, blood oranges, or red grapefruit. This cake is perfect served plain as a snack while it's still warm, but for a special treat try adding the sweet glaze. • **SERVES 6**

Step One: TOAST THE POPPY SEEDS

Toasting poppy seeds takes only a couple of minutes, and it really increases their flavor by releasing the aromatic compounds in the seeds.

½ cup poppy seeds (about 2½ ounces)

Heat a small heavy cast-iron skillet over medium-high heat until it is very hot. Pour the poppy seeds into the hot, dry skillet and stir with a spatula. Keep stirring until you begin to smell the aroma, which should only take about a minute. Remove the toasted seeds from the skillet immediately to prevent burning, and spread them out on a plate to cool.

Step Two: THE CAKE BATTER

2 cups all-purpose flour
1 teaspoon baking soda
1 teaspoon baking powder
½ teaspoon salt
2 large eggs, at room temperature, separated
1½ cups sugar
½ cup (1 stick) butter, softened
⅔ cup buttermilk
Zest and juice from 2 medium oranges
2 teaspoons almond extract

In a mixing bowl, sift or blend together the flour, baking soda, baking powder, and salt. Beat the egg whites with an electric mixer on high until foamy. Continue beating and gradually add ¼ cup of the sugar until the whites hold stiff, shiny peaks. Transfer the egg whites to a separate bowl and set aside. Add the butter and remaining sugar to the mixer bowl and beat on high speed until light and fluffy. Add the egg yolks and continue beating until thick and lemon colored. Add the buttermilk, orange juice and zest, and almond extract. Slowly add the dry ingredients and the poppy seeds to the egg mixture; beating on low speed until well blended. Gently fold in the beaten whites by hand until just blended. Pour the batter into a well-greased and floured decorative mold. Cover the mold with a tight-fitting lid or crimp a sheet of doubled aluminum foil over the top. Place the cooking rack in the bottom of the pressure cooker and add 1 cup water. Use foil helper handles to place the mold in the pressure cooker. Lock the lid in place. Bring to 15psi over high heat and immediately reduce the heat to the lowest possible setting to stabilize and maintain that pressure. Cook for 22 minutes. Remove from the heat and use the natural release method before opening the lid. Lift the mold out of the pressure cooker to a wire cooling rack and remove the lid. Let cool for 10 minutes and then turn the cake out onto a serving plate.

Orange Glaze

¼ cup thawed orange juice concentrate
1 teaspoon orange zest
1 cup confectioners' sugar
1 tablespoon thinly shredded orange peel, for garnish

Combine the orange juice concentrate, zest, and confectioners' sugar in a small bowl, stirring until smoothly blended. Spoon the glaze over the top of the cake in a thin layer, letting some run down the sides. After the glaze sets, additional layers may be added as desired, letting the glaze set after each addition. Sprinkle the orange peel shreds on top.

COOK'S NOTE: The decorative molds make a lovely presentation, but don't be put off if you don't have any fancy pan for your pressure cooker. Do what my grandma used to do, and convert any ordinary round insert pan of metal or silicone bakeware into a ring mold by placing an empty 4- to 6-ounce can in the center. Grease the outside of the little can, and weight it down with a handful of dried beans to hold it in place. Gently pull out the can before unmolding your cake.

---

chocolate-banana cake

Now, I like chocolate cake as much as anyone, but let me tell you about my dad. He adored the stuff. He was a true chocoholic . . . much to the delight of all us kids, who reaped the rewards of his insatiable chocolate craving. One of the few things that Dad could actually cook for himself was this simple chocolate cake. I have fond memories of him standing by the stove and carefully timing the pressure cooker as he made his midnight snack. The rattling noise of our old pressure cooker would soon wake us up, and one by one, all four children would find their way to the kitchen to find glasses of milk already on the table waiting for us.

As the story goes, my grandmother made an earlier version of this eggless cake when American cooks were scrambling to adapt traditional recipes to food rationing during WWII. Many common staples like sugar, butter, eggs, milk—all the cake-making necessities—were in short supply back then, so desserts tended to be low fat and almost vegan. Imported foodstuffs like bananas and chocolate were scarce, so her original ingredient list included applesauce, but Dad liked bananas better in his version. Serve this cake plain while it's still warm with a glass of cold milk, or add a scoop of vanilla ice cream. Of course, a bit of chocolate frosting makes a wonderful addition, too. • **SERVES 6**

- 1 tablespoon butter, softened, for greasing the cake pan
- 1 cup whole wheat flour
- ⅓ cup unsweetened cocoa powder
- ½ cup packed dark brown sugar
- ¼ teaspoon salt
- ½ teaspoon baking powder
- 2 tablespoons vegetable oil
- ⅔ cup mashed overripe bananas

Butter a cake pan that will fit within your pressure cooker. Mix together the flour, cocoa, sugar, salt, and baking powder in a mixing bowl. Add the oil and bananas and stir just enough to combine with the dry ingredients. Scrape the batter into the cake pan. Cover the cake pan securely with aluminum foil. Add ½ cup water to the pressure cooker and position the cooking rack in the bottom. Use foil helper handles to place the insert pan on the cooking rack. Lock the lid in place. Bring to 15psi over high heat and immediately reduce the heat to the lowest possible setting to stabilize and maintain that pressure. Cook for 18 minutes. Remove from the heat and use the natural release method before opening the lid. Cool in the pan for 5 minutes, and then invert the cake onto a wire rack to finish cooling.

Variation:

DOUBLE-CHOCOLATE BANANA CAKE

Fold ½ cup semisweet chocolate chips to the cake batter when you add the bananas.

double-lemon yogurt cake with crushed strawberry sauce

I'm always on the lookout for dessert ideas that will inspire a new pressure cooker recipe, and especially cakes and dessert breads because there are so few of them. This cake is very tender and moist, and it's elegant enough for a special dessert or that romantic dinner you keep putting off. It also makes a deliciously sweet treat for a lovely brunch or teatime. • **SERVES 6**

Step One: THE CRUSHED STRAWBERRY SAUCE

2 cups hulled strawberries
3 tablespoons sugar, or to taste
1 tablespoon fresh lemon juice
2 tablespoons Grand Marnier, Cointreau, triple sec, or orange curaçao

Combine all the ingredients in a blender. Puree until very smooth. Taste and adjust the sugar as desired. Cover and refrigerate until chilled. The sauce may be prepared a day ahead.

Step Two: THE CAKE

1 to 2 tablespoons butter, softened, for greasing the insert pan
2 cups all-purpose flour
1½ teaspoons baking powder
½ teaspoon baking soda
⅛ teaspoon salt
1 cup plain yogurt
⅓ cup unsweetened applesauce
1 cup sugar
Zest and juice of 1 large lemon
2 large eggs
Whipped cream, for garnish (optional)

Generously butter the inside of a 1½-quart metal ring mold, Bundt pan, or pudding mold that will fit within your pressure cooker. Grease the inside of the lid or a sheet of aluminum foil to cover the pan. Dust the inside of the insert pan with ⅓ cup of the flour, tapping out the excess. In a large bowl, sift together the remaining 1⅔ cups flour, baking powder, baking soda, and salt. Use a stand mixer with the paddle attachment to blend together the yogurt, applesauce, sugar, lemon zest, and juice. Add the eggs one by one, beating well after each addition. Slowly add the dry ingredients, beating until smooth after each addition. Scrape the batter into the prepared insert pan, filling about three-quarters full. Cover the insert pan securely with the lid or crimp the square of aluminum foil over the rim of the mold. Place the rack in the pressure cooker and add 1 cup water. Using foil helper handles, lower the mold pan into the pressure cooker. Lock the lid in place. Bring to 15psi over high heat and immediately reduce the heat to the lowest possible setting to stabilize and maintain that pressure. Cook for

(continued)

16 minutes. Remove from the heat and use the natural release method before opening the lid. Carefully lift the pan out of the cooker and remove the covering. Place on a wire rack to cool for about 10 minutes. Run a thin knife blade around the inside of the pan to loosen the sides, then place a serving plate over the top and quickly invert the pan to unmold the cake. To serve, place each slice of cake on a small dessert plate and top with the strawberry sauce and a mound of whipped cream if desired.

COOK'S NOTE: Substitute fruit-flavored yogurts, such as strawberry, raspberry, blueberry, or peach, to make a variety of different cakes. Do the same with the crushed fruit sauce, using the same fruit to match the flavor of the cake or trying a different fruit for a complementary or contrasting flavor.

---

banana-nut upside-down cake

If you think you can't make a scratch cake, or cook it in the pressure cooker, wait till you try this. This dessert is a very simple yellow cake with a top layer of caramelized bananas and nuts. This is a fantastic way to use overripe bananas. Not that you can't use the perfect-looking bananas, but wait a few days until they start to get soft and develop a few black speckles, and they'll taste and smell even more bananalike. To cook this PIP recipe, you will need a plain, flat-bottomed, stainless-steel insert pan that will fit within your pressure cooker. Serve this dessert with whipped cream or vanilla ice cream, if desired. • **SERVES 6**

Step One: THE CARAMEL LAYER

1 cup sugar
3 to 4 very ripe bananas
⅔ cup chopped nuts, such as walnuts or pecans

Put the sugar in a heavy skillet over medium heat to melt the sugar. Using a wooden spoon, begin stirring when the sugar starts to liquefy. Continue stirring and cook until the caramel becomes amber in color, 10 to 12 minutes. Watch closely, as the caramel can darken and burn very quickly at this stage. Using oven mitts, immediately pour the hot caramel into a stainless-steel insert pan, taking care not to let it splatter. Quickly tilt and rotate the insert pan, distributing the caramel evenly over the bottom and up the sides of the pan before it sets. Cut the bananas in half, and then cut each half lengthwise. Place the halves close together, cut side down, on top of the caramel in a spokelike pattern, or any other decorative arrangement you prefer. Distribute the nuts on top of the bananas, using the wooden spoon to press them into the caramel in the gaps between the bananas.

Step Two: THE CAKE LAYER

1¼ cups all-purpose flour
1 teaspoon baking powder
1 teaspoon baking soda
⅓ cup butter, softened
¾ cup sugar
2 large eggs
1 teaspoon vanilla extract
¾ cup buttermilk

In a medium bowl, sift together the flour, baking powder, and baking soda. In a large bowl, cream together the butter and sugar until light and fluffy. Beat in the eggs one at a time, then stir in the vanilla. Beat in the flour mixture alternately with the buttermilk, mixing just until incorporated. Pour the batter over the bananas. Cover the top of the pan with a doubled sheet of aluminum foil, crimping it tightly around the

(continued)

rim. Place the cooking rack in the pressure cooker and add 1 cup water. Use foil helper handles to position the insert pan in the pressure cooker. Lock the lid in place. Bring to 15psi over high heat and immediately reduce the heat to the lowest possible setting to stabilize and maintain that pressure. Cook for 12 minutes. Remove from the heat and use the natural release method before opening the lid. Test for doneness: A toothpick inserted into the center of the cake should come out clean. If needed, return to pressure for an additional 3 minutes and again use the natural release method. Transfer the insert pan to a wire cooling rack and run a thin knife blade around the sides of the pan to loosen the cake. Unmold the cake while it's still warm. Choose a deep, rimmed serving plate (a pie plate is good) to catch any melted caramel sauce; place it over the insert pan and quickly flip the setup over. Carefully remove the insert pan. Serve warm.

Variation:

PEACH UPSIDE-DOWN CAKE

Substitute 3 ripe peaches or nectarines for the bananas. Peel and slice the peaches into a bowl. Taste, and if the peaches are too tart add ⅓ cup (or an amount to your taste) light brown sugar. Arrange the peach slices in a decorative spiral pattern on top on the caramel. Omit the nuts if desired. Proceed with the recipe, but cook for 15 minutes rather than 12.

Variation:

PLUM UPSIDE-DOWN CAKE

Substitute 6 or 7 ripe plums for the bananas. Peel the plums, cut them in half, and remove the pits. Arrange the plum halves cut side down on the caramel in the insert pan in a decorative pattern. Omit the nuts if desired. Proceed with the recipe, but cook for 15 minutes rather than 12.

mango cheesecake with mango gelée and raspberry coulis

I love this cheesecake! It's so beautiful that it looks like it belongs on a magazine cover, and no one ever believes that it was cooked in a pressure cooker. It's not just lovely to look at, my dears, but it also tastes scrumptious, with the creamy cheesecake sitting on a gingersnap crust and hiding delicate bits of mangos, all topped off with that brilliant mango gelée and the delicious contrasting flavor of the vivid raspberry coulis. Now don't start hyperventilating and swoon over an innocent French word like *coulis*; it's just a fruit sauce—a thick, gorgeous, brightly colored and tangy fruit sauce that really complements the mango cheesecake, and many other desserts as well. • **SERVES 6**

Step One: THE CRUST

1 tablespoon butter, softened, for greasing the pan, plus 2 tablespoons, melted
⅔ cup gingersnap cookie crumbs

With the softened butter, grease the bottom and sides of a springform pan that will fit inside your pressure cooker. In a small bowl, mix the cookie crumbs and melted butter until just barely moistened. The crumbs should look grainy, not clumped together. Spread the crumb mixture a little thicker over the bottom of the pan, and make it a bit thinner as you pat the crumbs part of the way up the side of the pan. Use a small glass (a shot glass works well) to press the crumbs around the edges for a smooth, even base.

Step Two: THE FILLING

2 (8-ounce) packages cream cheese, softened
⅔ cup sugar, plus more if needed
2 large eggs
2 tablespoons fresh lime juice
2 teaspoons grated lime zest
1 teaspoon almond extract
½ cup diced fresh mango

Use a stand mixer with the paddle attachment to blend the cream cheese and sugar until smooth. Add the eggs, lime juice, lime zest, and almond extract. Gently fold the diced mango into the cheese mixture. Taste the filling and add sugar if additional sweetness is desired. Pour the cheesecake batter into the prepared springform pan. Crimp a square of aluminum foil tightly over the top of the pan. Place the cooking rack in the pressure cooker and add 1 cup water. Center the springform pan on a foil helper handle strip and lower it into the pressure cooker. Lock the lid in place. Bring to 15psi over high heat and immediately reduce the heat to the lowest possible setting to

(continued)

stabilize and maintain that pressure. Cook for 30 minutes. Remove from the heat and use the natural release method before opening the lid. Carefully lift the springform pan out of the pressure cooker, remove the aluminum foil cover, and move the pan to a wire rack to cool. Leave the cheesecake in the springform pan, cover the top with plastic wrap, and refrigerate for at least 8 hours and preferably overnight. When the cheesecake is thoroughly chilled, make the gelée.

Step Three: THE MANGO GELÉE

1 (¼-ounce) packet unflavored gelatin
1 to 2 tablespoons boiling water, or as needed
1 cup fresh mango puree
2 tablespoons fresh lime juice

In a small ramekin, dissolve the gelatin in a small amount of boiling water. Stir the gelatin into the mango puree and add the lime juice, mixing well. Gently spread the gelée over the top of the chilled cheesecake (still in the springform pan). Cover the springform pan tightly with plastic wrap and refrigerate until the gelée topping is firmly set.

Step Four: THE COULIS

2 cups fresh or thawed frozen unsweetened raspberries
2 tablespoons sugar (optional; the sauce should be more tart than sweet)
2 tablespoons Grand Marnier, Cointreau, triple sec, or orange curaçao

Puree the raspberries and any accumulated juice in a blender or food processor until smooth. Using the back of a large spoon, press the puree through a fine-mesh sieve into a bowl. Discard the seeds. Stir the sugar and Grand Marnier into the puree. Adjust the sweetness and liqueur to your taste. Cover and refrigerate until ready to serve. The raspberry sauce may be refrigerated for up to 1 week, and any extra may be frozen for later use.

To serve, carefully run a small thin knife blade around the sides of the pan to loosen the cheesecake. Unlock the springform pan and lift off the ring. Cut the cheesecake into serving portions. Make a 2-inch diameter puddle of coulis in the center of each dessert plate, and then make a fanciful pattern of swirls, dots, or zigzags around it. Place a slice of cheesecake in the center of each plate and serve immediately. Pass the remaining coulis at the table.

strawberry swirl cheesecake

Pretty, swirly cheesecakes have always intrigued me, and I just love the way they look— and taste, too. This is the perfect Fourth of July dessert, when strawberries are in season and it's way too hot to turn on the oven. Just watch the faces light up as you present this gorgeous treat. • **SERVES 6**

Step One: THE CRUST

1 tablespoon butter, softened, for greasing the insert pan, plus 2 tablespoons, melted
⅔ cup shortbread cookie crumbs

Butter a springform pan that will fit inside your pressure cooker. Mix the crumbs and melted butter until evenly moistened. The crumbs should look grainy, not clumped together. Spread the crumb mixture a little thicker over the bottom of the pan, and make it a bit thinner as you pat the crumbs part of the way up the side of the pan. Use a small glass (a shot glass works well) to press the crumbs around the edges for a smooth, even base.

Step Two: THE FILLING

11 ounces cream cheese, softened
⅔ cup plus 2 to 3 tablespoons granulated sugar
2 large eggs
1 tablespoon fresh lemon juice
1 teaspoon vanilla extract
1 cup fresh strawberry puree
6 large perfect strawberries, for garnish

Use a stand mixer with the paddle attachment to blend the cream cheese and ⅔ cup of the sugar until smooth. Add the eggs, lemon juice, and vanilla extract. Pour the cheesecake batter into the prepared springform pan. Add the remaining sugar to taste to the strawberry puree. Drop heaping teaspoonfuls of the strawberry puree at equal intervals over the top of the batter. Cover and refrigerate the remaining puree for the garnish. Cut through the drops of puree with a small knife, swirling it into the filling for a marble effect. Crimp a square of aluminum foil tightly over the top of the pan. Place the cooking rack in the pressure cooker and add 1½ cups water. Center the springform pan on a foil helper handle strip and lower it into the pressure cooker. Lock the lid in place. Bring to 15psi over high heat and immediately reduce the heat to the lowest possible setting to stabilize and maintain that pressure. Cook for 20 minutes. Remove from the heat and use the natural release method before opening the lid. Carefully lift the springform pan out of the pressure cooker, remove the aluminum

(continued)

foil cover, and move the pan to a wire rack to cool. Leave the cheesecake in the springform pan and refrigerate for at least 8 hours or preferably overnight.

To serve, carefully unlock the sides of the springform pan. Cut the cheesecake. Spoon some of the reserved strawberry puree on one side of a dessert plate and then smear it across with a rubber spatula. Position a slice of cheesecake in the center of the plate. Wash and dry the strawberries. For a fan shape you'll want to leave the cap (the green leaves) on. Make a decorative strawberry fan garnish by cutting thin slices in the berry from the bottom to the top without cutting through the stem cap. Carefully fan out the slices and place the beautiful garnish at the wide end of the cheesecake slice just before serving.

Variation:

BLUEBERRY SWIRL CHEESECAKE

Replace the strawberry puree with 1 cup fresh or frozen blueberry puree. Omit the strawberry fans and garnish with a few fresh blueberries.

apricot cheesecake with cranberry topping

Who doesn't love cheesecake? I know I do, and looking at all the comments and requests I've received about cheesecakes since my first pressure cooker cookbook was published, lots of my readers do, too. The gingersnap crust is filled with a rich apricot–cream cheese filling and topped with a tart and tangy whole-berry cranberry sauce. Why, oh why can't I eat the whole thing? I look for excuses to use my pressure cooker to make this luscious cheesecake in celebration of . . . oh, I don't remember them all, but July 30 has been unofficially declared National Cheesecake Day. You see how it is, my dears—if you need a good reason to put another cheesecake on the table, they abound! • **SERVES 6**

Step One: THE CRANBERRY TOPPING

1 cup canned whole-berry cranberry sauce
2 tablespoons Grand Marnier, Cointreau, triple sec, or orange curaçao

Combine the cranberry sauce and liqueur in a small bowl and stir until the mixture is smooth. Cover tightly and refrigerate until ready to serve.

Step Two: THE APRICOTS

8 ounces dried apricots (about 1½ cups)
1 cinnamon stick
10 whole cloves
10 whole black peppercorns
2 tablespoons fresh lemon juice
2 teaspoons grated lemon zest

Place the apricots in the pressure cooker and add ½ cup water. Tie the cinnamon stick, cloves, and peppercorns in a square of cheesecloth and push it under the water. Lock the lid in place. Bring to 15psi over high heat and immediately reduce the heat to the lowest possible setting to stabilize and maintain that pressure. Cook for 8 minutes. Remove from the heat and use the quick release method before opening the lid. Drain and discard the spice bag. Place the apricots, lemon juice, and zest in a food processor and blend until smooth.

(continued)

Step Three: THE CRUST

1 tablespoon butter, softened, for greasing the insert pan, plus 2 tablespoons, melted
⅔ cup gingersnap cookie crumbs

Butter the bottom and sides of a springform pan that will fit inside your pressure cooker. In a small bowl, mix the cookie crumbs and melted butter until just barely moistened. The crumbs should look grainy, not clumped together. Spread the crumb mixture a little thicker over the bottom of the pan, and make it a bit thinner as you pat the crumbs part of the way up the side of the pan. Use a small glass (a shot glass works well) to press the crumbs around the edges for a smooth, even base.

Step Three: THE FILLING

2 (8-ounce) packages cream cheese, softened
⅔ cup sugar
2 large eggs
1 teaspoon almond extract

Use a stand mixer with the paddle attachment to blend the cream cheese and sugar until smooth. Add the eggs, almond extract, and the apricot mixture, and beat until smooth. Pour the cheesecake batter into the prepared springform pan. Crimp a square of aluminum foil tightly over the top of the pan. Place the cooking rack in the pressure cooker and add 1 cup water. Center the springform pan on a foil helper handle strip and lower it into the pressure cooker. Lock the lid in place. Bring to 15psi over high heat and immediately reduce the heat to the lowest possible setting to stabilize and maintain that pressure. Cook for 30 minutes. Remove from the heat and use the natural release method before opening the lid. Carefully lift the springform pan out of the pressure cooker, remove the aluminum foil cover, and move the pan to a wire rack to cool for about 20 minutes. Run small knife around the rim of the pan to loosen the sides of the cheesecake, but leave it in the springform pan. Stir the cranberry sauce and spread it evenly over the top of the cheesecake. Reserve any extra sauce to pass at the table. Cover the top with plastic wrap and refrigerate for at least 8 hours, or preferably overnight so it is thoroughly chilled and the flavors have time to blend. To serve, remove the side of pan and cut into desired serving-size portions.

COOK'S NOTE: I have developed a fondness for gingersnap crusts with cheesecakes, but if the traditional graham cracker crust is more your style, any crumb substitution is fine.

---

chocolate cheesecake with tart cherry topping

To indulge my addiction to cheesecake, I don't have to work very hard to think of some likely ingredients that will make another awesomely delectable dessert. It seems like almost anything in my pantry will magically transform in the next "most awesome cheesecake recipe ever." I'm also quite the chocoholic, and I'm uncommonly fond of cherries, too. Isn't that a gorgeous combination? • **SERVES 6**

Step One: THE CRUST

1 tablespoon butter, softened, for greasing the insert pan, plus 2 tablespoons, melted
1 cup chocolate cookie crumbs
2 tablespoons sugar

Butter the bottom and sides of a springform pan that will fit inside your pressure cooker. In a small bowl, mix the cookie crumbs, sugar, and melted butter until just barely moistened. The crumbs should look grainy, not clumped together. Spread the crumb mixture a little thicker over the bottom of the pan, and make it a bit thinner as you pat the crumbs part of the way up the side of the pan. Use a small glass (a shot glass works well) to press the crumbs around the edges for a smooth, even base.

Step Two: THE FILLING

1 (8-ounce) can sweetened condensed milk (not evaporated milk)
2 ounces unsweetened chocolate, chopped or grated
2 (8-ounce) packages cream cheese, softened
3 large eggs
3 tablespoons cornstarch
1½ teaspoons almond extract

Heat the condensed milk in a small saucepan over low heat. Add the chocolate, stirring constantly until it's melted and blended smooth. Remove from the heat and set aside to cool slightly. Use a stand mixer with the paddle attachment to blend the cream cheese until smooth. Gradually add the chocolate mixture and continue to beat until smooth. Add the eggs one at a time, blending each one into the batter before adding the next. Add the cornstarch and almond extract. Pour the cheesecake batter into the prepared springform pan. Crimp a square of aluminum foil tightly over the top

(continued)

of the pan. Place the cooking rack in the pressure cooker and add 1 cup water. Center the springform pan on a foil helper handle strip and lower it into the pressure cooker. Lock the lid in place. Bring to 15psi over high heat and immediately reduce the heat to the lowest possible setting to stabilize and maintain that pressure. Cook for 30 minutes. Remove from the heat and use the natural release method before opening the lid. Carefully lift the springform pan out of the pressure cooker, remove the aluminum foil cover, and move the pan to a wire rack to cool for about 20 minutes. Run small knife around the rim of the pan to loosen the sides of the cheesecake, but leave it in the springform pan. Cover the top with plastic wrap and refrigerate for at least 8 hours or preferably overnight so it is thoroughly chilled and the flavors have time to blend.

Step Three: THE TOPPING

1 (20-ounce) can tart cherry pie filling
2 tablespoons fresh lemon juice
1 teaspoon grated lemon zest

In a small bowl, combine all the ingredients. When the cheesecake is thoroughly chilled, add the cherry topping. Reserve any extra to pass at the table. Leave the cheesecake in the springform pan until the topping is chilled and you're ready to serve. To serve, remove the side of pan and cut the cheesecake into portions as desired.

index

C

d

e

q

r

S

t

u

v

w

y

z